AF783669

SOFTWARE AND HARDWARE MANAGEMENT

ENCYCLOPAEDIA OF COMPUTER MANAGEMENT SERIES

SOFTWARE AND HARDWARE MANAGEMENT

Edited by

S.K. Goel

ANMOL PUBLICATIONS PVT. LTD.

NEW DELHI-110 002 (INDIA)

ANMOL PUBLICATIONS PVT. LTD.
4374/4B, Ansari Road, Daryaganj
New Delhi - 110 002

Software and Hardware Management
© Reserved
First Edition, 2000
ISBN 81-261-0345-0

PRINTED IN INDIA

Published by J.L. Kumar for Anmol Publications Pvt. Ltd., New Delhi and Printed at Mehra Offset Press, Delhi.

Contents

Preface

Management is defined as the process of achieving organizational objectives through the efforts of other people. Management is a process—i.e., management consists of a number of interrelated steps or function which, when satisfactorily performed, lead to the achievement of goals. The successful practice of management involves people working together in harmony to achieve desired results. The availability of quality information is, of course, a requirement for a smoothly functioning operation. The business manager is a practitioner of the art and science of management. It is his job to carry out the basic management functions necessary to attain company goals. Of course, the objectives pursued vary according to the manager's mission; however, the functions of *planning, organizing, staffing,* and *controlling* are performed by all managers. The planning function looks to the future; to plan is to decide in advance a future course of action. Thus, *planning* involves making decisions with regard to (1) the selection of both short-run and long-run business strategies and goals; (2) the development of policies and procedure which will help accomplish objectives or counter threats; (3) the establishment of operating standards which serve as the basis for control; and (4) the revision of earlier plans in the light of changing conditions. The organizing function involves the grouping of work teams into logical and efficient units in order to carry out plans and achieve goals. One aspect of the staffing consists of selecting people to fill the positions which exist in the organizational structure of the business. The staffing activity also includes the training of employees to meet their job requirements, the preparation of employees for promotion to positions of greater responsibility, and the reassignment or removal of employees when such action is required. Unlike planning, which looks to the future, the *control* function looks at the past and the present. It is a follow-up to planning; it is the check on past and current performance to see if planned goals are being achieved.

The process of management is a continuing one. In practice, however, managers carry out these functions simultaneously. Plans beget subordinate plans, old plans require modifications, and new plans develop while old ones are in effect. Thus, it is impractical to insist on a special time sequence for the various functions. Quality information could support good decisions; good decisions should lead to effective performance of managerial functions; and effective functional performance should lead to the attainment of organizational goals. It is not surprising, therefore, that the acquisition and use of a computer may have important managerial implications. We can consider this broad topic from at least three viewpoints. *First,* it is possible to look at the implications involved in *planning for computers. Second,* we can look at the impact of *planning with computers.* Finally, we can look at the computer-oriented *decision-making techniques* which are now gaining acceptance. In light of the importance of information in the decision-making process, it would be logical to assume that top executives have always actively participated in the planning and implementation of new systems which would influence their future decisions.

In short, many executive apparently felt that the introduction of a computer was primarily a technical problem. They were content to define the goals of the new system vaguely and then to turn the entire project over to data-processing specialists.

Top managers should realize that their serious involvement in planning for computers is perhaps the most important single factor determining the success or failure of a computer installation. They should also be aware of the magnitude of the problems which will have to be overcome. Firms which have been successful in making computers pay off have been through in the initial planning stages. Computer usage can certainly improve the effectiveness of managerial planning. But before leaving the subject of planning with computers, it should be emphasized that computers *do not* "make decisions." Rather, they follow program decisions made earlier by managers and programmers. Although experiments are being conducted by extremely able researchers attempting to improve the machines' ability to solve ill-structured problems, it is man who defines problems, selects strategies to follow, and formulates hypotheses and hunches. *Heuristic* is a word which means "serving to discover." Much of planning is judgmental or heuristic in nature, and man is far superior to machine in the heuristic area of intellectual work.

Editor

1
Concept of Software Management

A software project is very similar to other types of project. It consists of individual activities, it can be divided into phases, it uses organizational resources, it fulfils demands, it creates a product, and it has a deadline. These numerous points of similarity seduce managers into thinking of software projects in the same way as other projects such as construction projects. This approach is dangerous, however, as software projects differ from other projects in a number of important ways. It is difficult for outsiders to appreciate these differences unless they have developed software themselves, and this is why so many managers from other fields find managing software projects so difficult. They overlook these subtle differences, plan the project in the normal way, and then wonder why things have gone wrong. One of the first differences is how to represent results. If you are building a house, it is obvious when a wall has been built or a floor has been laid. The layman can recognize that progress has been made, even if a statistician is required to assess quality. This is not the case with software. It is often a question of interpretation whether a piece of software is finished or not, as a software developer can claim at almost any time that the partial product is finished, that a document or source member exists. It takes an examination by an expert to decide whether or not the document or source member can actually be put to use. Checking the quality of the partial product requires almost as much time and effort as its development. Project leaders therefore depend entirely on what their staff tell them; in general there are no simple, cheap ways of checking. Today there are even project management systems in widespread use which recognize a partial product solely on the basis of whether a source member exists, i.e. even if only one line of code has been written for it. The tool automates a rather superficial system of control.

The question of the 'manufacture' of software products therefore remains largely one of definition. As many developers are not sure what is expected from them, they are also unsure as to when the software is finished. Even good developers often think that they have finished when in fact they have not, as the task has not been defined clearly enough. Of course there are also developers who distort their rate of progress in order to gain time. This distortion of the state of the project is refined and passed onwards by middle managers in large projects until it becomes very difficult to determine the correct state of the project. This inability to establish the progress of a project objectively is one of the most serious problems encountered in software development.

A further difference between software projects and other projects is the nondeterministic nature of software development. As they progress from one task to the next, from one phase to the next, the developers build up more and more experience which can affect previous results. Any given partial product is therefore only finished in a limited sense. At the beginning of a project, we can never know how often the original concept will have to be reworked to make the program run. To this extent, the design stage is not finished until the test stage is complete.

The conventional phase concept breaks down at this point. Every phase result is only a temporary result which lasts until the end of the next phase, when we will have to come back to each phase in turn to make its results fit and new stage of development. For example, the technical concept is revamped after the system has been designed, after the programming stage and after tests have been carried out. Programs are altered after testing. This recursive way of working is what Barry Boehm calls the Spiral Phase Model. Tom Gilb prefers to speak of 'evolutionary software development. Any project plan which fails to take these internal cycles into account is only half a plan, as half the work in many projects is spent reworking results which are supposedly complete.

A third difference which should not be underestimated is that the work is indivisible. To solve a problem in software, a developer has to think hard about the problem. As much as 50% to 75% of this problem-solving activity is simply writing down the results of this mental activity. This makes it very expensive to transfer one employee's tasks to another, as the second will have to repeat this mental process, so wasting 50% to 75% of the previous work. This is why Professor Brooks says that introducing new manpower into a software project is like pouring petrol on a fire. The employees already on the project spend all their time training the new ones, thus neglecting their own tasks. The delayed project becomes even more delayed.

This phenomenon invalidates the calculations of network plans, which assume that tasks can be freely swapped between employees. In software development, however, we can never assume that one employee can take over the work of another; tasks are often too specialized. One task may demand particular technical skills, another particular database skills, and yet another particular language skills. It is rare that one employee is an expert in all these areas. Tasks can therefore be swapped only in theory, not in practice. Any expert leaving the project can only be replaced by another expert.

A final significant difference compared with other types of project is the high level of abstraction combined with a low level of standarization. Many decades of practice and international standardization have determined the nature of tasks and results in other engineering disciplines. Most experts agree on the results of engineering work and the steps necessary to achieve those results. This is not the case with software. Here there is no agreement as to the form and content of the desired results nor as to the best way to achieve them. It is true that there are some international and national bodies which have laid down standards, but they are largely unrecognized. The discipline is too young. As the results are all relatively abstract for example, an execution profile plan, a data structure and a test suite the definition of the form and content is open to interpretation. Furthermore, not only are there hardly any standards, there are also no uniform guidelines. Apart from the programming language, almost everything is contentious. It is astonishing that software projects can be successfully completed at all in the midst of this tangle of terminology, hypotheses and superstition. That they do is due more to the capacity for improvization and the determination shown by the project workers than to any bureaucratic management methods. The latter tend to hinder the work rather than help it.

As difficult to grasp as these characteristics of software projects may be, we must never give up the attempt to get to grips with them. A crude plan, constantly revised, is better than no plan at all. As long as the project management system does not hinder the work being done, it can be useful even if it is imperfect. It only becomes a nuisance if it reaches too deep into the project without taking account of the recursive and nondeterministic characteristics of software development.

If that happens, rather than illuminating the picture, a project management system will distort it and give the wrong results. In what follows, where we discuss the methods and means of planning, organizing and managing the progress of a project, it must be borne in mind that these methods and means cannot always be implemented fully, and that to attempt to do so can do more harm than good. The dividing line between harm and good depends on the situation, however, and every project manager must find it for himself.

Software project planning

Actual project planning should not be carried out until the project has been authorized and the estimated costs and time-scale have been accepted. At this point, the agreed scope and quality of the target system have been laid down, and the individual processes which are to be automated—along with the data to be held on computer are known, at least in outline. This is a prerequisite for determining the individual tasks, results and deadlines.

The tasks to be carried out are derived from the partial results, which in turn comes from the objects and processes planned. To this extent, project planning must be object-oriented. Intermediate states are established using the objects and processes as a starting point. One task has to defined for each intermediate state and for each partial result. Next the tasks have to be put into sequence over time, taking their mutual interdependence into account. Only once this has been done can the necessary organization resources be allocated, a decisive factor of course being their availability Finally, the project plan is drawn up and verified. Project planning thus proceeds in the following steps:

(1) Defining individual results.

(2) Determining individual tasks.

(3) Sequencing tasks.

(4) Documenting and validating the project plan.

Defining individual results

The objects and processes in the system definition are the project's individual results the documents, programs and test results created during the project. In addition, status reports and various management reports are written when results are measured. These partial results appear at the points where processes and objects intersect with the project phases. Objects and processes are the columns in a large table, and phase and subphases are the rows. Each system element therefore has an intermediate stage for each row.

In the *specification phase* each process and object has

- a rough specification document
- a refined specification document.

The *rough data specification* might consist of:

- object trees
- diagrams of relationships between objects
- tables of objects' usage
- verbal descriptions of each object.

The *rough function specification* might consist of:

- process trees
- process execution profiles
- data flow plans
- verbal descriptions of each process.

The *refined data specification* might consist of:

- example forms
- data structure trees
- tables of data usage

- descriptions of each data element.

The *refined function specification* might consist of:

- decision tables
- trees of function structure
- input-process-output diagrams
- descriptions of each function.

The *rough data design* might consist of:

- data base structure diagrams
- file descriptions
- report or mask descriptions.

The *rough program design* might consist of:

- process execution diagrams
- data flow diagrams
- program descriptions.

The *refined data design* might consist of:

- data description tables
- index keys
- descriptions of test data.

The *refined program design* might consist of:

- module interface diagrams
- pseudo-code module members
- module test frameworks.

In the *programming phase* there will be:

- a MAP or reporting macro for each information object
- a data description macro for each data object
- a source member for each module.

In the *verification phase* there will be:

- a test log for each module
- a test report for each module.

In the *delivery phase* there will be

- documentation of the quality of each process and object
- a record of delivery for each process and object.

Finally, the *system as a whole will* have:

- a user guide

- a certificate of quality.

Attributes such as content, form and standard of quality must be I down for each result, as different standards might apply to results of the same type.

Determining individual tasks

A project's individual results form the basis for determining the tasks involved in the project. For each result there must be a corresponding task. The following tasks are therefore listed for each object and each process

- drawing up a rough specification
- drawing up a refined specification
- drawing up a rough design
- drawing up a refined design
- coding
- generating
- verifying and validating
- documenting.

We therefore have eight tasks per object or process, and to this we must add at least six checks—one after each phase. An average system with only 100 objects and 50 processes would therefore have more than 1500 individual tasks. Beside the input and output results, attributes such as rules costs, time-scale and deadline must be laid down for each task.

Sequencing tasks

Network planning techniques are used to draw up a sequence for the task Tasks can be representedl either by the edges or by the nodes in a network plan. In the first case, the nodes are transitions from one task to another, a in the second case the edges are the transitions.

In either case, a task is started when its input results become available As these results are generated by other tasks, those tasks are predecessors the dependent task. Every task in the network, except for the first one, has conditional and unconditional predecessors. A predecessor is conditional if the same result could come from various alternative tasks. These dependencies lead to a number of parallel paths through the task network. The most expensive path is the one which uses the most man-days. The longest path is the one which lasts for the largest number of calender days. As some tasks are more complex than others, the number of tasks on a path is not the same as the number of mandays and calendar days. As some tasks can be divided up, the number of mandays is not the same as the number of calendar days It is therefore vital to estimate the duration of each task separately.

A tool to aid sequencing is worthwhile in all but the simplest projects.

Documenting and validating the project plan

Once the tasks and their relationships have been established, we can then evaluate them in various ways. One way is to draw up a Gantt diagram. This diagram shows when which tasks should start and end on a calendar. This makes it easier to gain an overview of how tasks are distributed over time and how they a dependent on each other's completion dates.

Another way is to document the sequence of tasks as a network plan. There are at least two methods:

- CPA (Critical Path Analysis) diagrams
- PERT (Program Evaluation and Review Technique) diagrams.

In CPA *diagrams*, the edges are tasks and the nodes are transitions fro one task to another. Several edges can have the same starting and even the same end node. The duration of tasks is noted on the edges, and the earlier and latest possible transition dates are noted at the nodes.

In *PERT diagrams*, the nodes are tasks and the edges are the transitions Several arrows or edges can lead to the same task node and lead from it other nodes. The duration of the tasks and the mandays required are not at the nodes. The transition dates are noted on the edges.

Both these network diagrams allow us to calculate the longest and the most expensive paths, along with the earliest and latest starting dates for each task.

These network plans can be very useful, particularly in illustrating the relationship between the individual tasks. On the other hand, it must be pointed out that the sequencing of tasks assumes no constraints on the availability of resources. If a resource is not available to a task, the whole path, and any paths depending on it, are held up. The network plan should therefore be checked against the availability of all types of resource—staff, hardware and software as soon as possible. Unfortunately, organizational resources are generally allocated after the network plan has been drawn up. If this is the case, the network plan should be revised after the project has been organized, and deadlines should be recalculated.

Project organization

Once the project plan has been drawn up, the necessary resources are allocated to the project. Individual tasks are allocated to individual members of staff, and the necessary hardware and software resources are provided.

Staff allocation

According to Daly, there are three ways of organizing a project:

- line organization
- project organization
- matrix organization.

Line organization means that the project is divided between the technical and the development departments, or between the client and the developers. The entire project is thus divided into two subprojects:

- an organization project
- a development project.

The organization project group comprises the organizers of the technical department, who draw up the technical concept and the rough specification, carry out any integration testing and write the user documentation. The development project group works on the refined specification, designs the system, codes and tests individual programs and writes the technical documentation. Responsibility is thus cleanly split between the user and the developer.

The *main advantages* of this type of organization are:

- the user shares responsiblity
- the user helps to design the system
- the user is responsible for testing the system
- actual development costs can be measured more easily, as basic development can be carried out at a fixed price.

The *disadvantages* are mainly the need for:

- an exact specification
- educated users
- a well-developed phase concept.

Project organization means that the project is taken on by a team consisting of organizers, developers and representatives of the technical department, the end user. The project leader has complete responsibility for the progress of the project. It is up to the project leader to distribute the tasks amongst the team members and to check whether they are carried out. It is important that the project team encompasses all the interests and technical fields involved in the project.

The *main advantages* of this type of organisation are:

- there is clear, centralized responsibility
- there is better communication between project staff
- a formal interface between technical and technological matters is avoided
- there is a mutual learning effect —technical staff learn from the technological staff and vice versa.

The disadvantages are:

- there are few mechanisms for control
- everyone depends on the project leader

- technical and technological problems are intermixed.

Matrix organisation means that the actual project group consists solely the project leader and a project secretary. The organizers, developers an other project staff still come under their respective departments. There is a organizational department and a development department alongside the technical department, and representatives of each department stay within that department. The project leader can allocate tasks to the various departments, but only via the departmental heads. It is up to the departmental head to ensure that the tasks are carried out. At soon as a member of staff has finished one task, the next one can be begun.

The *main advantages* of this type of organization are:

- project staff can stay in their home departments
- the concentration of specialists in their own groups
- increased transparency of projects
- projects are independent of line organization.

The most serious *disadvantages* are:

- Responsibility is split between the project leader and departmental heads
- the availability of specialists
- poor communication between project staff
- an increase in the effort required to coordinate the project.

Project support

Every development project has to be supported by specialists who are not directly allocated to the project, and the number of such groups rises continually with increasing specialization. Larger-scale development requires at least five groups of experts, namely:

- a systems programming group
- a database/data administration group
- a telecommunications group
- a methods and standards group
- a quality and product assurance group.

These experts work on a project as and when necessary. For example database administrators will be called in when a database is being designed or telecommunications experts when a distributed system is being designed These groups; are however not there merely to provide the project wit know-how.

The *systems group is* responsible for maintaining computing facilities They maintain the hardware and the operating system to ensure that the project groups have constant access to the computer.

The *database administrators* are responsible for setting up and managing the organization's data. This includes ensuring data is protected and secure Alongside the care of the database and the database system, they are also responsible for setting up the organization's data directionary, and they must therefore coordinate the data requirements of the individual project groups.

The *telecommunications group* is responsible for installing and maintaining the organization's communications networks. They must ensure that data is transmitted smoothly in-house. They support the design of data communications in the project.

The *methods and standards group* establishes organizational guidelines for development, sets out the phase concept and gives training in the necessary methods. They act as consultants to the project on questions of methodology. They are also responsible for acquiring and introducing software tools.

The *quality assurance group is* responsible for the quality of software produced. They must ensure that documents are formally correct, that programs follow programming conventions and that they are sufficiently well tested. These control functions mean that this group should reside outside the development organization.

Resource allocation

Modern software development demands ever more hardware and software resources. Many of a project's tasks can be carried out without computer support, but most tasks are completed with the help of the computer be it a host computer, a satellite computer in a cluster, or a workstation. The aim here is to match the computer to the type of task, e.g. a particular PC will be used for the specification of a form.

Alongside the development computers, we require a set of software tools, a software production environment, such as:

- a specification system for the specification tasks
- a design system for design tasks
- a testing system for test tasks.

Some software tools, such as the editor, are used in more than one type of task. The usage relationship between tasks and tools must be defined so as to allocate resources effectively. This will indicate which tasks need hardware and software resources and at what times. This resource requirement plan is used as the basis for planning capacity, from which the appropriate hardware and software resources will be acquired and made ready.

Project management

The best plans are useless if they cannot be implemented. The question arises, however, to what extent a plan can be followed. In software development, project plans are often used only as guidelines or as a measure of target progress for the project. The project's actual progress is only monitored in a superficial way. This is in crass contradiction to project monitoring in other disciplines, where the completion of every task, the quality of every result, adherence to all deadlines and accumulated costs a recorded exactly. Any deviation from the plan is immediately recognized and corrected. The reason for this could be that progress is easier to see other disciplines, whereas it is difficult to monitor in software development Problems thought to be solved have to be readdressed time and time again. The project seems to be stuck in a loop, causing many software project planners to give up and leave things to run their course. One final deadline and a total budget are enough, and corrective action is only taken once d deadline has passed or the budget has been used up. Asking developers how far they have got is a waste of effort, as the answer is always as vague as d question.

It is clear that this state of affairs cannnot be justified to the client. It should not come as a surprise if both the time-scale and the budget prove be far too small. It is a case of Parkinson's Law: software developers take must time and money as they are given. In addition, software developers are, in common with others engaged primarily mental activities, notoriously bad at organizing their own work. They can budget neither their energy nor their time and tend to be sidetraced by areas that only they are interested in. The main cause of this dilemma is to be found in the lack of clarity with which intermediate results are defined. For users, as for software managers, there is only one visible result of software development, namely a running system. Other intermediate results are beyond their comprehension and therefore not measurable, either in a qualitative or in a quantitative manner. While the project is in progress, they simply watch the clock and the money running out.

The key to monitoring projects effectively is therefore to define a large number of individual results which can be brought together as partial products. The first section of this chapter presented a scheme for dividing software products into partial products and individual results. This, or a similar, subdivision of products, from which individual results can be derived, is an indispensible prerequisite for proper monitoring of the product. Each individual result must have at least five charcteristics:

- quantity
- quality
- staff costs
- costs
- deadline.

Quantity is a framework for the number of items. It can be measured in pages, lines, statements, or function points among others. *Quality is* the value of the item. It can be measured on a scale from 0 to 1, where 0 denotes a total absence of quality and 1 denotes total fulfilment of quality demands.

Staff costs are the number of mandays necessary to produce the item.

Costs are the amount of money needed to produce the item. Besides personnel costs, these include the costs of computer time and the use of software tools.

The *deadline is* the date on which the item has to be ready. A large part of project management has to do with controlling those characteristics and with the measures introduced to bring the actual values of these characteristics up to their target values.

Monitoring quantity

Quantitative progress can be measured in a number of units, including:

- components
- lines and statements
- pages
- function points
- earned value points.

If the product is sufficiently well divided into subproducts, individual *components* can be counted. The technical concept could therefore consist of a series of individual documents such as function trees, data trees, example forms, execution networks, decision tables, data descriptions and function descriptions.

The system design could similarly consist of a series of individual design components such as database structures, product designs, test designs, process execution diagrams, program trees and pseudo-code members.

For their part, programs contain data description macros, procedure macros and code modules.

Each of these component types has several forms, each basic component having one form. Each basic component is an individual result. The advantage of component monitoring lies in the simple binary decision, finished or not. All components have equal status. That is of course the disadvantage too, that a complex module counts only as much as a simple one. If 50% of the components are finished, that does not necessarily mean that 50% of the project is finished, as the remaining components may take up 75% of the project's budget. In this respect component monitoring is the coarsest measure of quantitative progress.

The finest measure of a project's progress is counting the number of *lines and statements.* Text and programs consist of a certain number of lines and sentences. Each diagram consists of a certain number of symbols. Here a document is counted once for each line or symbol that it contains, and we are not measuring whether a code module is finished, but that a certain number of statements is finished.

Although this yardstick is useful in measuring productivity, it is hardly suitable for monitoring a project's progress. Lines, statements and symbols are often deleted or edited, so that they are an unstable unit of measurement. It is far too expensive to monitor their evolution.

Between these two extremes we have alternative measures of a project's progress such as:

- pages
- function points
- earned value points.

Counting *pages* is only a slightly more refined measure than counting components. Instead of declaring a document finished, its page count goes into the calculation. The same goes for programs and modules. Diagrams are counted as complete pages. Looked at in this way, a software product consists of an estimated number of pages which have to be filled in. A project's progress is equal to the percentage of pages completed.

Counting *function points* is an attempt to do justice to the logical complexity of the individual components. Not only are individual components such as objects, processes, files and programs identified, the components are also weighted in accordance with the number of interfaces or connectivity levels they have. This assigns a particular number of function points to each component. A software product with *n* function points consists of k partial products each having *n/k* function points. These function points in the partial products are, in their turn, distributed among the individual components. Once a component is finished, its function point tally goes into the calculation of how far the project has progressed. A project is 100% complete when all the function points have been finished.

Earned value points are also an attempt to weight individual components. Instead of counting interfaces, however, the cost of each component is estimated, its number of value points being derived from this estimate. One value point is equal to half a manday.

A document or module which is estimated to take four mandays thus has eight value points. The developer earns value points by completing a component. It is only once all the value points have been earned that a partial product is said to be finished. TRW in America even use this measure for staff; in principle, any measure of productivity could apply to staff, In Europe, however, strict control of individual people is not acceptable and so productivity is measured at the team level.

There are numerous ways of representing a project's progress, including

- Gantt diagrams
- progress tables
- progress cards

These graphic techniques show the current state of results obtained compared with the total number of results required for a phase or for the project as a whole. The progress curve can also be projected over a target curve to clarify any variances. The difference between the target and actual states is sometimes called 'slippage'. A project can be delayed by a year if i slips day by day and the variance between target and actual increase continually. This can easily be seen on a progress card.

Monitoring quality

Every software component, be it text, a diagram, a table, or a source member, has not only a quality score in terms of lines, pages, function points, earned value points etc., but also a quality score on a scale from 0 to 1. In chapter 4 we discussed various ways of measuring this quality score. What we need to do in a project is to determine the quality of all the individual results of partial products at the end of each phase.

The specification phase is followed by the delivery of the specification, the design phase is followed by an evaluation of the design, the programming phase is followed by program checking and the test phase is followed by test revision. Results whose actual score is at variance with their target score are sorted out and noted. The project's management then has to decide whether these results should be accepted or whether more work is necessary on them. Even if they are accepted, it is important to know where the qualitative weaknesses of the software product lie. For example, the aim may be to achieve a 95% success rate, but only 85% is achieved. This indicates that the module is less reliable than was desired, and, so, more errors than usual are to be expected. The same is true of programming. If a static analysis shows that a program is neither modular nor structured, higher expenditure on testing and maintenance is to be expected. Again, the management must decide whether to accept the program so as to progress more quickly or not. In any case, it is important that the discrepancy between the actual and the target quality becomes evident as soon as possible.

Tables and cards can clarify quality variances. They portray the percentage of software components falling below a certain quality standard in a graphical manner. This helps to identify projects with an above average quality shortfall quickly.

Monitoring staff costs

Staff costs are relatively easy to measure in comparison with quality and quantity.. Here it is simply a question of counting mandays taken up by individual tasks and phases. Mandays must be recorded at the task level to do this, and at that level they can be compared with the number of mandays planned.

Staff costs—target and actual can be plotted in just the same way that project progress and product quality can. One well-known way of doing this is to use a 'rate chart.

Monitoring costs

If at all possible, project costs should be recorded at the task level. Here we are dealing with computing and tools costs, training costs and the costs of other resources, alongside personnel costs. As each task has one and only one result, costs can easily be traced back to components so that the cost of each component can be exactly determined. Accumulated costs can be shown as target and actual cost curves measured against time in calendar months.

Monitoring deadlines

Finally we have to keep an eye on adherence to deadlines. Every task has an ideal deadline and the latest possible deadline. A phase is complete once the last task in the phase is finished. Deadlines can be checked at regular intervals during the project. Deadlines that are not met must be summarized in a deadline report, which can also indicate the percentage of deadlines not met as a proportion of deadlines due so far. If this percentage is too high, it is a sure sign that the project is in difficulties.

Corrective measures

What should a project leader do if reports show that the project is slipping in quantity or quality, is costing too much or is taking too long? In general, there are only a few courses of action. If quality is slipping, the project's member of staff can be warned or trained better if necessary. This however takes up time which is precious. The project's standard of quality might be lowered in agreement with the client. It is important that the user is consulted quickly. If the project is slipping in quantity, the situation is more difficult. Warnings are of little use. The project leader can of course ask for more capacity, but new members of staff will have to be introduced to the job first If possible, the best course is to work overtime. If that is not possible, the only alternative left is to reduce the planned scope of the project. Promise must be broken, and objects and processes will have to be deleted. Again, i is important to consult the user.

Software project costing

Software project costing is based on comparing the contradictory aims of software development. The four aims, represented by the four corners of a square, are:

- quantity
- quality
- time
- costs.

These aims compete for the limited capacity and productivity available in an organization, represented by the innermost square. This square is of a given size, and although it can be stretched in one direction or another, this brings with it a consequent shortening of one of the other sides. At any given point in time, productivity in terms of statements, components, function points or other measures is a fixed quantity which is dependent on various productivity factors, and which can only be changed by altering those factors.

There are then five parameters in all for software costing. They are grouped together as follows:

arguments
- quantity (system, size)
- quality (system 'worth')

constants
- productivity

results
- time
- costs.

Of these variables, time and costs are the dependent variables. They can always be changed by redefining the system. It is only possible to calculate time and costs after the quantity and quality of the system, and the organization's productivity, have been established. Here we must take factors specific to the project into account as they could influence productivity.

If the calculation shows that costs are too high or that the project will take too long, the system must be redefined by reducing quantity, quality or both. The costing calculation therefore requires five steps:

- establishing productivity
- isolating specific factors
- calculating costs
- calculating the project's duration
- calculating maintenance costs.

Establishing productivity

Before we can estimate costs, we must establish the level of productivity. There are three factors involved in determining productivity:

- hardware
- software
- staff.

The formula is:

Productivity = Hardware factors x software factors x staff factors

The *hardware factor is* composed of:

- compatibility between the development computer and the target computer
- computing conditions during development
- availability of the development computer
- size of the development database
- the response time of the developmental computer

- equipment available in the work place.

The *software factor is* composed of:

- the phase concept
- methods used
- tools used
- quality assurance.

The *staff factor is* composed of:

- the developers' level of education
- the, developers' experience with applications
- the developers' knowledge of languages
- the developers' familiarity with the DB-DC environment.

The weights and values assigned to these subfactors gives us a productivity table which is updated after each project.

Each estimation technique can have its own productivity table. For example:

- a statement table for COCOMO (Constructuve Costing Model)
- a function point table for function points
- a component table for components.

The productivity table can relate to a whole organization, to an application area, or to a single project. Whichever the case, it is an integral part the cost calculation.

Statement table

The statement table shows the exponential relationship between kilo statements and

- man-months
- computing hours
- costs.

Function point table

The function point table shows the relationship, as an S-curve, between function points and

- man-months
- computing hours
- costs.

Component table

The component table shows the arithmetic relationship between components and man-months computing hours costs.

Isolating specific factors

Beside the factors of productivity themselves, there are numerous factors specific to the project that we must take account of. Different estimation techniques involve different factors, which may drive costs either upwards or downwards. COCOMO factors are multiplicative, function point factors are additive, and component analysis factors have an averaging effect.

COCOMO factors

The twelve following factors have to be taken into account in the COCOMO

method [1]:

(1) Compatibility between the development and target computers:
full = 1. 00
partial= 1. 15
non = 1. 30

(2) Computing conditions during development:
online = 0. 90
mixed = 1. 00
batch = 1.10

(3) Availability of the development computer:
high = 0. 80
average = 1.00
low = 1.20

(4) Size of the developmental databases:
large = 0.90
average = 1.00
small = 1.20

(5) Phase concept being used:
detailed= 0.90
general = 1.00
none = 1. 10

(6) Development methodology used:
full = 0. 80
partial= 1. 00
none = 1. 20

(7) Support from tools:
full= 0.75
partial= 1. 00
none = 1.25

(8) Project-related quality assurance:

automated= 0.90
manual = 1.05
none = 1. 20

(9) Developers' level of education:
high = 0.75
average = 1.00
low = 1.40

(10) Developers' applications experience
wide = 0.80
average = 1.00
little = 1.20

(11) Developers' knowledge of languages:
good= 0.95
average = 1.00
poor = 1.15

(12) Developers' familiarity with the DB-DC environment:
high = 0.90
average = 1.00
low = 1.10

The overall factor is obtained by multiplying the individual factors together.

Function point factors

The function point method is subject to the following 14 factors.

(1) Communications facilities

Data top be processed by the application is sent and received by the communications facilities.

(2) *Distributed data processing* (DDP)

The data is managed or processed in line with the DDP concept.

(3) *Response time behaviour*

A short response time has a high ranking.

(4) *System load*

The target computer is already heavily loaded by other tasks.

(5) *Transaction rate*

Design, implementation and maintenance are all affected by a high transaction rate.

(6) *Online data capture*

Data is input online

(7) *Use of dialogue*

Data input and output is controlled by dialogues, and a transaction is built up in several processing streps.

(8) *Real-time updating*

Files and databases are updated online.

(9) *Complexity*

Processing is complex, including a large number of links, decision logical and mathematical calculations and exceptions.

(10) *Reusability*

The ability to reuse programs in other applications should be taken in account during development, implementation and maintenance.

(11) *Ease of conversion*

Ease of conversion should be taken into account during design and implementation.

(12) *Ease of use*

Particular interface procedures should be provided for later ease of use.

(13) *Portability*

Design and implementation must take into account that the application will be installed at a number of sites.

(14) *Editability*

Development allows users to change system functions.

Apart from the ninth factor, which is measured on a scale from 0 to 50, all these factors are measured on a scale from 0 to 5, where

0 = no effect

1 = occasional effect

2 = small effect

3 = average effect

4 = noticeable effect

5 = strong effect.

The overall factor for a project is the sum of all 14 factors, after applying a normalizing factor of 1.64

Component analysis factors

There are five factors affecting project costing in the component analysis method:

(1) Amount of hardware
large = 1. *20*
average = 1.00
small = 0. 80.

(2) Amount of software
large = 1.*20*
average = 1.00
small = 0.80

(3) Quality of staff
good =1.20
average =1.00
poor =0.80

(4) Degree of organization
high =1.20
average=1.00
low =0.80

(5) Familiarity with applications
high =1.20
average=1.00
low =0.80

These individual factors are averaged to arrive at the overall score. Factors specific to the organization can also be included in this calculation.

Measuring quantity

We can measure quantity in various ways, three of them being:

- by the number of statements
- by the number of function points
- by the number of components.

Measuring statements

The COCOMO method uses the statement or the statement line as a yardstick. For a language like PL/1, statements are counted, whereas for COBOL, lines of code are counted. Statements have a higher weighting for 4th generation languages such as SOL or Natural. In all these cases we must distinguish between processing statements and data description statements:

Statements = Processingstatements + data description statements

The number of data description statements is derived from the definition of the project's data areas. The data area definition lists each object with its type and the estimated number of data elements. In addition, the level of the object's integration is given as one of:

- high
- average
- low

Finally, there is a flag showing whether the object has to be created, changed, or remain as it is.

Highly integrated information objects have three times as many data description statements as data elements, average ones have twice as many, and low ones have one data description statement per data element. Highly integrated data objects have four times as many data description statements as there are data elements, average ones have three times as many, and low ones have twice as many.

Real objects are not taken into account here. New objects have a score of 100%, changed objects of 50%, and old objects 0%.

The number of processing statements is derived from the project's application definition. Each process appears in the definition along with its estimated number of functions and its type, one of:

- real
- batch
- online.

In addition, the level of the process's complexity is given as one of:

- high
- average
- low.

Finally, there is a flag showing whether the process is new, changed, or old.

For highly complex batch processes the number of processing statements is 60 times the number of functions, for average ones it is 50 times, and for not very complex ones it is 40 times the number of functions.

The number of processing statements for all types of online process is equal to the number of functions.

Highly complex 3rd generation language processes have 80 times as many processing statements as functions, average ones have 60 times as many, and low ones 40 times as many. Highly complex 4th generation language processes have 40 times as many processing statements as there are functions, average ones have 30 times as many, and low ones 20 times as many.

Real or manual processes are not taken into account. New functions have a score of 100%, changed functions 50%, and old functions have a score of 0%.

The final figure is then:

Number of data description statements+ number of processing statements

Measuring function points

The function point is a language-independent measure of complexity.

The number of function points is measured separately for:

- data objects
- information
- processes.

Information is also split into inputs and outputs.

Highly integrated data objects are given 15 function points, average ones are given 10 function points, and poorly integrated ones 7 function points.

Highly integrated input information is given 6 function points and average input information 4 function points.

Highly integrated output information is given 7 function points, average output information is given 5 function points, And poorly integrated output information 4 function points.

Highly complex online processes are given 10 function points, average ones 7 function points, and not very complex ones are given 5 function points.

Highly complex batch processes are given 8 function points, average ones 5 function points, and not very complex ones 3 function points.

Function points for new objects and processes are included in the calculation at their full value, those for changed objects and processes at half their value, and those for old objects and processes are left out of the calculation altogether.

The quantity of a project's objects and processes is the sum of all the function points which affects them. The strength of the function point method is that user interfaces determine quantity rather than the scope of the code.

Measuring components

The yardstick used in the component analysis method is the software component or the configuration element. Software components comprise:

- documents
- code objects
- test procedures

Documents can be subdivided into:

- specification documents
- design documents
- user documents.

Code objects can be subdivided into:

- modules
- data records
- command procedures
- MAP or DBD macros.

Each of these objects is a component which has to be coded.

Test procedures can be subdivided into:

- module testing procedures
- data testing procedures
- system testing procedures.

Each test procedure is a component which has to be specified and executed. We can derive the number of data-related components from the definition of the data area. Each object can have the following components:

- specification
- design
- data records
- MAP and DBD macros
- test data procedure
- description for the user.

From that, we have five components for each data object, three components per data view and six components for each piece of information data. These components are included in the calculation at half their value for objects which have to be altered. Old objects are not included in the calculation at all.

We can see the number of program-related components from the definition of the application. Each process can have the following components:.

- process specficiation document
- program design
- module design
- dialogue design
- module code
- module test procedures

- command procedures
- description for the users.

From that, we have at least eight components for each online process and seven components per batch process. Altered components are included in the calculation at 50% of their value, and old processes are excluded altogether. When expressed in components, the quantity of a project is the sum of the components for all objects and processes within the project's scope.

Measuring quality

Software quality is determined by the factors of quality that the user specifies. Each data area and each application in the system definition have their own quality characteristics.

The eight main characteristics of quality are:

- reliability or integrity
- security
- user friendliness
- time efficiency
- space efficiency
- maintainability
- portability or data independence
- extensibility..

There may be additional characteristics specific to a data area or application.

Each characteristic is given a target score on a scale from 0 to 1, fro which a multiplication factor between 0.75 and 1.25 is derived. The COCOMO multiplication factors can serve as a guide here, but do not have to be adopted. The overall quality of a data area of an application is the product of the weighted multiplication factors for each data area or application. A project's quality is the product of the individual qualities of each application and data area affected by the project. This assumes a multiplication factor 1. Calculating the project's cost involves multiplying the quality by this factor. If this factor is greater than 1, the quality score for the project rises accordingly. This means that quality has an impact on the work to be undertaken.

Estimating costs

There are three approaches to estimating the cost of a project, corresponding to the three measures of quantity:

- the COCOMO method
- the function point method
- the component analysis method.

The COCOMO method

The starting point for the COCOMO method is the number of statements, and the cost in man-months is derived from it in three stages. First, the number of statements is multiplied by the product of the weighted quality factors for the data areas and applications in question.

Second, the number of statements is multiplied by the weighted factors from the COCOMO table of factors specific to the project.

Third, the smoothed number of statements is used as an index into the productivity table to find the corresponding statement interval, interpolating if necessary. The number of man-months, the relevant costs and the number of computing hours required are read from the table.

The COCOMO formula is:

Man-months = MF (quantity x quality x factor)^{EX}

where MF = multiplier, EX=exponent .

MF and EX are read from the productivity table. They can be changed by drawing up new productivity tables so that different tables can be used for batch, online and mixed projects.

The standard values are as follows:

Batch system

MF = 2.40

EX = 1.05

Online systems

MF = 3.00

EX = 1. 12

Mixed systems

MF = 2.70

EX = 1.09

The function point method

The starting point for the function point method is the number of function points, and this method also has three stages. First, the number of function points is multiplied by the product of the weighted quality factors for the data areas and applications affected.

Second, the number of 'statements is added to the sum of the factors. Third, the smoothed number of statements is used as an index into the productivity table to find the corresponding function point interval, interpolating as necessary. The number of man-months, the relevant costs and the required number of computing hours are then read from the table.

We can use IBM's standard function point table as a basis for illustration.

The component analysis method

The starting point for the component analysis is the number of components or documents, code members and test procedures. It too involves three steps.

First, the number of components is multiplied by the product of the weighted quality factors for the data areas and statements affected.

Second, the number of components is weighted by multiplying it by the average value of the individual factors. Third, the sum of the components is used as an index into the productivity table to find the corresponding component interval, again interpolating if necessary. The number of manmonths, the appropriate costs and the computing hours required are read from the table.

Estimating project duration

There is only one formula, taken from the COCOMO method, for estimating the duration of the project. The parameters for this formula are:

- system type
- development cost in man-months.

First, therefore, we have to calculate the cost and here we must distinguish between:

- batch systems
- online systems
- mixed systems.

The formula for *batch systems is:*

Time = 2.5 $(\text{manmonths})^{0.38}$

The formula for *online systems is:*

Time = 2.5 $(\text{manmonths})^{0.35}$

The formula for *mixed systems is:*

Time = 2.5 $(\text{manmonths})^{0.37}$

Estimating maintenance costs

Maintenance costs are also estimated on the basis of a COCOMO formula. The parameters for this formula are:

- system type
- development cost
- average number of changes
- quality score.

The result of this calculation is the yearly maintenance cost in terms of man-months.

The formula for *batch systems is:*

MM_W = (MM_E x change rate) x (1. 5 - quality score)

The formula for *online systems is:*

MM_w = 1. 2_E (MM X change rate) x (1. 5 - quality score)

The formula for *mixed systems is:*

MMw = 1. 1 (MM_E x change rate) x 1.5 - quality score)

where MM = manmonth, W = maintenance cost, E = developmer' cost.

Software environment

The computerization of America is reaching epidemic proportions. Demand for software to perform ever-expanding computer applications is outgrowing the industry's ability to produce it. This gloomy outlook stems from the fact that writing workable software to meet established requirements historically has proved to be costly and time-consuming. It has consistently resisted the kind of cost-saving breakthroughs that have characterized the hardware side of the computer business. Even though there has been significant progress in software methodologies and disciplines, software development remains substantially a labor-intensive and unpredictable effort. After years of attempts to harness the software problem, creating software is still more of an art than a science.

Much has been written about the creative process of computer programming, and various structured methodologies and procedures for converting algorithms into programs have been devised. This book has presented an important component of the equation, an effective management control methodology. Part of this software development methodology is the environment in which the technical teams and managers must work.

Software organization

The following figure shows a representative software functional organization similar to the matrix-type organization described by Daly. Such an organization can provide a concentrated and controlled environment for building, supporting, and safekeeping a growing base of software assets.

Software development

The software development function supplies the skill resources required to plan and execute software development projects and software product lifecycles. This includes defining the software problem, detailed planning, time and resource estimation, proposal writing, functional analysis and specification, environment analysis and specification, design, development, and prerelease testing. Managers of projects that are primarily software in nature fall into this group. Team leaders responsible for supporting projects managed from outside the software area may also fall within this function. Standards for documentation, programming, testing, and quality control of software that is to be applied to the software development effort may be generated within this function, with exceptions justified on a project or product basis.

Software product support

Two major differences between hardware and software warrant a modified organizational approach to software production and support efforts. First, each time software is "maintained," the design is changed. Software does not "wear out" as hardware does; there are no "replacement parts." Second, one would usually not build into hardware the complex systems built into software. Hardware is too difficult to change. Software is used because it is relatively easy to change. Statistics on successful software products indicate that 60 to 90% of the software maintenance support resources are spent on enhancements to the functional capability. This process can continue for 5 to 15 years for a given product. Personnel turnover is a major consideration, along with protection of the assets (embodied in the documentation, program, and test libraries) as they constantly undergo change.

A breakdown of the software product support function is briefly described in the following paragraphs. A more detailed discussion is given in Chapter 9.

Customer interface. One of the product support activities is a function for receiving customer or internal problem reports, resolving actions to be taken, and soliciting solution recommendations for the reported problems from the technical support functions. Problem reports are translated here into change orders to the software libraries and then are diligently tracked until finally solved. The interface function is also responsible for the distribution of new releases of software products to the existing customer base and the installation of new customers.

Responsibility for customer training on the use of the products may also reside within this functional area. Entry- or junior-level software and clerical skills normally are sufficient for this function, supported by ample knowledge of the application.

Software library. Another important software support activity is a facility protecting the basic software product assets (e.g., the document library, program library, test library, version and release control records, and configuration control). With proper procedures and standards in place, the library can be realized by a high-level clerical function supported by lower level software backup skills when necessary.

Technical support. This function maintains a pool of skill resources to provide technical support across software product lines. It provides the technical expertise needed to interpret difficult problems, recommend changes, implement approved changes and generally to support the previously discussed functions as needed. This function should be a core group of medium to high-level software technical persons responsible for doing but not controlling. Technical persons newly assigned to the software area may start in this function to gain familiarity with a software product before assignment to new development projects. Organizational flexibility should also exist between this function and the software development function so that skill resources can easily be allocated based on need priorities.

Software operations

This function is responsible for the maintenance and operation of the physical computer facilities required for development and support of software products. Planning, aquisition, maintanance, controlling, and scheduling of computer facilities are typical activities of this function. Knowledge of available computer vendor hardware and support software, telecommunication facilities, and peripheral products are important attributes of this function's personnel. In addition to in-house computer facility management, this function may also supply rental of time-sharing services where they can be shown to be cost effective. Heirarchical library storage facilities and security interactive edit, compile and test, and symbolic debugging facilities provided by this function may cut manpower costs significantly, may speed up development, and may improve overall control of the software development process.

System software

This function often serves three purposes. First, it provides the special' software expertise when changes and interfaces to the standard operating system (OS) are required for a development project. Second, the selection or creation of OS-related development support tools (e.g., precompilers, librarians, self-test aids) may also require the same special expertise. Third, this function is a convenient consultation center for problems relating to the usage, performance, or service features of the standard software operating systems used by the software development projects. Although people with such specialized skills could be placed within the software development and operations support functional areas, there are personnel attraction and retention considerations that may warrant separate grouping.

Quality control

Quality control typically is a review and audit function. The only "doing" type of task normally found in this function involves participation in the modification of standards and procedures. This function is normally attached at the staff level of the software area, but should have a direct reporting channel to higher management to ensure its functional independence.

Software technical environments

The term "software" is an all-encompassing word covering a wide variety of programming products. Development and maintenance effectiveness for may types of software products largely depends on the software development environment provided for the technical staff. An efficient software development system improves productivity by liberating programmers from unnecessary routine work, by automatically coordinating the program development efforts of different persons on the same project, and by providing systematic means for producing high quality software and supporting documentation. The specific configuration of a software environment must be closely tied to the nature of the software products to be developed in order to be most cost effective and to afford maximum support to the technical staff. One important consideration in establishing an efficient software development environment is an emphasis on in-house support software to support the development and maintenance of the end product applications software.

A host computing system is one on which an application software product is developed and is necessarily fully equipped with a wide range of support and utility software. The host is also the system necessary to fix or modify an application's software product. A target system, on the other hand, is the system on which the application's software is to ultimately operate in the end user's environment. In some cases, such as commercial computing centers, schools, scientific research centers, or any large-scale mainframe installation, the host and the target systems may he the same. In other environments, such as commercial "turnkey" systems (point of sale systems, air line reservation systems, small accounting systems), process control systems, or military field computers, the host and the target systems are often considerably different. For environments in which the end user's target system configuration is compatible with the vendor's host system, a full range of support software can be provided at the end user's site that will permit software updating and maintenance in the field. Such environments also permit the end users to develop their own applications software if so desired. In a turnkey computer environment, it is usually not desirable nor economically feasible to provide facilities within the target system for field development or maintenance. Often the end user of such systems is not knowledgeable in computer usage or programming; the systems are deliberately designed to be used within the context of their intended applications in the same way that an automobile is designed for use by a driver rather than a mechanic. In fact, the support function can fix the software without going near the user's installation.

Software development tools and facilities

A host computing center should have all the sophistication with respect to system software capabilities, software development tools, peripheral hardware devices, and languages necessary to make the most efficient, highly productive use of the technical talent available. A typical modern, medium-scale development environment is shown in Figure 10.3. A centrally located host computing system is provided that can support a community of real-time, interactive terminals located at remote programmer work stations. The host also has the capability to communicate with and download programs to a target system. The host software is capable of simultaneously supporting the interactive terminals in the foreground and a batch job stream in the background. The conversational timesharing nature of the interactive terminals typically provides each development programmer with a problem-solving work station, complete with system control commands, a library of time-saving development and debugging tools, a word processing facility for program documentation, a selection of program language compilers, and a prompt-driven help system.

A comprehensive host system configuration is only part of the story. A software "craftsman" must have the proper tools to perform efficiently and effectively. The state of the art is currently far beyond the historical software development approach of manual debugging, wholly dependent on the wits and deductive skills of the programmer, with little use of the computer for debugging assistance. Today's "tools" permit extensive use of the host computer to carry out the clerical work necessary to build software properly and to eliminate the inherent guesswork. Some of the generic software "tools" available to today's software practitioners are:

- Structured program design languages (PDL) to clearly map a design. This is the latter-day successor to the classical flow chart
- Structured application-level languages to facilitate structured programming methodologies and to minimize the need for assembly coding
- Interface documenters to generate complete and clear cross-reference documentation at the object module level, thus minimizing interface errors and improving productivity
- Symbolic debuggers to provide interactive debugging facilities at the work station and to accelerate software testing
- Tracing, testing, and optimization tools that can allow management to establish, facilitate, and enforce methodologies and standards for software tracing, testing, and optimization and to provide an audit vehicle for quality assurance
- Word processor to expedite the uniform documentation of source programs and to provide an easy facility for keeping software documentation abreast of software code development
- Productivity library to facilitate the use of data structures in structured programming and to allow the use of prefabricated sections of code
- Memory management package to provide the software developer with a selection of dynamic memory managers that minimize the amount of data space required
- Library of preprocessors to facilitate the generation of portable programs between dissimilar machines

  Configuration control facilities to assist in the orderly and consistent management of software revisions and releases. This facility can also support automatic backup and archiving of software modules and programs

Conventional approaches to software development in the past generally have made little use of the computer to assist the programmer in developing quality software products. Today's software tools, on the other hand, make extensive use of the computer to carry out many of the clerical tasks inherent in the development process and, thereby, eliminate much of the guesswork and costly rework that have plagued the software industry in the past.

Data processing (DP) users are becoming more and more confused about the different approaches to producing and maintaining their software systems. Some talk of expensive methods within the framework of a strict phase concept, others of simple, friendly user languages which will satisfy users' requirements simply and cheaply. What is the case of this apparent contradiction? The answer is readily at hand. The field of data processing has become ever larger and, as with everything which grows, has split into subfields. Contradictory tendencies develop for the different application areas, and the user, depending on which area he is currently concerned with, things that the approach used there is the only correct one. One firm quite often has three different application areas, namely:

- technical and scientific processing
- process data processing
- commercial data processing.

Technical and scientific processing

Here great emphasis is placed on creating a prototype of the product. The developer and the user are often the same. There should be as few formalisms as possible, and a strict phase concept is not adopted. Most programming is done in FORTRAN. The most important factor is the static and dynamic analysis of programs. Osterweil's TOOLPACK" toolkit package is characteristic of developmental approaches in this area.

Process data processing

Here the emphasis is on a valid processing concept with accompanying quality control of the project. Here the specification and verification of programs should be as formal as possible, and so specification languages and test techniques are very important, as critical control processes must be correct and reliable. This need not be overly expensive, as such process control usually has only limited amounts of data and functionality. Programs are written in languages such as PASCAL, PEARL and ADA. Lauber's 'EPOS' system and Alford's 'REVS' system are characteristic of the developmental approaches in this area.

Commercial data processing

There are two different approaches to commercial data processing. On the one hand, increasingly high-level languages are becoming available which allow the user or the developer to program, test and get applications running quickly and easily without too many formalities. This tendency goes alongside decentralization of corporate data processing. It is supported by PC systems such as DBase-III and Open Access as well as by 4th generation languages such as NATURAL, RAMIS, FOCUS, IDEAL and MANTIS. What all these systems have in common is that they offer users a relatively simple interface for defining their ideas. The developer can therefore be a layman. These widely varying approaches come within the framework of individual data processing. On the other hand, there is much discussion of software engineering and the software life cycle. Here expensive methods such as HIPO, MJSD, SADT and Structured Analysis are used and programming is done in languages such as COBOL or PL/1. The development process is divided into phases and is subject to strict control. Developers are professional programmers and analysts.

The nature of software engineering work is subject to numerous conditions. Almost half the cost goes on documentation. The other half is taken up mainly by systematic testing. The actual programming is the smallest part. The basic difference between these two subfields of commercial data processing consists in their opposing objectives. In individual data processing the system is simply a willing and more-or-less intelligent 'slave' of the individual person. The user can do with it what he wants. He can input data in various forms, store it, and view it on demand. The user is self-sufficient, that is, he can solve his problems quickly and cheaply, independently of anyone else.

There are, however, complex applications which cannot be implemented in terms of a short dialogue between the user and the computer. These are mainly applications involving a number of people, primarily automated processes such as stock control, job processing and payrole management, which have to be planned and specified just as carefully as process data processing and programming, which must maximise their use of available resources.

Individual data processing programs are thrown away once they are obsolete. They are designed to be disposable from the start. Automated processes are different. They are maintained and developed over many years., Maintenance represents more than two-thirds of their costs. This leads to the emphasis on the systems' maintainability and extensibility, highlighting such characteristics as modularity, flexibility and ease of maintenance. It should not, therefore, be surprising that the development costs of such a system are many times higher than those of individual programs. It is in the nature of the beast. Management of corporate software development must therefore include, as a prime requisite, a typology of software systems in the company. On the one hand we have the classical division into:

- technical and scientific systems
- production control systems
- commercial systems.

We should note that these systems may overlap considerably. On the other hand we have the newer division into:

- individual, short-lived programs
- complex, long-lived systems.

Different methods and tools are necessary for each of these types of system. The dream of a uniform procedural model for all software development in a company is just as unattainable as the dream of a single model of society. This is the first lesson that a software manager must learn. He must also, like a good politician, be in a position to make compromises between, and even coordinate, conflicting interests and working practices. That is the true art of software management.

Software system types

The typology of software systems gives us three types of software system in all application areas:

- throw-away systems
- static systems
- evolutionary systems.

Throw-away systems

Throwaway systems are the result of individual data processing. In general, they are implemented by one person at the site of their application for one quite specific purpose. They are of only local importance and can be written inside six months are minimal costs. According to Gumaraes, their average lifetime is less than two years. They are neither maintained nor developed further. When they are obsolete, they are thrown away. Such systems can be likened to daily newspapers, which are of only transitory value.

Static systems

Static systems are integrated operational applications in a well-defined area of application. While they are of universal importance, they can be written within two years. After that they are maintained and developed to only a limited extent. Their annual rate of change is less than 10%; in other words, they are relatively static. Once developed, they remain in use until they become obsolete on technical grounds.

Evolutionary systems

Evolutionary systems are systems which come into being step by step through iterative repetitions of the software life cycle. Each passage through the life cycle expands the available system and makes it more complete, so that the development of such a system can last many years. The system will pass through several intermediate states or versions during its development. Applications for such systems are not sufficiently precisely defined and/or they are constantly changing, so that the development process is never completely finished. Maintenance and further development can hardly be distinguished from one another. The cost of the first version is of course only a fraction of the total cost of the system. It is therefore very important to plan and document these systems carefully.

The software life cycle

The 'software life cycle' is a central concept in software engineering. This encompasses the view of the software development as an iterative process or as a loop, in which each iteration builds on the results of the previous iteration. There is no final result, as the applications that the software represents are themselves always in a state of flux and the technical environment in which the software exists is also changing. A software system is therefore maintained as long as it is needed and is not obsolete. Software becomes obsolete to the extent that it can no longer be adapted to the changes in the application. Software systems are similar to biological systems in this respect. They arise out of a painful birth, require intensive care at the beginning, slowly mature, reach their state of maximum benefit after several years, become increasingly inflexible and difficult to suport, die, and leave behind experience from which grows a new generation of systems. This birds-eye view of software development is one of the most important prerequisites for successful software management. The project manager must always be aware that his project is only one iteration in a series and that his results are the starting point for the next project. Each software element should therefore be constructed such that it can be changed or extended at any time with minimal effects on other elements. For the purposes of project management it is worthwhile dividing the development of complex systems into three stages:

- primary development
- further development
- maintenance.

Initial development

Initial development is the first iteration of the software life cycle. It derive from a limited system, perhaps a prototype developed beforehand to serve as a model of the production system. On the other hand, the system might, first be formally specified by modelling the application which is to be automated. In any case, the system passes through several phases in which the operational requirement is translated into an executable and reliable product. Finally the product is introduced into the company according to the agreed delivery criteria.

Further development

Further development represents those iterations of the software life cycle which follow the operational introduction of the first version and where the system is extended and made more comprehensive. Static systems undergo no further development, only maintenance.

Evolutionary systems may however pass through numerous cycles of further development until the system is fully mature. Each passage through the phases of the life cycle gives rise to a new version of the software. Each version enhances and completes the previous version. The rate of change can be as high as 5% to 25% from one version to the next. This change entails the simultaneous updating of all the software elements, the specification and documentation as well as the programs and test suites. A software system quickly becomes obsolete if all its components are not compatible with each other. This step-by-step further development of a complex software system makes considerable demands on both the software developer and the software manager. Discipline and systematic ways of working are essential here.

Maintenance

Maintenance denotes keeping a system in a functioning form. This includes correcting faults and, in addition, adapting the software to changes in the technical environment. Changes in component systems, such as database systems, graphics terminals and operating systems must be catered for immediately. Critical errors must be corrected or avoided. Functional changes are only undertaken where previous performance has to be maintained. For this reason, the cost of maintenance is sporadic and so difficult to plan. It is therefore ad hoc in nature and should not be confused with the planned phases of further development.

Software development phases

A project is a passage through the software development cycle. In consequence, a software product is a version of a system, one stage in the automation of an area of application. As projects can take up to two years, they last too long to allow effective project control. Management, however, needs to be able to measure the progress of a project. In addition, many individual activities in a project must be structured, and to this end projects are divided into phases.

There are many different phase concepts, typified by those of the DoD, ACM, IEEE and IBM-FSD. Almost every company that produces software has its own phase concept with its own terminology for the phases. One of the best-known phase concepts in Germany is ADV-Orga's ORGWARE concept.

What almost all phase concepts have in common is that they differentiate between implementation and planning. Implementation involves producing the kernel of the software the programs themselves. Planning involves designing the system as a whole. A distinction is also usually drawn between application-oriented and technical planning. Application-oriented planning leads to an application concept, whereas technical planning leads to the technical DP concept. There is often a difference, too, between programming and testing in the implementation stages. Finally, there is a phase at the end of the project to allow for delivery and introduction of the new product. Hence we have the following five project phases:

- application specification
- system design
- programming
- testing
- delivery.

Application specification

In the application specification phase, the requirements of automating an application are established, analysed and assigned priorities. They then serve as a starting point for the rough specification using a function model and a data model. The external users' view and the internal data structures are drawn up from the data model, and program structure and decision logic are drawn up on the basis of the function model. Finally, all the data and function elements relevant to the application are catalogued. This phase should result in a comprehensive, formal, consistent and plausible concept for the application.

System design

During the design phase the application concept is translated into a technical DP concept for the particular target environment. This involves converting the logical data model into a physical database schema, the logical function model into a program outline and the user views into physical masks, reports and so on. A test environment is designed at the same time. In this phase developers use data description languages for the relevant database systems and use program specification languages to design the programs. The aim is to standardize the data structures and to ensure that the programs are modular and structured. This phase should result in a system design that is ready to be implemented.

Programming

In the programming phase the design elements are coded into a particular compiled programming language and/or a database language. This should bee the least problematical phase of all, as program coding has recently become highly automated. This phase should result in executable programs and accessible databases.

Testing

The first part of the test phase is to run the individual program modules in a test framework, checking their logical correctness. This involves testing each branch of a module, validating all results and confirming that all the parts of the module work together as they should. Here the programs are being checked against their specification. Next the databases are fed test data, terminal interfaces are simulated with test masks and the programs are tested in combination with one another and with the databases. Here the interfaces are being checked. Finally the programs are tested in this latter environment with actual users and under real production conditions. Here the system's interaction with the user and with the technical environment are being validated. This phase should result in a fully tested program system.

Delivery

In the last phase, the fully tested system, complete with the application's documentation, is handed over to the end user or installed at the end user's site. At this point the programs may be checked again to ensure that they conform to their guidelines and to the application documentation. This phase results in an automated or semi-automated application.

Aims of Software management

In a narrow definition, software management has two main aims:

- to increase software productivity
- to improve software quality.

In addition to these purely technical aims, the software should serve the following corporate financial aims:

- the automation of all corporate application
- machine storage of all corporate data.

These four aims are of course interconnected, and so it is not possible to pursue one aim without affecting the others. In the final analysis, everything is related to everything else.

Increasing software productivity

Software productivity is measured in units produced, be they statements, function points, components, data elements, decisions or a combination of these elements. What is important is quantifiability of productivity. Without being able to quantify productivity, we cannot measure it. Without being able to measure productivity, we cannot measure the extent to which we have achieved our aim. Software is, of course, a multidimensional product. Individual phase results — the application concept, the system design, the programs, the test environment, the user documentation are in one dimension. In the other dimension we have the measures of the phase results, such as the number of:

- objects, procedures, functions, data, decisions and relationships in the application concept
- databases, DC-interfaces, data records, data fields, processes, programs, modules and pseudo-code statements in the system design
- database descriptions (DBDs), maps, modules, branches, paths, arguments, results, predicates and statements in the programs
- test cases, test data, test procedures, test drivers and test stubs in the test environments
- pages of text and diagrams in the user documentation.

Improving software quality

Software quality is measured by a variety of characteristics, such as:

- reliability
- security
- efficiency
- user friendliness
- maintainability
- adaptability
- portability.

Here, too, we must quantify quality. For example, reliability can be measured by the relationship between the number of errors and the number of test cases, or maintainability by the relationship between the cost of maintenance and the cost of development. Quality is of course relative to the user's expectations. For some users, security is everything, while for others it is efficiency, and for yet others user friendliness is the most important factor. Quality characteristics must therefore be weighted according to the user's criteria.

Automating corporate applications

The degree to which corpoarte applications are automated is measured by the extent to which the firm's functions are supported by machines. I measure this of course implies that we need to know the firm's function Only then can we determine which of these function are automated.

Functions requireing physical energy should be carried out by robots and functions requiring mental energy should be carried out by programs. This means that the application is completely automated once no-one working in the pure application area.

Automating corporate data

Automation of corporate data is measured by the percentage of the firm' data which is stored on a machine and can be processed by machine. Her too we must of course know what data the firm needs. We can determine this from an analysis of corporate data, and at the same time we can establish which of these data items are stored on machines. Stored on machines mean that the data exists in a codified, machine readable form which programs can access without human interaction.

Software management tasks

With regard to the aims stated above, software management is responsible for a series of related tasks ranging from analysis of the firm's operation through to management of existing software systems. In particular, this includes:

- establishing and documenting corporate applications (both actual an target)
- establishing and documenting corporate information requirement (both actual and target)
- defining and costing DP projects to meet requirements
- planning and managing DP projects
- managing DP systems in operation
- advising users on the use of the DP systems on offer.

It should of course be borne in mind that, alongside these mainstream activities, software management has numerous peripheral activities such as looking after corporate users, advising corporate managers and extending the actual production environment. The introduction of modern software technology is in itself a far-reaching project which demands many resources without, bringing immediate benefits. Benefits are only gained in the medium term from the firm's own software production and improved quality. Nevertheless such support tasks are indispensable for the achievement of the main aims.

Establishing and documenting corporate applications

To achieve the aims of automating corporate applications, the software manager must know to what extent current applications are automated and to what extent they should be automated in the immediate future. He must therefore examine the firm's procedures and data flows, identify individual processes and determine the level of automation. This actual situation must be documented and at the same time a projected target situation must be modelled incorporating a higher degree of automation of existing applications. This should be done by using procedural analysis methods.

We should mention at this point that on-line data processing is only a temporary state of automation, a state of semi-automation. What many proclaim as progress, namely tying the user to a terminal screen, is for others a new form of salvery. The user is forced to react to the machine and to serve it as part of the on-line access to a system, be it a PC or a host.

Establishing and documenting corporate information requirements

An analysis of information requirements goes hand in hand with the analysis of corporate applications. here we have to establish which data is used from existing applications, how it is used and in what form it is stored. Once this is done, the next task is to establish future information requirements on the basis of the applications planned, i.e. how the corporate data is to be structured, stored and used. Here information analysis methods should be used. It ought to be obvious that total automation of a firm's operations presupposes machine capture of all corporate data.

Analysing corporate requirements

The demands made on data processing arise out of the difference between the actual and the target state of affairs, both in automating functions an storing data on machines. It is incumbent on the software manage measure this difference and to define various levels of automation. E level should be achievable within two years. In addition, the demands should be categorized by subject area. The demands can then be divided their respective subject areas and time units.

Evolutionary software implies hauling oneself up from subject are subject area and from level to level. Automation is therefore implemented in many small steps instead of in one large jump. The demands are dealt one after another.

This of course presupposes that all the data processing demands can precisely formulated, identified and recorded. That is the task of demand analysis.

Defining and costing DP projects

A DP project is a bundle of tasks having a time limit. The aim of the tasks to achieve a higher level of automation. A project may encompass on more demands. Defining a software project involves determining the scope of the target software system which is to be produced or altered. Software systems defined in terms of their quantity and quality. The quantity of a system i sum of all the affected elements in the system plus the sum of their relationships. The quality of a system is the product of its quality characteristics.

Costing a software project involves calculating the expense and duration of a project. The quantity and quality factors are accompanied by productivity factor. To be able to cost the project, the software man must be able to establish the productivity of his software developers and to compare quantitative and qualitative demands with the time and cost constraints. The result is what is feasible for the project.

Planning and managing DP projects

Once a project has been evaluated and authorized, the software man has to plan and manage the implementation of the project. Planning a software project involves dividing it into phases and phases into tasks. At the same time the product is divided into p products and the partial products into individual resuls. Then a time-scale for the tasks must be drawn up and their interdependencies must be explicit. Finally, corporate resources must be allocated to the tasks.

Managing a software project involves monitoring deadlines and cost as well as progress and quality and, if necessary, making corrections or altering plans. Deadlines and costs can be derived from an acounting system. The project's progress can be measured form the number of tasks completed. Product quality can be determined with appropriate machine aids as well as from reviews and inspections. Planned deadlines, tasks, progress and quality are regularly compared with their actual counterparts to establish any variances from the plan.

Introducing and managing finished systems

Developing a complex DP system is one thing, introducing and managing it is another. Introducing the system entails allocation of necessary corporate resources, training users and often reorganizing the areas affected. It is obvious that this is not a painless operation. It is not only staff that have to be systematically prepared from a new system; the corporate organization must also be adapted, particularly as far as communication with neighbouring systems is concerned. This is a difficult corporate economic, sociological and technical task.

Once a new system is in use, the software manager has to maintain the software components of the system. To do this, he must use the techniques of configuration management. ALl the software components and documentation in use must be identified and recorded. The state and location of the software must be tracked and responsibility must be regulated. In addition, error reporting and changes must be kept up to date. The software manager is responsible for recording all reported errors and changes and for ensuring that they are included as new demands. This requires a certain software 'bureaucracy'.

Looking after software users

A final, but no less important, task of the software manager is to look after software users. As long as there are people who have to interact with systems, there will be problems with man-machine communication. It is therefore incumbent on the software manager to make staff available in a user support centre —who can advise and help users in carrying out their daily tasks. This is just as true for systems developed in house as for systems acquired from outside.

The support staff must, of course, themselves have been trained in the use of the new systems as well as in dealing with users. This support task is becoming more and more important as automation increases.

Software project planning

Phase 1: Project definition and planning

Staffing: The anticipated project leader and his or her manager should work closely to develop the documents required for completion of Phase I, calling on technical expertise as needed. External assistant may be required.

Problem definition: Entry into Phase I assumes that user requirements or a market study provide general project justification, or at lease Phase I justification. The first step in initiating any project must be describing the general problem to be solved. The result should be a brief but formal problem definition.

Initial project Plan: After the user (marketing manage-ment) agrees with the written problem definition, the next step is to develop an overall project plan showing critical path developments and a brief description of each research and development (R and D) problem that must be solved. Reasonably detailed cost estimates on Phase II must be prepared, possibly with minimum and maximum limits.

Review: It is necessary to conduct a formal review of the general project definition and plan as well as required changes by developer and user. Copies for reading and time for commenting should be provided before scheduled meetings. If the effort is justified, changes should be incorporated and the project should proceed to Phase II. Review should not terminate without countersignatures representing user and developer management agreement.

Phase 2: Functional analysis and specification

Staffing: Phase II requires the experience of people knowledgeable with the problem of user/costomer interface. User personnel must be dealt with carefully at all levels, and the analysis team must be groomed for marketing purposes. This is not the time to show off individual technical expertise or cleverness. The user must believe that his or her problems are in the hands of people who sincerely want to help. The use of outside expertise knowledgeable in the particular application area can be vital.

Analysis of overall system functional requirements: Unless the user constrains particular hardware specifications (for example, a particular printer, modem, and so forth), hardware should remain unspecified. At this time the user should be encouraged to be completely open as to what is desired ideally as well as realistically. Obviously, the final system must lie between the present system and the ideal system.

Development of Overall System Functional Specification

This specification, in conjunction with the initial documentation set, should completely define the user functional requirements. No reference should be made to specific hardware types unless constrained. This must be a joint development effort with user personnel who will be involved in operating and using the existing system.

Continuation plan: With the functional specifications completed, the overall project plan should be revised or refined, along with cost estimates and a detailed plan for Phase III.

Review: The last step of Phase II is to review specifications, plans, changes, and cost estimates with user /management, ensuring that total functional requirements are well defined and explained and that the plan is acceptable. If the effort is justified, changes should be incorporated, and the project should proceed to Phase III. Incremental movements from each phase to another through a formal review "gate," enable potential project problems to be adjusted.

Phase 3: Environment analysis/specification

Staffing: Emphasis during this phase must be on the enlistment of highly qualified technical personnel, particularly in the advanced systems area. At least one person should be aware of the latest technology available. Real-world experience in a similar application area is also vital.

Technology analysis: Existing hardware/software technology, applicability, and trade-offs should be analyzed to meet overall system functional specifications.

Hardware environment synthesis: The system hardware environment should be synthesized, on a building-block basis. For example, computer processors and peripherals for both the development and field environments should be selected.

Software environment synthesis: The system software environment should be synthesized, on a building-block basis. For example, operating system, language, and support software should be, selected for both the development and field environments.

Hardware/Software System Specifications: These specifications should reflect the hardware/soft ware synthesis requirements as stated above.

Preliminary documentation set: A detailed user's manual should be completed, along with the remaining detailed functional documentation, including system outline, output formats, database descriptions, and input formats.

Continuation plan: A more detailed project plan should be developed, nailing down any unresolved R and D elements along the critical path. A more detailed cost estimate should be developed, particularly for Phase IV.

Review: Specifications, documentation, changes, and estimates should be reviewed with user/ management, ensuring a clear understanding of approach. If the effort is justified, changes should be incorporated and the project should proceed to Phase IV.

Phase 4: System design

Staffing: Programmers who are expected to write code for subprograms called for in the system outline should be selected to help write the corresponding detailed program documentation. In addition, particular staff members should be given specific responsibility for coordinating each of the following areas: total system documentation, detailed test procedures and full cycle test implementation plan, and quality control standards and procedures.

Detailed Program Documentation: The detailed design and corresponding documentation of each program module must include detailed narratives on each subprogram and specifications of all references, both internal and external to each module.

Detailed test plan: This must include detailed test schedules and a description of the required data sets needed to test each subprogram as part of a regression test set.

Quality control plan: Procedures should be developed for maintaining, refining, and enhancing the system, ensuring system identity and integrity of the product libraries as changes are developed and implemented.

Continuation plan: The final detailed continuation plan should include formal specifications, documentation, and cost estimates for the critical design review.

Critical design review: The critical design review evaluates the continuation plan and required changes. At this point the user must be made to understand the potential level of difficulty of incorporating changes once program development (Phase V) is under way. A reasonable amount of time should be allowed for this review/revision period because of (1) level of complexity of the decisions at this time, (2) volume of documentation and corresponding effort for changes, and (3) fermentation period to allow review of how changes propagate through the system.

Phase 5: Program development

Staffing: After the written, detailed system software documentation is reviewed, it may be desirable to shift personnel assignments. This is a critical decision step. It is most desirable that those designers who have written satisfactory documentation remain to supervise writing of the corresponding code. Poor documentation will generally indicate lack of understanding or the inability to supervise or write good code. Also, the personnel resources required to produce an adequate test set should not be underestimated.

Program development/integration: It will be necessary to coordinate emphasis on the development of critical path programs to facilitate proper test plan implementation. For example, it is necessary, to ensure construction of input edit and database update programs before accessing the database for processing and output.

Hardware facility coordination: Scheduling of required hardware facilities for compilation and testing may be crucial, depending on the environment for this phase. It is easy to accumulate day-by-day slippage owing to improper coordination of hardware test facilities, conversions, and so forth.

Test set development: As compilation gets underway, programming personnel should have gained sufficient knowledge and should have been provided sufficient time to develop detailed test procedures. In any event this time period must be planned in advance, with emphasis on input interface and database maintenance programs to ensure database integrity. It is imperative at this time to isolate personnel responsibility for the coordination of detailed test procedures and materials for a regression test set to be used in whole or part each time the system is modified.

Continuation plan: A detailed plan should be developed for operational testing (Phase VI), and plans for future phases should be refined. A detailed cost estimate should be developed for operational testing and for future phases. Sufficient resources should be included to ensure integrity of specifications and documentation for project intracommunications as well as user review. Plans for long-term system/product support and distribution should be developed at this time.

Review: Specifications, documentation, changes, plan, and estimates should be reviewed with user/ management, ensuring clear understanding of system operation and the approach to projected effectiveness of the operational testing plan.

Phase 6: Operational Testing

Staffing: Direct management responsibility for coordination of operational testing should be assigned to a specific individual. The objective is the development of a set of full system tests with effectiveness that is satisfactory to both user and developer management. The responsibility for operational testing must be kept separate from completion of final documentation and coordination of user requests for review and modification.

User personnel training: The user personnel training period provides the opportunity to "shake down" the documentation--for example, the user's manual and the operations manual--as well as the system itself. This period usually generates requests for modifications that should not be introduced without following formal procedures.

Full-Cycle acceptance testing: Final full-cycle acceptance testing must be performed with user personnel (or the equivalent) under simulated real-world conditions in order to be effective. For software products, initial versions usually can be given out at no cost to friendly users to accomplish real-life operational testing. Such user installations generally are known as alpha and beta test sites.

Quality control procedures: Formal distribution and support procedures should be implemented. Finalized procedures for processing requests for corrections, refinements, and enhancements, must ensure a thorough understanding of both user and developer management regarding the generation of new versions and releases.

Final documentation: Additions to the documentation set that depend on final program construction must be incorporated at this time. Assignment of this function to someone other than the originating programmer can be an effective method for review of internal documentation, programming practices, and skill, as well as the detailed external documentation.

Continuation plan: A detailed plan should be developed for cutover to installation and support (Phase 7), and any future plans should be outlined. Cost estimates should be included for steady-state operation as well as for the initial period. Allowances for formal modification procedures should be included as should recovery procedures to cover (1) on-site restart and (2) abort and return to operational testing phase.

Review and acceptance: This is the final review and acceptance of documentation, changes, plan, and estimates for installation and support with user and developer management. Emphasis is on recovery, maintenance, and modification procedures. Written approval and schedule to proceed should be obtained.

Phase 7: Installation and support

Staffing: Staff considerations during Phase VII include users in selecting any additional personnel required beyond those participating in operational testing, shifting present personnel where desirable, and selecting personnel for user training. The developer should assist the user in selecting user interface as well as on-site or on-call personnel for system support and in evaluating requirements for implementing and controlling product library changes. Ample time should be allowed for this step and the next before system production begins.

User personnel training/guidance: Off-site as well as on-site classroom sessions should be provided for all personnel, both user and support. Ongoing training for new and backup personnel should be considered.

Full operation implementation/product release: Timing and coordination usually are critical. Plans must include abort timing and corresponding personnel activity or nonactivity. Revovery procedures should be well documented and understood.

Quality control implementation: Formal support procedures are required to determine responsibility for system errors and the corresponding correction process. Notification for correction requests can be initiated by the system support agent as well as the user. The divergence of identity of multiple fielded systems can prove catastrophic in most applications; its avoidance depends on well-disciplined support procedures to ensure congruence. Formal procedures for processing requests for system refinements and enhancements are necessary to ensure that required resources are scoped properly and that allowance is included for preserving system identity and integrity of the product libraries. Accumulating modification requests is desirable as long as the system remains operable so that total documentation and program modification efforts can be grouped into new releases. Quality control procedures should be strictly followed for all modifications that are under direct management responsibility for process and approval. The objective is to ensure reliable operation within an effective test bed, simulating real-world conditions before each new release. Continual refinement of the regression test set and corresponding documentation will afford procedures that are easily implemented and controlled.

Continuation plan: The level of continuation planning required depends on the level of activity and scope of modification requests. Plans will fall into three basic categories: hold, implement, and major system rewrite. Major modifications should be initiated at an effective phase and developed in accordance with successive phases as applicable. Major system rewrites should start back at Phase I.

Review: The level and formality of reviews depends on continuation plan activity. In any event, formal user/management reviews should be undertaken at least once annually.

Software maintenance

System management entails planning, controlling and monitoring software maintenance. The question is, though, what is software maintenance, and what happens in the maintenance phase? The maintenance of software is fundamentally different from that of hardware. Hardware components wear out and thus no longer deliver their original level of performance. Defective hardware components have to be identified and replaced by new ones. It is therefore important to build hardware in a modular fashion so that worn-out components can easily be replaced. With software the situation is different. Software does not wear out. Many components do have defects built in from the beginning, but that is another story. Software does, however, age to the extent that it can no longer meet the demands of its environment. To understand that, we must first understand the nature of software. Software is a representation of a model of reality. Data records are representations of data objects, which in turn represent real-world entities. Programs are representations of processes, themselves representing actual events or business operations. If the operations or information requirements change in real life, the model must change too and software with it.

Obsolete software is therefore software that has not kept up with the physical environment.

This physical environment can be viewed in two ways. On the one hand, there is the technical or business application that the software is supposed to support. This may be a manufacturing process, stock control or a corporate information system. Changes in the application necessitate changes in the software, which may involve simply redesigning the VDU screen layout, bringing a new file on-line, or changing the decision logic. On the other hand, there is the software's DP environment. Every application is part of a particular DB-DC environment, running under a particular operating system, on a particular computer. There are usually numerous interfaces between the application and this environment. If the environment changes, e.g. the database system is enlarged or the method of data communications changes, the application software must be adapted to suit the new conditions. The software systems that the users develop are therefore sandwiched between two moving layers, the application above and the technical environment below. It has to be updated continuously to remain current.

Apart from the necessity of keeping software up-to-date, software differs from hardware in two other respects:

- defectiveness
- time and space efficiency.

Software defectiveness

In general, hardware is tested much better than software. The amount of testing carried out on normal applications programs is shockingly low. It has been shown that programs have around 1.5 errors per 100 lines; the programmer will recognize around 50% of them. That leaves approximately 0.75 errors per 100 lines still in the program. A 10 000 line program would therefore have 75 errors in it. Only some of these errors are discovered before the software goes into use. Many are spotted only once the software is in production, and the resulting costs are considerable. The localization and correction of such errors is termed maintenance.

Time and space efficiency

Newly installed software systems are not only unreliable, but in general they also gobble up resources, i.e. they use more time or space in carrying out their tasks than is actually necessary. Programs are seldom optimized before they are first released. This led Michael Jackson to formulate the motto, 'First structure, then optimize'. Optimization therefore comes under maintenance as well.

Looking at a software system that has been released clarifies the nature of software maintenance; it entails:

- corrective measures

- progressive measures.

Corrective software maintenance

- stabilizing (removing errors)
- optimizing (improving performance).

Progressive software maintenance

- making alterations
- expanding the system.

We can turn to much of the literature to support this definition:

- *Ogdin* describes maintenance as keeping the system up-to-date and modifying it: 'Maintenance is the continuing process of keeping the program running or improving its characteristics. Program modification has as its objective the adaptation to a changing environment.

Riggs defines maintenance as 'the activity associated with keeping operational computer systems continuously in tune with the requirements of users, data processing operations, associated clerical functions and external demands from governmental and other agencies'.

Mooney sees maintenance as the interdependence between the three activities 'repair, revisions and enhancements'.

Swanson divides maintenance into three categories:

(1) corrective — dealing with processing, performance or implementation
(2) adaptive responding to anticipated change
(3) perspective enhancing processing efficiency, performance or system maintainability.

Boehm distinguishes only between 'software update' and 'software repair'. In the first case, the demands change, in the second, they do not. Gilb defines the notion of' evolutionary software development'. The represents a software development strategy in which complex applications systems are developed step by step.

The first release of a system is seen simply as a prototype or test version which is designed to stimulate a dialogue with the user the so-called zero version. The first production system is released afterwards, this being the first version that the user can actually work with. This does not however mean that the user's requirements have all been met, for new requirements appear as the system is used more and more. The system is constantly expanded from version to version, from level to level, in an iterative and incremental way. Weaknesses are removed and new functions are added. The system slowly becomes more mature. This sort of evolutionary software development sees no difference between development and maintenance. We can however make the distinction between:

- stabilization
- optimization
- changing functions
- extending functions.

The term 'maintenance' is misleading.

The importance of maintenance depends greatly on the nature of the application. End-user programs written in a language such as SQL, APL, BASIC or NATURAL do not create any maintenance problems, as there is no maintenance they are throwaway programs. They are written quickly and cheaply to meet a momentary need. When the need changes, a new throwaway program is written. Throwaway programs have a maximum life expectancy of two years. The situation is different with integrated systems designed to automate organizational procedures. These systems have to be planned and developed in an engineering manner. If the application is well defined and relatively stable, there will be a development cycle and a maintenance cycle. During the development cycle the system is specified, programmed and tested. During the maintenance cycle, the original version is corrected and improved slightly.

Applications that are difficult to define or are very dynamic obey the laws of evolutionary software development, where the system is simultaneously maintained and developed. In this context, maintenance is equivalent to further development.

The attention that has been paid to maintainability therefore depends greatly upon the type of application:

- End-user systems are hardly maintained at all; they are replaced instead. Their maintainability is therefore irrelevant.
- Integrated applications developed over a period of up to two years and expected to last up to seven years will almost certainly have to be maintained, as they will change by up to 10% a year during their lifetime. These systems must be designed to be maintainable and extensible from the outset. This means that the programs must be as modular, as standardized, as structured and as parameterized as possible. It falls to software quality assurance to guarantee that this is the case. What is skimped in development will be paid for many times over in maintenance.

Evolutionary applications which take from two to five years to mature and last over seven years require a high level of maintainability, portability and extensibility. Quality assurance plays an even greater part here. If the system is not modular, flexible, portable and well-structured, it will never mature properly. We therefore need constant configuration management to keep an eye on any permanent changes. To a very large extent it is a picture of reality and so is subject to changes in reality. It is quite different from simple static systems and requires central control and ongoing quality assurance.

Categorizing software systems properly and then planning them accordingly is a management task with far-reaching consequences for life cycle costs. Anyone who tries to develop an evolutionary system with the methods and tools of throwaway systems will have to pay dearly later on.

Software configuration management

The term 'software configuration management' describes all the activities relating to the checking and maintenance of existing software systems. Until now, 'software development management' has been at the forefront of research, but increasing maintenance costs have meant that configuration management is becoming more and more important. Lientz and Swanson's latest surveys show that 53% of costs are devoted to maintenance, as against 47% to development; the maintenance of existing systems has become the largest factor in software costs. It has also become obvious that the management of software maintenance obeys laws different from those of software development. It therefore requires a different management technique, a method concentrating on maintenance. Configuration management has arisen in response to this need. We need to answer the following five key questions:

(1) Why configuration management?
(2) What is being managed?
(3) How is it being managed?
(4) With what is it being managed?
(5) Who should manage it?

The first question addresses the purpose of configuration management. Why has it become an indispensable part of software engineering?

The second question deals with the definition of software configuration. What is it that is being managed, what is the subject of configuration management? The third question relates to the method of system management. What activities does the new discipline entail?

The fourth question is devoted to the tools of configuration management. Which tools are needed, to manage software systems efficiently and cost-effectively? Finally, the last question is one of organization. What form of organization is best suited to managing existing software systems?

Purpose of configuration management

Configuration management is part of software engineering and, like much in that discipline, stems from the field of hardware production where it is used to identify and describe individual parts, as well as to monitor their assembly and maintenance.

In a conventional production process, project managment encompasses:

- planning
- organization

- management
- control.

Configuration management makes the control function operational. As such, its purpose is to make the production and maintenance of complex systems more transparent so that these systems do not get out of control. Configuration management plays a similar role in the field of software production. A software system, like a hardware system, consists of a large number of individual parts whose quality and quantity are critical to the functioning of the whole. The whole is only as good as its weakest part.

The number of elements is particularly high in software production. This is not only because software systems contain a large number of parts, but also because each element appears at least twice and sometimes three times:

- as executable code
- as a formal development document
- as an informal user document.

Configuration management has to ensure that all three incarnations are current and agree with each other. Every change in the code must filter through to the development and user documents.

This strict control is necessary to avoid the software becoming obsolete or breaking down prematurely. A software system can be compared to a biological system. It grows slowly, reaches a stage where it more or less works, increases its functionality and, sooner or later, reaches a point where it is no longer adaptable and starts to die. Any defect in its development causes it to age more quickly. The consistency of its parts can be guaranteed, and its functionality prolonged, only by disciplined and systematic working. This is extremely important in view of the enormous costs of software development. The purpose of configuration management is therefore to bestow the longest possible life on the software system. In contrast to system development, it is a discipline of preservation.

Subject of configuration management

The subject of configuration management is the software system. Until now, software has been understood to mean, more or less, the programs which contain the executable code. The software configuration, however, comprises two component types:

- non-executable
- executable.

What is executable and what is non-executable code has not yet been defined. Pseudo-code that the processor can work with is also quasi-executable, and the same is true of test data assertions. The non-executable components must therefore be subdivided as follows:

- formal
- informal.

A function description written in English is an informal document. The same function in a design language is a formal document. 'Formal' denotes everything that can be processed by another program.

We should remember that software configuration deals with three component types:

- executable code
- formal documents
- informal documents.

These individual components can be grouped according to their level of abstraction, their usage, or their common objects.

As far as abstraction and usage are concerned, we have:

- a specification or technical concept
- a design or technological concept
- the programs themselves
- a test concept
- an integration concept.

The *specification* or *technical concept* includes all the formal and informal documents describing the system from the application view point, i.e. the data and function requirements.

The *design* or *technological concept* consists of all the formal and informal documents describing the implementation from the view point of the virtual machine, i.e. the data organization, program structures and interface designs. The *programs* are made up from the descriptive and executable code pieces, i.e. the data description and procedures.

The *test concept* includes all the documents formal and informal describing the test environment, the test data and the test procedures, along with the test data and results themselves. The *integration concept* contains all the documents necessary for the system's integration and introduction, including the user documentation and instructions for use.

This is the horizontal or phase-oriented view of software. There is also a vertical or function oriented view. For example, all the documents, program pieces and test data relating to a particular process can be brought together in one software group. The same is true of data objects.

Software components can be grouped in different ways, depending on the point of view. As far as configuration management is concerned, it is only important to identify clearly each component, each document, each section of code and each test data procedure and to be able to put them in order. This is the prerequisite for configuration management.

Methodology of configuration management

Any method of software configuration managment must take the software system life cycle concept as its starting point. This concept envisages the system passing through particular phases before it matures completely. The system thus develops slowly in different stages of functionality. Each passage through the life cycle results in an executable, but incomplete system with additional functions and data objects. In principle, then, the system is never finished; it simply reaches higher levels of functionality. The system is only finished when it is not worth investing any more time or money in it. This process is also called evolutionary software development.

At each stage of development the development passes through the same phases. The phases themselves are still debated, but in general they are as follows:

- *definition phase,* where new requirements are evaluated and the scope of the next stage of expansion is laid down (planning)
- *specification phase,* where the new, extended, technical concept is worked out in detail (technical conceptualization)
- *design phase,* where the implementation concept, the database design and program designs are drawn up (DP conceptualization)
- *programming phase,* where the data descriptions and modules are coded(implementation)
- *testphase,* where the programs' static form and dynamic behaviour are examined (verification and validation)
- *integration phase,* where the components of the system are brought together and installed in their target environment (introduction)
- *maintenance phase,* where the latest stage of the system is stablized and optimized.

These or similar phases are a vital prerequisite for manageable software development. Configuration management *per se* cannot be used without them. Configuration management has the following four major functions:

- configuration identification
- configuration control
- configuration tracking
- configuration checking.

Configuration identification is the clear recognition and description of each software element. Every process and function including their associated modules and test procedures along with every data object and data element including their related data descriptions and test data— has to be identified and described. This requires a naming convention and a central catalogue, a project library in which to record these elements.

Configuration control is the process of accepting, recording, checking and authorizing all error reports and changes desired. This is where all software system requirements are dealt with. No changes may be made to the system without passing through this control process. This of course means that the necessary organizational and technical measures must be taken, such as setting up a change request committee and designing a suitable request form. To categorize requirements better, we can subdivide them into:

corrections
changes
extensions.

Configuration tracking means that the effect of every correction, improvement, change, or extension to the existing system is measured to see what its impact on the software components is. Here we want to establish which software elements are affected, and by how much, and which new software elements are added. We must be able to trace all the ramifications of any change from the technical concept, via the DP concept, through to the actual code and to the user documentation. Every change leaves a long trail through the software configuration. Configuration tracking aims to find this trail and to follow it.

Configuration checking consists in checking whether the corrections, changes etc. carried out are reflected in all the parts of the system, i.e. in all the documents and code sections affected. A module must not be changed without the corresponding design, specification and test procedures being changed as well. The different software components must agree with each other at all times, otherwise the configuration becomes inconsistent. Configuration checking should ensure that code and design are maintained at the same time, for failure to do so can lead to the system's downfall.

Tools for configuration management

Appropriate tools are an important prerequisite for configuration management. These tools must be rather more powerful than traditional programmers' aids, for not only are programs being managed, but specification and design documents and test data and procedures are too. In addition, error reports and change requests should be automated as much as possible. A configuration management toolkit must therefore provide a whole series of different tools.

Configuration management is based on the project database or project library, where both formal and informal documents and programs are stored. Here we need rapid and accurate access to programs and documents, a friendly editor and some way of recording any changes made. At least six tools are necessary:

- a text editor for managing informal documents and user documentation
- a data dictionary system for managing programs
- a program library management system
- a test system for managing test data and test procedures
- a project management system for managing requests and error reports
- a revision system for comparing partial databases.

The *text editor* stores textual documents and allows them to be changed. It is important that the system records any changes so that they can be understood later.

The *data dictionary system* stores the elements and relationships in the specification and design. This system is different from the text editor in that the designs are stored as discrete elements with pre-defined attributes and relationships. The actual design documents are generated on demand. This system must also allow the user to change designs easily and to recognize what changes have been made.

The *program library system* stores macros,, source segments and object modules. Here too an editor is important for editing source code. Different program versions must be listed here to aid configuration management, and the differences between versions are marked and recorded. The *test system* stores the test data, test procedures, drivers and stubs. It must also provide a means of bringing the test environment up-to-date and recording any changes made to it.

The *project management system* stores error reports and tracks their status. This system must allow regular reporting, must enable the user to find out the status of requests, and allow the developer to change their status.

The *revision system* compares partial databases with each other so as to report any differences. This tool exists to ensure that the software configuration is consistent.

Organization of configuration management

The key to success in configuration management is finding the right form of organization even more so than in development. Responsibility for configuration manage-ment must be clearly distributed on the basis of expertise, and everyone must know what they should do when.

Configuration management demands an *authorization department for configuration control.* This may be a working group, a standing committee or one individual, but in any case the department must be able to decide whether, and in what order, to carry out:

- error corrections
- improvements
- changes desired.

This department therefore needs secretarial assistance to collect, record and store requests.

Next there should be a department which *checks the implementation of requests*, such as a quality control department. On no account should this be the project leader or the developer, however, as the point of the checking would then be lost.

Finally, the developers who maintain the software configuration, i.e. make corrections, changes and improvements, should be organized along the same lines as the configuration. Each subsystem should be allocated to a particular developer, and there should be a chief developer responsible for the system as a whole who coordinates the subsystems. It is important to adapt the maintenance organization to suit the software configuration, as this makes it easy to determine who is responsible for which errors, changes or extensions.

Configuration management is not fundamentally new. Similar procedures have existed for a long time in other fields. It is only new in the field of software because we could not define what software configuration was before now. Once we have done that, the other steps the procedures, the tools and the organization follow automatically. One thing is certain: the more software is developed, the more will have to be maintained. Too little attention has been paid to software maintenance for some time now. The task of configuration management is to rectify the situation.

2
Quality Control

All of the foregoing management methods for project definition, estimation, design, and documentation are precursors to the task of writing the code or programs. Therefore it is imperative that the same attention be given to programming standards and practices as was given to the previous development phases. Programming standards typically follow lines prescribed by Ledgard and Cave. Specific choices, of course, depend on the particular characteristics of the programming language being used and the requirements of the project under consideration. Recent experience has demonstrated that the economics of development, integration, and, particularly, the support of software is enhanced by using certain new approaches to writing code. These new approaches include top-down programming, structured programming, and GO TO-less programming. After one has used these new approaches sufficiently, their usefulness becomes obvious. In addition, the resulting standards are easily enforced.

Considering the acclaimed impact that programming languages can have on the economics of software development and support, relatively little has been done to scientifically measure the effects of one language versus another on the software lifecycle cost curve. We have located only two papers that deal directly with productivity as a function of language. The conclusion is not surprising: Productivity is highest when the language is closest to English. What is surprising is that COBOL, which was designed to be an English-like language, was not considered in any of the comparisons. Literally hundreds of programming languages exist today, each emphasizing certain types of capabilities, features, or applications. Software vogues are constantly changing, with some languages at times appearing to enjoy higher popularity than others. Languages such as BASIC, Pascal, and "C" are currently popular in the microprocessor field. However, published statistics show that the majority of software for production usage is written in COBOL, with FORTRAN used second most. Both languages have been around for a long time and therefore carry longevity. So, too, have ALGOL and PL/1.

We acknowledge the many other languages that exist and the theoretical reasons why they should be in the number-one spot. Certainly they will be used if they are good. However, as we stated in the Preface, we are addressing only those methods and techniques that have proved themselves in the competitive software product market environment. Therefore we limit our discussions to COBOL and FORTRAN.

On the positive side, neither of these two languages is standing still. COBOL enjoys the National Bureau of Standards acknowledgement as the only language that provides the basis for complete standardization and portability. This is because in COBOL, all data is specified in terms of number of characters or digits. FORTRAN 77 provides many of the features desired for structured programming, and it has extensive support facilities for scientific calculations. FORTRAN is used as the base language for many special-purpose languages because of its natural expression of algebraic relations. Both FORTRAN and COBOL enjoy the strong support of standardization efforts that are prerequisites to their use for a major software product to be rehostable.

Overview

The standardization approaches presented here contain principles that at first may appear controversial because they rule out the use of many "sacred" concepts used in programming. These principles are:

1. The readability of programs is the most important programming factor affecting the economics of the lifecycle cost curve, particularly the cost of long-term support.
2. The transportability of software from one machine to another makes it much more valuable.

Although it is clear that writing quality programs requires more effort and deeper thought, the overall economics will repay the practitioner. The thrust of this chapter is to suggest guidelines for good programming practice as well as rigorous standards for writing quality programs. Developing rigorous programming standards is not easy, for the rules should be unambiguous, of sufficient merit so that a programmer will not be unduly stifled by their adoption, and, ideally, machine testable.

The importance of developing such standards is clear. There is great value in adherence to uniform rules so that programmers may more easily read and understand programs written by others. There is a need to use coding techniques that reduce the complexity of programs and ensure portability from one machine to another. There is the need to control the entire programming effort. Ultimately, program standards should be automatically aided and enforced.

No standard can attempt to cover the particular aspects or operating environment of a given programming project. In fact, many features are ruled out to remove ambiguity and ensure transportability and supportability. For those issues not covered, one must trust that a wise programmer will distill the spirit of standardization and apply creativity and good sense to the program at hand. Finally, no attempt is made to consider the consequences on efficiency. If a particular implementation causes inefficiency in the adoption of standards, then this may be due cause for revocation. However, one of the major roles of a manager during the coding process is maintaining a vigilance against the sacrifice of economic effectiveness for coding efficiencies.

Cobol standards

The following is a sampling of standards based on the COBOL language.

General rules

1. For each installation and project application, there should be a standard set of user-defined words. The rationale here is to develop a well-accepted set of naming conventions and to reduce the time spent by programmers in devising good (but different) names. Having a standard set of words will promote a high degree of readability of programs and will Prevent confusion over different names for the same objects. Enforcement of standard names is best accomplished by using the copy library of COBOL to define standard data descriptions and procedures, and the data element dictionary. These can be inserted in programs using the COPY verb described later in this chapter.
2. Columns 1 through 6 are used for statement sequence numbers, right-adjusted if unfilled. Columns 8 through 72 are used for COBOL statement contents. Columns 73 through 80 are used for system/module identification. Certain interactive systems provide attractive but contradictory features, discretion must be exercised. Under no circumstances, however, should the statement length exceed 65 characters. The rationale here is to maintain independence from a particular compiler, editor, or librarian.

Identification division rules

1. The AUTHOR paragraph must be given in every program. In the program development phase this must include the names of all persons who have written or changed code for the program. The rationale here is to allow quicker access to the originators of a program should problems arise during program development.
2. After a project is beyond the program development phase, as changes are being made comment lines following those for program identification must be updated by appending a brief comment that refers to the software change authorization (SCA) corresponding to the change being made. This comment should contain the following:

- SCA numbers corresponding to the changes
- Date that changes actually were made
- Name of person making changes
- Any comments relating to the differences incorporated in that particular version of the module

If other equivalent documentation facilities exist (for example, through the use of an automated librarian), pertinent comment lines may be inserted. The rationale here is to make error detection in operational programs, easier. As is often the case, a change made to a program can introduce errors in other program sections. The modification record is a valuable aid in detecting such errors. In addition, as changes are being made, various versions of a given module can be generated. The programming standard will provide for the identification of those versions.

Data division rules

1. All database descriptions contained in the database specification must be maintained in a copy library, external to the processing programs. These descriptions can then be copied into place using the COPY statement. The rationale here is to place all shared database descriptions in a common library so that all programs that access the data will use correct descriptions with uniform naming conventions.

Procedure division rules

1. All input/output is to be done in separate paragraphs, allowing only one READ statement for each file and only one WRITE statement for each different length and kind of output record. This procedure is enforced by putting all input/output statements within a separate input/output section. For example, use

```
    PERFORM UPDATE-SCAN-TABLES.
    IF (NOT ABORT) OR (NOT END-OF-INPUT)
       PERFORM READ-INPUT.
    IF END-OF-INPUT
       PERFORM SCAN-WRAPUP.
I-O-SECTION.
READ-INPUT.
      READ INPUT-FILE
              AT END MOVE 'E' TO INPUT-FILE-STATUS.
      IF      NOT END-OF-INPUT
              ADD 1 TO LINE-COUNT
```

The rationale here is to isolate those portions of a program that interface with external files.

2. If there is any possibility that the type or value of data that is input external to the system is not correct, and thus can cause an error in subsequent processing, the input must be followed immediately by a test that edits and validates the type or value of the input data. The rationale here is to detect input data errors as soon as they enter the system.
3. The maximum length of any paragraph is 55 lines. The rationale here is to have the length of each paragraph limited to a page of printed text.
4. GO TO statements are not allowed. With some practice, programming without GO TOs becomes quite easy. When you think you need to GO TO, consider: (a) restricting the algorithm, (b) performing blocks of code, (c) copying in a piece of code, (d) repeating a condition previously tested, or (e) reversing a condition to its

negative. The rationale here is to force the programmer to think ahead and use only 1-in, 1-out control structures. In COBOL this means using the PERFORM, IF, and PERFORM-VARYING-UNTIL constructs for flow of control.

5. The THRU option for PERFORM statements is not allowed. The rationale here is to make the program logic independent of the physical placement of paragraphs.
6. Nesting of IF statements may be three levels deep at most. If deeper nesting is desired, separate procedures should be used.
7. The IF verb can be used for a "multiple-choice" or "case" statement of the form:

```
IF CONDITION - 1
        STATEMENT - 1
ELSE IF CONDITION - 2
        STATEMENT - 2
        .
        .
        .
ELSE IF CONDITION - N
        STATEMENT - N.
```

The statements within the case construct must be simple and may not include additional IF statements. The rationale here and in 6 is to avoid having confusing conditional constructs.

8. STOP RUN or EXIT PROGRAM may occur only as the last statement of the main program (that is, the main paragraph or section of the program). The rationale here is to make the logical exit of a program identical to the lexical end of the main program.
9. Parentheses must be used to specify the order of evaluation for the individual conditions of a complex conditional expression. For example, use

```
IF (NOT QUIT-STATE) OR DISPLAY-STATE
   PERFORM RESET-INPUT-BUFFER.
IF ((DISPLAY-LINE-NUM LESS THAN MAX-
   DISPLAY-LENGTH) AND
   (MSG-LENGTH LESS THAN FIELD-SIZE))
   OR UP-CURSOR
      PERFORM PROCESS-MSG.
```

not

```
IF NOT QUIT-STATE OR DISPLAY-STATE
PERFORM RESET-INPUT-BUFFER.
IF DISPLAY-LINE-NUM LESS THAN MAX-DISPLAY-
        LENGTH AND
  MSG-LENGTH LESS THAN FIELD-SIZE OR
```

```
UP-CURSOR
PERFORM PROCESS-MSG.
```

The rationale here is to make logical operations visible without relying on the often confusing precedence rules.

10. Wherever possible, conditionals should be defined using 88-level definitions in the data division, rather than logical expressions within the conditional procedure statement. The rationale here is to structure the condition details separately from the higher level conditional procedure.

Cobol alignment standards

For displaying the logical structure of a program, the organization of well-spaced programs is critical. Because the time required to space programs may sometimes be laborious, the ultimate solution is an automatic preprocessor for respacing programs according to alignment standards. A sample of such standards is given here.

General rules

1. Between each division, section, or paragraph place a sequence of blank lines that is longer than the maximum sequence of blank lines within the previous division, section, or paragraph.
2. Use at least one blank line between a division header and the first nonblank line of the division.
3. Place division and section headers on a line by themselves starting at column 8.
4. Place paragraph headers on a line by themselves starting at column 8.
5. Do not break words or numeric literals across lines.
6. Indent continuation ines four spaces from the starting column of the initial line.

Environment division

1. Start the computer names of the CONFIGURATION section, the SELECT-NAMES, and I-O CONTROL paragraphs on separate lines starting at column 12.
2. Place subordinate clauses of the SELECT statement and other similar paragraphs on separate lines indented four spaces.

Data division

1. Separate the independent data division aggregates--that is, FD entries along with their following data description entries--by a sequence of blank lines longer than the maximum sequence of blank lines within the previous aggregate.
2. Place at least one blank line before each 01 level data description entry.
3. Start level indicators (FD and 01 level numbers) at column 8.
4. Indent the level numbers of immediately subordinate items of a group item at least two columns (four when possible) from the starting column of the level number of the group item.
5. In an FD entry with multiple clauses, place each clause on a separate line, indenting each clause four spaces from the starting column of the entry name.

6. Do not split nonnumeric literals of a VALUE clause onto a continuation line.
7. If the descriptive clauses of a data description entry do not fit on one line, attempt to indent the starting columns of continuation lines at least two spaces from the starting column of the last descriptive clause.

Procedure division

1. Do not place two or more statements on one line. The only exception is for lengthy sequences of short statements logically grouped in pairs or triples on one line.
2. Align the starting columns of the statements making up a sentence and the sentences making up a paragraph. The general rule is to align logically parallel constructs.
3. Align the word ELSE in a conditional statement with the corresponding word IF. Indent the statements in the IF part and the ELSE part at least four spaces.
4. Place phrases such as AT END, WHEN, INVALID KEY, GIVING, USING, TALLYING, VARYING, UNTIL, and AFTER on separate lines, indenting the start of each phrase at least four spaces.
5. List each procedure (level 2) performed by the main program (level 1) immediately after the main procedure. Subsequent procedures (level 3) performed by a procedure in level 2 must be listed just after level 2, and so forth. Within levels, the order of listing is up to the user. Two exceptions are allowed: (1) procedures called from several levels and (2) procedures that logically are related (for example, 1/0 routines). These may be grouped as desired by the programmer.

The COPY Feature

One of the most effective features of COBOL is the COPY verb. In brief, the COPY verb allows the insertion of program text from an external library. This feature has many advantages for writing large systems.

The format of the COPY statement is simple:

```
COPY TEXT-NAME {      } LIBRARY NAME
```

The effect of compilation of a COPY statement is to replace the COPY statement by text written in the COBOL library. The COBOL library may contain three types of entries:

1. Entries for the identification or environment division giving security comments or equipment oriented information.
2. Entries for the data division giving descriptions of files, reports, a working-storage items.
3. Entries for the procedure division giving procedures or sections for commonly used routines

The advantages of using the COPY verb backed up by a suitable library are many:

1. Descriptions of external files may be copied into place, thus ensuring that all programs that use the files have identical descriptions. This also ensures uniform program names for objects in the files.
2. The use of standard user-defined words for a given project can be enforced by copying their description into working storage.
3. The use of standard procedures for input/output, file updating, and so forth, can be facilitated.
4. Writing of programs can be simplified, as the user need not type in segments of code given in the library.
5. Errors can be reduced, because once the library entries are correct all accessing programs will be correct.
6. The entire programming effort can proceed more quickly as the library facility grows to handle more cases.

Thus with a sufficiently developed library, the COPY feature can significantly upgrade the entire programming process, allowing the rapid development and cost-effective support of high-quality programs.

The foregoing standards are a sample effort to promote high-quality COBOL programs. This concern is a familiar one to all managers and programmers who face day-to-day problems in the development of software systems. Although the adoption of good programming conventions is only a part of the effort to produce high-quality software, we believe that the standards given here are a solid step in the right direction.

Fortran standards

FORTRAN is the grandfather of algebraically oriented languages; its use was already established as early as 1958. Over the years it has evolved into a standard language for scientific programming projects. An official standard issued by ANSI in 1966 has enjoyed wide acceptance by the computer industry. This standardization made it possible to transport FORTRAN programs developed on one computer to another computer without significant modifications. Gradually, FORTRAN applications broadened from strictly numerically oriented problems to more general applications involving character and file manipulations. This evolution made it necessary to extend the capabilities of the FORTRAN language. In 1977 ANSI issued an enhanced FORTRAN standard that includes the 1966 standard as a subset. Today both FORTRAN 66 and FORTRAN 77 are used, depending on the particular compiler version supported by various operating systems.

Transportability criteria

Transportability is one of the most attractive aspects of any standard language. The maturity and wide acceptance of FORTRAN makes it particularly attractive as a portable language. In certain cases, however, total transportability is not actually realized. There are usually some machine dependent aspects to be considered when a language is moved from one machine to another. The ability to divide machine-dependent and independent attributes into separate entities by subprograms greatly enhances the transferability of programs. Furthermore, the ability to compile these entities individually aids in the speedy checkout of transferred modules. Programs may be written as a collection of smaller routines, compiled and tested individually, and put together in building-block fashion into' large assemblages without recompilation. In this way, machine-dependent code may be economically isolated into separate modules. Typical machine-dependent functions may be:

- Precision of variables
- Special input/output
- Error checking and recovery
- Operating system interfaces
- Particularly stringent real-time applications

Coding techniques and rules

Paradoxically, the more clever the programmer, the less likely that transportable code will be produced. That is, many commonly used techniques or "tricks" in FORTRAN programming are severely detrimental to program transportability because of implementation differences inherent to individual compilers. The following is a list of some practices of techniques that generally should be avoided to assure the generation of transportable code.

1. A DO loop should not be terminated with a complex statement as an IF. Many compilers that allow termination of DO loops of IF statements disclaim the predictability of results.
2. One terminal statement for several nested DO loops should be avoided. Some compilers put special restrictions on nested DO loops that terminate on one statement. For example, a particular compiler may only allow the innermost DO to transfer directly to its termination point.
3. Compilers may have inherent table size restrictions on character length. Therefore, literal strings of length greater than 255 characters should be avoided.
4. Altering a DO parameter within a loop may produce varying results depending on particular compiler mechanization of the DO. Therefore, it is generally a good practice not to alter a DO parameter within a loop.
5. Testing for floating-point zero is a risky practice and should not be done. Example:

```
IF (X. EQ. O. O) GO TO 10.
```

Because of inherent inaccuracies of floating-point representations, a test for a specific number may fail when it actually should pass.

6. Ambiguous statements such as

```
N = N+FUNC (N) N
```

where FUNC(N) alters N depending on the particular implementation of the compiler's scanning algorithm. If the original value of N is not stored in another temporary location, FUNC(N) may destroy it.

7. Compiler implementation of division by zero may vary. Division by zero may result in values zero, 10^{39}, and so forth, or may generate an error condition depending on the system. It should not be assumed that some finite value will result from division by zero.
8. Most compilers do not allow recursive subroutines. They usually are difficult to support and should not be used.
9. Some compilers will not handle missing arguments (variable length) in a subroutine CALL successfully. Generally the number of arguments is assumed to be fixed. Therefore, it is generally wise to avoid variable-length argument strings in subroutine CALLS.
10. Incremental compilers cannot handle scattered type, dimension, and DATA statements.
11. Do not assume a loop is always executed once. Example:

    ```
    DO 10 I = 4, N
    ```

    where N=3. Loops of the form DO 10 I = K, J, where J K may or may not be executed once depending on where the test for completion is implemented.
12. Using large numbers as DO indices may cause problems in compilers in which the DO loops are implemented in index registers, thereby setting an upper limit on index values. Example:

    ```
    DO 10 I = 1, N
    ```

    where $N = 2^{17}$.
13. Never transfer into a DO range. Most compilers do not guarantee the results of transfers into a DO loop.
14. Do not assume that an incorrect computed GO TO variable will result in a default condition such as "falling through." Some compilers generate code for testing the computed GO TO arguments. The last statement label or next statement becomes the error condition default.

Some additional rule-of-thumb guidelines are:

1. Avoid usage of extensions to the standard being used. This includes avoiding FORTRAN 77 capabilities that are not part of FORTRAN 66, if that is the standard to be used.
2. Document extensively all dialect variations and machine-dependent code, functions.
3. Modularize programs into machine-dependent and -independent sections.
4. The FORTRAN external procedure permits interfacing to a non-FORTRAN

subprogram. This provides the capability of allowing subprograms written in assembler language (or another higher level language) to be referenced by a FORTRAN 77 program unit. Such interfacing should be done by strict adherence to FORTRAN 77 procedural rules. In the use of FORTRAN 66, it is good practice to avoid assembly language code interfaces.

5. Do not use programming tricks that depend on machine idiosyncrasies.
6. Design magnetic tape outputs for general compatibility. Avoid complicated blocking or binary outputs.
7. Always initialize storage; never depend on the system to do this for you.
8. Always assume the character set is variable. Do not make programs dependent on the internal character representation of a particular machine.
9. Plan to end the implementation phase with a test package (that is, a regression test set) that can be used in future transfers.
10. Estimate the range of data values and document them. The precision of integer and floating-point arithmetic in FORTRAN is machine and software dependent. If other systems to which the program is to be transferred have fewer bits assigned to the mantissa in floating-point representations, for example, the current data may generate over or underflows. These could go undetected, causing an inherent "gremlin" in the transferred program.

Software testing and quality control

Effective computer software testing and quality control procedures require the same level of management control as does writing the software. Software must be tested to identify faults and to confirm the correctness of its performance--*before the system is m ode operational*! Quality control (with emphasis on control) is the process by which operational software is built and maintained at an acceptable level of quality. Every aspect of a system's development and operational use must be handled with appropriate care, with no exceptions for these two supporting functions.

This chapter also advances a secondary theme, that test requirements can be identified as natural extensions of the system's design requirements. In addition, a system's test library is a principal tool of the quality control procedural package. The chapter addresses the subjects of software testing and quality control within the framework of the incremental method. Thus considerable detail has been applied to management control over incremental development and use of software testing to establish and maintain quality control.

There are far too many examples of data systems that do not provide the service required by the system's users. Each of these faulty systems fails, to some degree, to perform in terms of the following qualitative definitions:

- *Availability:* to provide the functions and services requested by the users
- *Reliability*: to provide accurate and dependable functional outputs required by the users
- *Maintainability*: to provide services supported by rapid recovery after failure

A system's inability to meet any of these performance measures usually can be traced to one of the following: faulty design, improper development, or inadequate maintenance provisions. These deficiencies often are not discovered until the system is operational, owing mainly to lack of appropriate testing and inadequate quality control planning during the system's development. Software is particularly vulnerable to poor performance when it is inadequately tested. It's effectiveness has proved difficult to verify within the system development process. Successful software testing is tied directly to design of the system. Quality of the design is likely to have greater impact on project success than quality of work at any other stage. The following design elements are essential:

- Documentation of each module must be prepared in depth and must be complete before programming is begun.
- Software testing plans and procedures must be developed in the same phase as the system design.
- Test data required to test the software must be meticulously selected as representative of the full range of live data.
- Preliminary correctness of each module is the responsibility of the programmer. Final certification, however, must be performed by someone other than the original programmer.

The means for proving software effectiveness must be prepared in conjunction with the software design. Also, the facilities to support software maintenance and future changes must be built into the system; therefore, planning for quality control must start no later than the design phase. If a top-down approach is employed in the software design and development, the preparation of tests and quality control procedures must track this top-down process.

A measure of software quality

As an aid to defining the lifecycle control problem, we subscribe to the measure of software quality described by Cave and Salisbury. Although this is a more quantitative approach than that of Wilbur, many of the conclusions are the same. Software quality, as defined here, can only be measured after IOC in a live operational environment. Before IOC, software quality can be predicted and controlled by measuring factors that affect it; however, the measure of quality offered here is considered essential in correlating the effects of such factors.

The measures of quality offered are not intended to be absolute. Their shortcomings, such as interdepen-dencies among functions, can be overcome by good judgment in determining the levels of availability. If one keeps a log of individual values of functional availability, then one can compute a new set of quality factors on changing the relative weights of functional importance; however, the significance of the measures lies with their interpretation. Note that availability can be improved by shortening the time it takes to bring a reduced level of availability back to unity; however, such efforts can increase the cost of maintenance and thereby offset potential improvements in the overall measure of quality.

Software testing and quality control planning

This section presents guidelines for defining the requirements and plans for both testing and quality control within the context of the incremental method. Statements on individual test plans and quality control procedures are presented in sequence with the corresponding phases. The assumption is that, during each succeeding phase within the incremental method, a more refined understanding of the testing and quality control requirements can be gained. This is a cumulative process.

Project definition phase

Activity during this phase yields the documented definition of system objectives, constraints, parameters, strategy, and preliminary system development plan.

Testing and quality control considerations

1. *Initial identification*: It is appropriate at this time simply to review the problem definition and identify areas within the preliminary system description that will require some form of testing. For example, if the system is to have real-time capability, a corresponding plan can be set for real-time testing.
2. *Related systems*: It may be appropriate during this phase to review other operational systems considered to have similar objectives and applications. Identify and note the methods used to test and maintain these systems.
3. *Development plan*: The preliminary system develop-ment plan requires only identification and gross scheduling of subsystem tests, full-system tests, and parallel tests.

Functional specification phase

Activity during this phase yields a set of system functional requirements and an updated system development plan.

Activity during this phase yields the documented definition of system objectives, constraints, parameters, strategy, and preliminary system" development plan.

Testing and quality control considerations

1. *Test criteria*: Before the functional specifications are documented, it is necessary to interview user personnel about their current and desired information-handling capability. Most responses to interview questions affect the testing and quality control requirements as well as system design requirements. Consider that each functional requirement can also be translated into a "test-to" criterion. For example, if the user's present system is automated, ask about the response-to-

inquiry time. The new system, when tested, ordinarily will have to equal and probably beat the old response time.

2. *User environment*: Determine how the user's present system is maintained and enhanced. This information will help identify constraints that may be imposed on the maintenance and change control procedures by the user's organization and operating environment.
3. *Requirements*: Because no individual or group can possibly remember the various potential test parameters and constraints required of a large system, it is best to record this information as it is uncovered. Test parameters and performance constraints form a major part of the functional specifications. Quantitative criteria may be necessary to further delineate the system's functional specifications. Examples of quantitative criteria are desired mean time between failure and desired mean time to repair.
4. *Plan update*: The updated system development plan should include any specific notations that can be made at this time about testing and quality control procedures. Activity titles in the plan should correspond to the terms used as testing and quality control procedures.

Environment specification phase

Activity during this phase yields hardware/software environment specifications, an initial system documentation set, and an updated project plan.

Testing and quality control considerations

1. *Test environment specification*: The testing environment must be described in precise terms. Considerable evaluation must precede the selection of hardware, system software, and the development support software environment. Virtually the same level of effort must be made to evaluate and trade off the test environment. Additional parameters and environmental constraints, such as the computer capacity and application language, must be included in the evaluation. Refer to the following section, "System Design Phase," for additional considerations.
2. *Walk-throughs:* The information gathered in the preliminary documentation set provides the first opportunity for a paper evaluation or "walk-through" of the system specifications against the test parameters and the operating environment constraints. The objective of this walk-through is to determine the adequacy and relevance of the test parameters and constraints. Separate individuals should determine whether there is one or more tests for each functional specification and whether each test is expressed in relevant, quantitative terms.
3. *Quality control comparisons:* A similar comparison can be made between the initial documentation set and the proposed quality control procedures.
4. *Review of technical approach*: Another reason for performing these walk-throughs is to raise the user's level of confidence in the technical approach selected. The

system's analysts should be able to state convincingly that they are sure of how to satisfy the user's needs. The results of these walk-throughs should also reinforce the justification for entering the system design phase.

From project definition through environment specification, the activity related to system testing and quality control have involved requirements definition, comparison, and evaluation. This cumulative process is required to minimize technical oversight. The results of these activities will be used in the next phase, system design.

System design phase

This activity yields a complete external system documentation set, a detailed test plan, an initial quality control plan, and a detailed program development plan with "build" schedules.

Testing and quality control considerations

1. Three important considerations should be mentioned first:

The system test library must be documented as precisely as the final software documentation. Change control procedures must be developed and imposed at the outset of the design phase as the first and principal element of quality control. Changes in functional or environment specifications must be initiated only for justifible cause and executed under tight management control.

The following outline is general and must be tailored to the specific application.

2. *Development test plan*: The development test plan and supporting activity schedule should complement and be as formal as the software development plan and schedule. As a minimum, the test plan should identify:

- The system by title and nomenclature, with appropriate cross-references to the external documentation set and development plan.
- The organization/personnel responsible for preparing the plan, the organization responsible for implementing and executing test, and the organizations that are to evaluate and approve the test results.
- A general overview or test philosophy that includes: testing objectives in terms of software performance, constraints imposed by the system's configuration, equipment and software availability, contractual considerations, and the methods selected for performing and verifying the tests.
- The identification and sequence of the various tests, identification of the product, and the report or activity milestone that signifies the end of each test.
- Listings of computer test tools, equipments, testing procedures, and physical locations for conducting the tests.
- A detailed statement on specification change control procedures.

The test plan is to be used as one of the principal references for developing the test library and quality control procedures.

3. *Test schedule*: The testing schedule should be prepared in conjunction with final review of the system documentation. By producing the test schedule before the program development or "build" schedule, the sequence of programming activities is brought into perspective directly. The rationale is that specific modules, programs, and supporting subsystems must be available to perform a test. It follows that these items must be identified along with their availability schedules in order to meet the test. Again, dates and durations of individual developments and tests must be included in the program development and test schedule when changes are considered. The development and test schedules are also management control documents.
4. *Testing process*: The testing process from the user's viewpoint is the reverse of the top-down development process. The general sequence is as follows:
   User requirements definition
   System design
   Subsystem design
   Module design and code
   Module test
   Subsystem test
   System test
   User operations

   The objective of this process is to identify errors early in the sequence, where they can be corrected with the least expense. The basic philosophy is build, prove through testing, fix if faulty, add to, and test with the previously proven modules and programs.
5. *Walk-through:* The best guard against incorporating an undetected error into the design is the walk-through. It is invariably less costly to spend the time and effort to confirm the soundness of a system's design than to rework the system after it has been built. The walk-through, performed on a group or unbiased individual basis, is an excellent test of the design before the design phase is terminated.
6. *Test library:* A major feature of the incremental development concept is the test library described in the next section. Briefly, the test library is the computer-assisted test tools plus the complete documentation of test parameters, tests, their limitations, and reported results for every module and subsystem. The test plan is the cornerstone of the test library development. The test schedule is obviously both the chronicle of past events and a forecast of the future. Growth of the test library must reflect the testing plan and process in the following manner:

Phase	*Test*	*Activity*
Development	Module	Individual program modules machine tested and debugged

	System	Total system integrated to check integration out under volume transactions and to determine capacity and dynamics
Operational	Parallel	Total system installed under an testing environment parallel to that planned under live operation, with the use, if possible, of live input to track a true parallel operation
	Acceptance	Full-cycle tests conducted to demonstrate performance in terms of operating capability, availability, and dependability
Support	Regression	Full-cycle regression test library maintained and ready to go for each new change

7. *Quality control plan*: Quality control is the planned and concerted effort to maintain system integrity and identity, along with service, at an acceptable performance level and an affordable cost. Like the development and test plans, a quality control plan must be tailored to the system it supports. During the design phase, an initial control plan must be prepared.

Four activities within a system's lifecycle must be controlled to assure the system's performance:

- *Development*: design and construction of the software
- *Operational maintenance*: fixing programs that fail during normal operation so that they will provide the service intended
- *Software refinement*: modifying programs to improve the performance of one or more existing functions
- *Software enhancement:* modifying existing programs or creating new programs to support one or more new functions

8. *Plan contents*: The quality control plan should have the same attributes of formality and compatibility as the other plans and schedules. It is to be used as the principal reference for writing quality control procedures. As a minimum it should identify:

- The system by title and nomenclature
- The organization/personnel responsible for directing the quality control program and for the training user and support personnel, together with the qualifications for training and the job descriptions for the support functions
- A general overview to include: quality control objectives as they relate to the particular system, with a careful definition of development, maintenance, refinement, and enhancement in terms of the system's needs

- Use of the system documentation libraries and test libraries to perform error detection and analysis, with emphasis on the pertinent areas (e.g., recovery procedures, etc.)
- The functional specification and documentation change control procedure
- The test library maintenance procedure
- The operational/performance audit procedure and attendant reports
- Quality control training and implementation schedules

Program development phase

During this phase individual program modules are coded, tested, integrated as functional programs, and retested. Coding is accomplished in response to the objectives and sequence prescribed in the development plan. The test library is constructed. Testing is accomplished in accordance with the test plan and schedule. The hardware, communications, and peripheral equipment are acquired, installed, and checked out. The system test plan is updated for the operational test phase.

Testing and quality control considerations

1. *Change control implementation*: The efforts put into test library planning, development, scheduling, and quality control procedures are challenged during this phase. First, change control must operate properly at the outset, or program rewriting efforts will result in chaos. It is assumed that better planning will result in fewer changes. It must also be assumed that some factor has been overlooked and that changes will occur.
2. *System test library*: The system test library must be developed and documented during this phase in conjunction with program coding. This is the ideal time for this activity because the responsible programmers now will have the opportunity to tune test procedures to the software as well as the system documentation. The object is to develop sequential procedures that will exercise and demonstrate the system's capability to respond to both partial and complete functional requirements. The procedures, when used, should show predictable results using both good and bad data as well as good and bad operating methods. Refer to the detailed description of the system test library and techniques in the prior section.
3. *Operational test plan*: During the latter part of the development phase, the test plan and procedures should be evaluated to determine their effectiveness for the operational test plan. Any revisions that are required should be made. This review is to aid in preparation of the operational test plan, which is the cornerstone of the operational testing phase. It fully specifies the acceptance test sequence, required personnel training, equipment deployment, and system activation. If the previous plans and results have been documented adequately, the final writing should involve no more than a recompilation of the pertinent "test-to" requirements, development scenarios, test reporting formats, and acceptance requirements.

Particular attention should be given to testing the modules and subsystems that have been subjected to change during development. It must be verified that the full-cycle regression test library has been maintained and that changes have been properly integrated.

Operational testing phase

During this phase, selected user operating and support personnel are trained for participation in the tests. Full systems tests are conducted, and quality control procedures, system documentation library, and test library are finalized.

Testing and quality control considerations

1. *User's exposure to system:* If this phase could be conducted within totally ideal circumstances, system capability would be demonstrated to show anticipated results and they simply would be accepted. In practice, it is common for the user to finally see (at this late date) exactly what services the system is designed to provide. The user then realizes what he must pay in terms of revised organization, policies, and procedures. Although he previously may have been told what to expect, now he can see the process for himself. The sequence of tests should be conducted in such a way that the user is given ample opportunity to observe, gain understanding, and comment on the demonstrated service. A vital consideration for successful testing and imple-mentation is early exposure of the user, who must be assisted to appreciate the system's limitations as well as its advantages.
2. *Test bed:* If operational tests are performed in a test-bed environment, the final acceptance tests should be performed on the target operating facilities. There may have been some technical accommodation (such as a translator) made to simulate "live" operations on the test bed that are not required in the operating environment. There may be a difference in software performance on the two facilities. These differences must be resolved in favor of the "live" operating system.
3. *Quality control plan:* The initial quality control plan, prepared during the design phase, is formalized now. The procedures incorporated in the plan must be executed and evaluated during operational tests. Those procedures that pass the evaluation are formally documented and included in the training programs for operating and support personnel.
4. *Quality control during tests:* Often there is a temptation during this phase to make changes in an expedient manner to gain the system's acceptance. Not every system requirement, however, will be met during the acceptance test. It can also be anticipated that additional functional capabilities may be requested just before or during the tests. Any major deficiency must be resolved before final acceptance. Action on minor deficiencies and additional capabilities should be deferred until after testing because knowledge of the whole picture may modify the changes. In both situations quality control procedures must be enforced to assure the system's

overall performance and integrity. Only after formal test and acceptance can the system be considered ready for live operation.

Installation and support phase

During this phase the system is installed and activated according to the implementation plan and schedule. Production (operations) control procedures are implemented under an appropriate operations coordinator or system manager. A system continuation plan is prepared and maintained as the reference document for controlling system operation, performance evaluation, system change, and ultimately the transition form the current system to its replacement.

Quality control considerations

1. *Implementation*: Between the time a system is accepted for installation and the time it is phased out, production and quality control are the two major functions of the system's manager. Under an operating philosophy, the maintenance, software refinements, and software enhancements are subordinated to the quality control plan. Software modification efforts, including the full range of testing and formal release for use, are to be considered a logical extension of the change control procedure. The system's test library is one of the tools that support these modifications. As changes are incorporated, the test and documentation libraries must be maintained accordingly. The significant concept of quality control is that both availability and quality of the system's service must be deliberately managed.
2. *System performance log*: Adequate documentation of system performance should be maintained during the system's operating life. A performance log, the system's performance specifications, performance audit report, operations status reports, and those change requests that were not acted on will provide an excellent source of information for defining the current status.

General considerations

1. *Testing philosophy:* A testing philosophy lays down the rationale for identifying test requirements and for developing and executing tests. The obvious but often neglected rationale for testing is:

- User requirements will change.
- The system will have errors.
- Revisions and modifications will occur before all of the system requirements are met.
- Changes will introduce new problems and errors.
- Errors can be costly during live operation.

System test requirements, which must be specific, grow from three simple propositions:

- Functional specification: What must the system do?

- Performance requirements: How frequent and fast must the system perform these functions? What are the tolerances, if any?
- Environment specifications: What constraints are imposed on the system's development/operating environment? When can testing be done? What equipments and support software can be used?

The system test should demonstrate:

- Functional performance with acceptable error
- Performance in time with acceptable degradation
- Suitability of the testing environment

Ground rules for conducting a test are:

- To qualify as valid, a test must be repeatable under prescribed conditions and testing environments.
- A test is not complete until all requirements are satisfied--that is, a go-no go condition, pass or fail.
- Tests are to be conducted as formally as possible, with the testing activity visible to everyone concerned.
- All test slippages must be reported, together with an analysis of the cause and, if necessary, the planned remedial action.

2. *Staffing*: Personnel assignments for system testing should be divided on the basis of three areas of responsibility:

- Preparation of test requirements in accordance with the functional and performance requirements; preparation of the test plan and requirements for test data
- Preparation of the detailed test data, scenarios, and documentation in response to the requirements and in conjunction with the design; maintainance of the test set
- Testing of the program modules after they are coded; reporting the results. Testing and exercising of the integrated subsystems to measure performance against the capabilities of the integrated system (which should be done independently from 2 above)

Major errors stem from improper interpretation either of functional requirements or their translation during the design phase. Such mistakes do not stem from coding logic errors. As a result, software for an interactive, database system requires comprehensive testing conducted under well-conceived and controlled procedures to minimize the risks of major errors and poor integration of programs.

These systems are complex because of a high degree of user interface, sophisticated systems software, communications, and concurrent processing of multiple transactions based on random demand. Variations on the following procedure can be devised to deal effectively with these complexities:

1. *Module or program testing*: The purpose of these tests is to search for and correct module logic/coding errors.
2. *Integration testing*: These tests are applied to integrated modules, or to programs to check out subsystem logic and operation of one or more complete system functions, including indicated errors.
3. *Single-thread testing*: A single input data stream is added to the system, and single transactions are sequentially entered and processed to further check out and verify the system's logic and individual functions.
4. *Multithread testing*: These tests require multiterminal simulation for entering multiple inputs concurrently to detect errors arising from simultaneous processing of a variety of transactions. Database update and inquiry modules will require input in both correct and incorrect order to properly exercise editing and control procedures.
5. *Volume testing*: A simulator can be used to apply a heavy volume of representative transactions on the system. All the file processing and other functions must be exercised to ensure that the cumulative results are correct. These test runs must simulate actual operating cycles, including system failure and recovery.
6. *Field testing*: Remote entry and receiving terminals must be installed to check out data-communications networks in all transmission modes. The terminals must be operated by both project and user personnel under near-actual conditions to check on the system's ability to handle variations and errors caused by the operators.

Techniques

1. *Top-down testing*: The testing process may appear to be bottom-up because input control modules must be developed before any testing can be started. These modules may include state control, input edit, transaction validation and control, and database updates. Such modules may require support programs that simulate the input of data and inquiry transactions. These modules must be designed and developed to the point that at least sequential functions or transactions can be processed. They should contain program exits or stubs for those modules that will be added in the future. Once these major modules are adequately tested and debugged, subordinate modules are added to the major modules and tested. It is this process that must be performed top-down.

At this point we should put to rest the issue of top-down versus bottom-up testing. Certainly Sherr's approach to testing satisfies what generally is considered the best way to construct and test a system during the program development phase. Yet, Sherr calls this method "bottom-up" and clearly justifies it. On the other hand, this approach as we have interpreted it satisfies the common definition of top-down testing. The discrepancy is easily explained: It merely depends on the viewpoint taken--that is, the functional (user) viewpoint or the implementation (developer) viewpoint. Design must be top-down from the functional standpoint, starting with the major outputs the user desires. Testing, on the other hand, must be top-down from the implementation standpoint-that is, top control and input modules first, reporting last. As it turns out, this approach appears "bottom-up" from the user viewpoint, which is Scherr's stance for both design and testing. Because the top-down testing sequence is a mirror image, in reverse order, of the top-down design process, it is obvious that implementation/testing cannot start until the design is complete.

2. *Regression testing*: Regression testing is a fault isolation technique that has proved successful in assuring software integrity while additional functions are introduced. The technique should be considered as a formal testing procedure. It is consistant with the top-down approach.

The regression principal is to rerun previous successful tests (before adding new functional tests) to measure the effects of a software modification once it has been integrated. In practice, new modules that have been individually tested are compiled with the previously tested major modules. First, the previous functional (regression) tests are run to determine if the presence of the new modules causes any problems. After the anticipated results are obtained, the functional tests for the new modules are applied in conjunction with rerun of the previous tests, or "tested base," to ensure the integrity and capability of the total system. The regression test sequence is a natural course to use with a top-down approach.

To recap, the scheduled sequence for adding functions should be:

- Build and test next level of modules.
- Integrate these modules.
- Perform regression tests with tested base.
- Test new function with rerun of augmented regression tests.
- Repeat procedural cycle until all functions have been added and accepted.

This "growing" procedure is carried over to the system's operational phase to be used in conjunction with the total system test set to support software quality control.

3. *Benchmark testing*: Performance requirements or comparisons are best measured using a set of benchmark tests. Benchmark tests should be designed to provide a clear measure of system response to input and processing functions that cover the time spectrum. These tests should be extensive enough so that their results define the crossover points of system response versus requirement satisfaction
4. *Test scenarios*: Test scenarios of single and combined functions have proved useful as structured test procedures. A script is prepared that identifies the user and operating environments. It prescribes the transactions, initiation, input, throughput (including file identification), and output. A good scenario instructs the test conductor to make a variety of errors, as well as to correct inquiries. The survey information gathered on the potential user's personnel, operations, current system, and tests applied to similar systems should provide a good basis for writing

realistic scenario scripts. These scenarios, refined after use in the testing environment, are useful as training tools and as part of the quality control package for use in regression tests.

5. *Walk-throughs*: Walk-throughs, as discussed in prior sections, are an economical technique for determining the validity and completeness of the specifications and planned tests. They can be accomplished in a variety of ways. One type of walk-through is simulated by a group of people working their way through the functional specifications, system documentation set, and program code, using a test case or scenario. Creating a matrix by listing the system functions on one axis and the modules in logical order on the other axis also may be desirable. The matrix then can be filled in to show where the modules implement and support each function. In addition, one may require the listing of inputs and outputs and a comparison of the lists to the code to derive cause-effect relationships. To avoid excessive and costly reruns, walk-throughs also should be required practice during the trouble-shooting of operational failures. These walk-throughs can be done if one has access to a computer-generated error report, a printout of the affected modules showing the status of the transaction when a failure occurred and the system documentation library.

6. *System test library:* The following test library items and documentation should be available for testing and quality control for each module and subsystem.

- A specification title page, with the date of preparation and signatures of the analyst and programmer
- The latest test output, dated, with the name of the person performing the test and containing listings of the printed transaction outputs with all controls
- The most recent specification change and release notices, with test requirements and test data
- Pertinent preceding test output sets and specification changes in reverse date order
- The most recent complete documentation for the module, with program listing, interface specifications, test requirements, and test data
- The control language listing for the operating system

If testing is conducted in a uniform manner, it is likely that any differences in output or any software failures can be attributed to the last "fix" or specification change.

7. *Testing aids*: There are almost as many testing aids as there are application systems. Available aids developed for previous applications will not work precisely for the next application, no matter how similar, without some adaptation. If existing computer equipment, attendant supporting software, and a proven compiler language are selected for a new system, the development risk is moderate. If, on the other hand, new unproven equipment and software are to be used in an application, or any of the applicable aids must be highly modified or newly developed, the risk goes up.

Among the variety of aids available, some are especially useful if a test bed is to be maintained to support the operational system.

Software product support

Many authorities state that 80% of the efforts devoted to software are expended on existing product support. This is because successful software products are constantly subject to change and evolution. The economic reality of software lifecycles is that requests, which necessitate changes and revisions, will be made by the users throughout the life of the product. As the product matures and user experience broadens, enhancements to the product will be introduced continually. The software end product, usually represents the major assets of a software company. These assets must be protected in the same manner as any highly valuable assets to ensure that their value is maintained and, in the case of software, continually enhanced. To accomplish this, all changes must be carefully documented and controlled.

System action requests

After a software product is installed into a customer's site, problems will arise that will necessitate vendor action. This situation will occur regardless of the preinstallation testing rigor. Some reported problems will be deficiencies within the software, for which remedies will be necessary. Other reports will result from misunderstandings, improper user operations, and so forth. As the product matures, most requests will be for improvements in system functional or performance capabilities. The basic objective in dealing with such requests for support is to satisfy the customer in a timely and efficient manner. Initial requests for action directed to the software support organization are defined herein as system action requests (SAR). These requests can be divided broadly into three categories: correction of deficiencies, refinements, and enhancements or change of function scope.

Correction of deficiencies

Requests for correction of deficiences result from errors encountered in the software. This implies that the software does not respond in the manner described in the user's manuals (the functional specification). Certain user predicaments may warrant "quick fixes" to the software, at the customer's site, without waiting for a new release. Such quick fixes must be handled with extra care. Corrections of deficiencies normally do not affect the functional specifications or design documentation.

Refinements

A second category is concerned with requests for refinement of current software. This type of change includes such objectives as performance improvement (e.g., speed), memory utilization (e.g., size requirements), and program structural changes to improve maintainability. Refinement requests generally will not affect the functional scope of the subject software, but will affect the design documentation.

Enhancement

Software changes may also be instigated by a request for new features, an expansion of existing features and functions, or an accommodation for a new application. These requests generally imply a change in scope, and many have extensive impact on the existing version of the software product. Initiation of the change usually is preceded by a formal plan and change authorization.

Software support overview

Software support is basically a two-step process, from initiation of a system action request until the change is incorporated into a new operational release. The first step requires analysis of the request, determination of the best solution, and authorization of prescribed changes. The second step starts with the software change authorizations and contains all steps necessary to ensure reliable implementation in a future release. These processes are best described in the context of a typical software support organization.

Software functional organization

Two functional sections report to the group manager: product development and product support. In addition, a quality control function reports directly to the group manager, which keeps it unencumbered by either of the functional sections.

Customer interface functions

The customer interface team is responsible for three basic support areas, each having in common an interface function with the product customer base.

Customer request control. The customer request control function receives or generates system action requests (SAR) from customers and tracks their dispositions. This function analyzes the requests and determines appropriate solutions. It also has the responsibility to respond promptly to the customer regarding the request. A standard SAR form, is the primary vehicle for recording and monitoring progress of reported requests.

Product change control. The product change control function authorizes work for all changes to be acted on by technical operations. Product control will also consider implementation priorities for software enhancements or features requested from marketing. A standard software change authorization (SCA) form, shown in Figure 9.5, normally is provided to track program change decisions and status.

Each software change is classified in terms of the type of change and the urgency. Each then is assigned an implementation priority based on descending order of urgency. The change authorizations then are passed to the technical operations function, with the implementation queue being on a first-in, first-out (FIFO) basis according to assigned priorities.

Distribution and configuration control. This function handles all of the shipment and installation support of software packages to the customers. To fulfill an order, the distribution function requires two basic inputs:

1. A configuration form from the user defining all features and system configuration parameters (i.e., the customer's order)
2. A software package "manufactured" by the software library containing the latest release on specified media and the required supporting documentation

The distribution function prepares a packing list of all deliverables, including a letter of transmittal, and it ensures that newsletters accompany all new releases. This function also maintains a file of all customer installation configurations and revision levels. Such a file (or database) serves two purposes:

1. To provide a convenient status reference for determining which customers should or should not be automatically updated by new releases
2. To provide a reference file when system action requests are received

Technical operations function

This function is a resource of experienced analysts and programmers who receive the software change authorizations from the product change control function. The team must be staffed with a permanent cadre of personnel who have in-depth knowledge of the product being supported. Several temporary people also may rotate through this function as they are needed and available. In general, the technical operations function provides a good training ground to introduce new employees to software development.

Software library

The software library is responsible for protecting and controlling the software assets of the company. Protection of these assets generally consists of three control functions:

Documentation control
Program control
Test control

Documentation control. This function is responsible for setting up and maintaining a control and storage center for all external software documentation. The documents under control by this function include:

User documents
Technical support documents
Standards and procedures
Technical reports

Documentation control must provide a catalog numbering scheme for all documentation, procedures for controlling the official revision level, and control procedures for distribution of the documents.

Program control. This function is responsible for maintaining a control and storage center for all software media. In general, this consists of a set of master files with backup for each standard software product containing:

Source modules
Production modules
Listing files
JCL files

Program control maintains an appropriate catalog number scheme for controlling the released revision levels of each software product in the library. It also establishes and implements a procedure for "manufacturing" deliverable software packages according to a standard configuration request.

Test Control. This function is responsible for setting up and maintaining a control and storage center for all test programs and procedures pertaining to the product. This includes all formal test experiments and benchmarks, and the standard regression test library.

Operations and procedures: The product support cycle

To illustrate the operation of the product support cycle, the following discussion traces the resolution of a typical problem reported by a customer. Each SAR received passes through a five-phase cycle of processing.

	Processing Phase	*Responsible Support Function*
I.	Registration	Problem control
II.	Evaluation and response	Product control/problem control (with assistance from technical operations)
III.	Resolution and testing	Technical operations/quality control
IV.	System integration	Technical operations/library
V.	Distribution	Distribution

Phase I: Registration

When the problem control function receives an SAR, registration should proceed as follows:

1. Assure that all the following data is entered on the SAR form:
   Identification of the customer (or problem source)
   Date of the initial request
   Name of the person receiving the request
   Statement of the request
   Special consideration relating to the request
   Preliminary analysis of the request (probable action)
2. Assign a control number to the SAR.
3. Assure that the SAR is accompanied by supporting documentation (e.g., printouts, etc.) when applicable.

4. If data is incomplete or is unclear, contact the customer (or reporter) for further information or clarification.
5. Initial the SAR as duly registered and entered into the problem control function. Enter a copy of the SAR into the log file, including support material.
6. Provide a quick response to the customer or problem reporter. The written response should be made within (14) days, acknowledging that activity has been initiated.
7. Pass the registered SAR package on for preliminary problem analysis, priority assignment, and solution scheduling. The package consists of:
   Original SAR form
   Supporting documentation
   SCA forms

Phase II: Evaluation and response

In this phase, problem control does a preliminary analysis of the problem, consulting with the technical operations function if necessary, to clarify priorities or technical questions. If the computer system configuration is at hand, an attempt should be made to recreate the reported problem. The SAR form then is submitted to product control for detailed analysis and implementation scheduling.

The Product Control function considers implementation techniques, system cutin priorities, and scheduling of the pending problem solutions. At this point the software and documentation changes necessary to satisfy the SAR are sufficiently understood so that each change can be precisely described on the software change authorization (SCA) form. Changes imposed by each SAR may generate one or many SCA forms.

Each software change is classified in terms of the type of change and the resolution urgency. Three types of changes are defined:

Type	*Definition*	*Affected Documents*
Functional	Change that alters the functionality of the subject software maintenance	User documents Program documents
Imple-mentation	Change that alters the method of implementation, etc. (e.g., design changes)	Listings Program algorithms, speed, storage, maintenance documents Listings
Coding	Change that alters the coding of software (no function or design alterations)	Listings

Problems scheduled for action are passed to the technical operations team for implementation and test; deferred problems are placed on a follow-up list. Each change is assigned an implementation priority based on descending order of urgencies and on a first-in, first-out basis according to assigned priorities. Typically, priorities will be assigned according to the following criteria:

Priority	*Criteria*
A	*Urgent*: A critical system malfunction that seriously impedes the customer's use of the product (a problem not previously reported and not part of a planned release). Temporary "patches" between releases also will be considered within this top priority.
B	*As soon as possible*: A system malfunction, not previously reported or part of a planned release, which is not seriously impeding the customer's use of the product.
C	*Background*: A problem previously reported and part of a planned release, or a low-grade problem that causes difficulties only under special conditions. This priority is implemented when resources are available.
D	*No system problem*: A reported problem that is determined to be operator, error or documentation error.

At this point, a second written response is sent to the customer delineating the preliminary analysis of the problem and an estimate of the schedule revision in which the resolution will appear. If on-site software patching for an isolated installation is deemed advisable, the customer will be requested to sign a "waiver of procedures" form by which the customer accepts responsibility for software regression due to the patching operation. The status of all change authorizations is tracked by product control, and periodic status reports are ussued for management.

Phase 3: Change resolution and regression testing

The technical operations function further analyzes the proposed changes in terms of detailed implementation approaches, updates the affected documentation, implements the change, and devises adequate test procedures and routines to assure that the solution does indeed correct the original problem. Changes first are tested with the applicable regression test programs to assure that they have not caused problems elsewhere. Additional test programs, when necessary to verify the solution, then are systematically added to the regression test library. A typical procedure is:

- Run a modified program with the original appropriate regression test.
- If satisfactory, run a modified program with the modified regression test.

When the technical operations function is satisfied that the solution is correct and that the overall system performance has not regressed, the solution package, including the SCA and pertinent updated documentation, is submitted to the quality control function for verification.

Testing criteria. Software testing is defined as a preplanned, structured activity in which prescribed experiments are systematically performed on the software to measure its quality against a specified standard. The standard is a controlled body of test programs called the regression test library.

Regression testing is a mechanism for assuring that the previously established quality for the software is not degraded (or regressed) by changes introduced. The regression test library is a body of test programs derived from the test sets used initially to establish the quality level of the software product. The regression test library must be adaptable to the characteristics of modifications made to the subject software. There are several possible causes for such changes:

- Problem reports from customers
- Enhancements or feature additions required by marketing
- Configuration changes due to changes in existing equipment or to a new system
- Configuration or logical changes·

When such changes are approved and implemented, generally it will be necessary to add tests to the regression test base to verify the changes and to assure that they have not degraded the overall system. When quality control (QC) is satisfied that the changes and additional tests have not compromised the integrity of the system, a regression test revision release is made to the test library. The new regression test base then becomes the testing standard for all software delivered to the field.

At any time, the regression test library must be considered the official, reliable benchmark standard that all software packages must meet before shipment to a customer. To assure this, the master regression test library must always be in the possession of the library function. Copies are maintained and must be signed out of the library for a test run and returned to the library immediately afterward. A system verification form, attesting to the successful running of the test, will contain the library number of the regression test used, the date run, and the signature of the tester. The library function must permit no additions or deletions to the master regression test library unless authorized as official.

When additional tests either are added or deleted from the existing base, thereby creating a new reference base, the former base level is retained in the test library for backup purposes. It is recommended that at least three levels of backup be retained. Each time a revision is made to the regression test complement, the library must require appropriate documentation updates to accompany the change.

Phase I4: System integration

Within the control environment of the software library, a system of present, past, and pending revision masters are maintained. At any time, the current master is the only version of the software product from which deliverable copies can be derived. As each change is accepted by the software library, the librarian systematically integrates the change into the pending new release. Test programs associated with each change, which were part of the technical operations validation process, are also added to the new release master regression test.

Release generation. The product review board oversees the condition of the product at all times. It determines the date of a new release and the software changes to be included in that release. The librarian then implements the release generation procedure, including successful running of the regression test authorized for the new release. The pending master then becomes the official master as release $n + 1$; the former master is saved and submitted to archival storage as backup. A new pending master will begin to be built as additional changes come into the library. In summary, the versions of the software product that can exist at any time are as follows:

Revision Level	*Status*
Previous release	Archival storage
Current release	Authorized for distribution
Pending release	Revision in process

Following the regression testing of the new master, the librarian issues an official release notice, authorizing the new master for the generation of deliverables and for distribution.

Phase 5: Distribution

The distribution function handles all of the shipment and installation support of software packages to the customers.

New Customer Deliveries. The following is a step-by-step description of a typical delivery procedure to a new customer:

1. An order comes to the distribution function with a completed configuration sheet.
2. The order is reviewed for standard or nonstandard handling (e.g., special installation or acceptance requirements, etc.).
3. The configuration is reviewed for completeness.
4. The distribution function requests the software library to prepare the appropriate deliverables.
5. The library assembles the required deliverables, tests the software package, updates the customer file, updates the status file, and prepares a packing list.
6. The distribution function verifies that all deliverables are ready for shipment and authorizes the librarian to ship.

Customer updates and support. Following the generation of a new release, an updating schedule is established for the warranted customer base. The following is a step-by-step description of the update procedures:

1. Each configuration is reviewed by the distribution function to resolve any potential problem the new release could create.
2. The distribution function prepares a general memo, stating the features of this new release.
3. The distribution function requests the software library to prepare the appropriate deliverables for each authorized update.
4. The library assembles the required deliverables, tests the software, updates the customer file, updates the status file, and prepares a packing list.
5. The distribution function verifies that all deliverables are ready for shipment, and the librarian ships the deliverables, including a cover letter, feature memo, and possibly a newsletter.
6. The distribution function follows up to assure that the update is successfully installed and tested at the customer site.

Monitoring and review functions

The following functions shown are not part of the normal processing sequence. That is, each provides a monitoring and review of the normal work flow.

Quality control. The basic responsibility of the quality control function is to assure that the established quality level of the released software is maintained or improved when changes of any kind are introduced. Using audits and the regression test standard as a vehicle, QC will certify that the system, as modified by the technical operations team, meets its criteria. To maintain control of quality, the total package--including documentation, source code, object files, listing files, and test sets--must be kept under library control.

Product review board. The product review board (PRB) functions as an overseer. Its purpose is periodically to review the workflow through the problem control/product control function of the product support cycle and to consider implications to other related functions and/or marketing interests. In essence, the PRB has advice-and-consent responsibility for the workflow through the product support cycle. The board consists of representatives of the development and support groups as well as the responsible QC person. It must be chaired by the responsible marketing product manager, with the software product manager serving as deputy. If consensus cannot be reached, the decision must be left to marketing.

Product maintenance

This section discusses the methods and procedures for controlled updating and maintenance of a software product and its documentation. To maintain the integrity of the software and documentation, the user and maintenance documents must be reviewed and modified prior to modifications to the software. The approved updated documentation then will be part of the approved change package submitted to the library. A documentation update will always accompany a software release; occasionally, document updates may also occur between releases.

Document change control procedures

The general steps involved in the documentation library change control are outlined below.

1. Technical operations requests duplicate copies of pages of documentation that need changing. The librarian is requested to log the initiation date and the description of the changes to be made, indicating pages to be changed, on the appropriate change record forms.
2. Technical operations makes the required changes to their private copy.
3. Changes are submitted to the appropriate level of management for final approval.
4. SCAs with approvals and supporting documentation are submitted to the librarian for update of the documents.
5. The librarian incorporates the changes into the working copy directly and updates the change record accordingly.
6. The librarian sends the change control packages to a word processing or typing facility to get new originals cut at specified intervals.
7. The librarian incorporates the new pages into the original and working copy files and updates the change record and document control number accordingly.
8. At specified times the librarian releases (temporarily) originals to the distribution function.
9. Distribution coordinates reproduction of updated pages and cover sheet as well as the new documentation set.

Document change record

The document change record provides an instantaneous "snapshot" of where each document stands with respect to changes since the last formal release of that document. This record contains a log of changes, from the date of initiation of a new release of the document. It contains the date of initiation of the change, pages to be changed, a brief description of the change, the date the working copy was updated, and the date the originals were updated. When a new release of the document is generated, all open items are transcribed to a new change record to cover the next release.

Program change control procedures

Procedures for controlling changes to the program library depend highly on the computer hardware and software environment in which the program is maintained. The procedures defined here are designed to minimize the time and cost of program maintenance while achieving sufficient control over the program library. These procedures address control of program changes between releases as well as control over generation of a new release.

Program changes can occur in a "steady-state" fashion between releases. Ideally, procedures to be followed by the program librarian and programmers making changes to the software should be independent of release generation procedures. This provides three advantages:

1. If the release generation time spans a number of days, work can proceed to modify programs for the next release during the generation period. Programmers need not wait for completion of release generation to get back to work.
2. Final determination on inclusion of certain changes can wait until release generation is under way.
3. The release generation period can be shortened if certain policies are set down regarding the methods for testing changes as they are made.

The following overview describes the elements needed to make up a library.

1. *Coded media library*: The existing and prior release backup generally is kept on tape and consists of the following:

Current Release

Source modules
Object modules
Load modules
JCL files
Test files

Safekeeping. Safekeeping, as used here, implies storage of the most recent prior releases, including the current release, for immediate recovery from an unexpected loss (usually due to a disaster). Safekeeping storage would be located at other than the current physical library location, most likely in a vault. The following should be stored:

Current release: source modules, object modules, load modules

Prior Releases: source modules

Regression test library

Archives. Archives, as used herein, implies storage of prior (historic) releases that are still required to support the existing customer base. Considerations are as follows:

Source may be required to back up special configurations or to ensure that problems have not occurred because of customers' modifying the source.

Source should not be given to customers.

2. *Current system disk.* This disk (or set of disks) contains the current working version of the product in preparation for the next release. The procedures written here assure that this disk gets backed up on a regular basis--at least weekly, and daily during heavy change periods.

Released version. Files containing the released version must be read-only for everyone except the librarian, who will have write privileges. They will contain the following:

Source Modules released (R),	Only those being changed since last release; will be stored as however, and will remain unchanged
Object modules the system	All modules for the subject product; will be maintained in library and in a private library (possibly on tape) for backup
Load modules	As needed, stored in the R files
JCL files	As needed, stored in the R files
Test files	As needed, stored in the R files

Current development version. Files containing the current development version must be read-only for everyone except the librarian. They contain only those modules that have changed since the last release and that have achieved a high degree of confidence via regression testing. They contain the following:

Source	Only those modules that have been changed (these correspond to the pending release object modules).
Load modules	As need to test the development version, stored in the D files
JCL files	As needed to test the development version, stored in the D files
Test files	As needed to test the development version, stored in the D files

Private library versions. If a programmer wants to test a change in a given subroutine, then he or she must modify a copy of the latest source and must create a corresponding copy of the object and load module files. If the development version is to remain unchanged during this process, then such changes must constitute a "private" version. It is the ability to create these private versions that provides isolation between changes introduced by different programmers. Therefore, multiple private libraries generally will exist at any given time. The private library versions contain the following:

Source	Only those modules undergoing change by that programmer. Because only one programmer should be working on a given module at a time, only a single copy of changed source modules should reside in the private library area at a given time. When sufficient regression testing is done to warrant confidence that the module is ready for release, then the module is moved to the development (D) library, compiled, and tested again. Upon completion of these tests, unless further work is to be done immediately, the module must be erased from the private library.

Object modules private version	Only those modules needed to link and test the
Load modules version	Only those modules needed to test the private
JCL files private version	Only those files needed to test the
Test files private version	Only those files needed to test the

Source listings. Any routine that has been modified since the last release must be "finally compiled" during release generation. The resulting listing must be put under control of the librarian to be kept in the library of source listings that represent what was just released. Listing of old versions should be moved to the archives or thrown out.

Change control procedures. The following set of procedures are defined for controlling "steady-state" changes to the program library.

1. Technical operations receives change authorizations previously generated in support of SAR solutions.
2. Technical operations requests the librarian to make the latest versions of source to be changed available on disk.
3. If source to be changed already exists on disk, technical operations is notified. Otherwise, the librarian schedules mounting of current release tape and puts required source into R files on disk.
4. Technical operations copies source to be changed into the private file and

- Makes changes to source modules as required
- Compiles source to private object file
- Links the new object modules from private object files to development library and system library, creating a new load module.
- Tests changes using appropriate regression tests and procedures and gets preliminary certification from QC

5. On preliminary certification, the librarian moves the modified source to the D files, compiles and moves the new object to the development library, links appropriate load modules in the development library, and deletes original copy of source from R files.
6. Technical operations deletes private files no longer needed.
7. If it is determined that tests are failing because of a changed module in the development library, the librarian will be requested to delete that module from the pending-release object library so that testing can proceed with the current-release library version.

8. The librarian must obtain authorization from management before deleting modules from any of the following: system library, development version library, R files, or D files.

Release generation procedures

The product review board will define what level of change must be achieved to generate a new release. It will also set a target cut-off date, after which no new changes will be made to the development version of the system. The librarian will be notified of this cut-off date.

The following steps must be performed by technical operations in coordination with the librarian to generate and accept a new release of the software product. Most of the procedures listed can be automated using JCL files for copying, deleting, and compiling routines.

1. Copy the current released version of the object from tape to a private library. Recompile all D file routines and move the resulting object modules into the private library.
2. Link object modules from the private library, yielding all new load modules that contain them.
3. Copy modified JCL and test data into the private library files.
4. Run the release acceptance tests and gain initial sign-off.

Test library change control

Tests are conducted to ensure that a desired software functional capability exists and provides correct and timely output. When a test is modified, the conclusions that can be drawn regarding functionality generally are modified. The purpose of a regression test is to ensure that when the software is modified, system quality has not regressed. The purpose of controlling changes to the regression test library is to ensure that the ability to test system quality does not regress.

By its nature, regression testing affords a reasonable degree of control over test modifications. This is due to the underlying concept of a growing test base. This test base can only regress if, when modified, a desired test is eliminated. The normal consequence is that after a new system release, reports from the field indicate that a function that previously worked is no longer available. And, this was a function for which a test previously existed.

When a particular test program is modified, the change control procedures must ensure that no desired test is reduced, inhibited, or eliminated. When a test is created to determine whether a problem (error) in the software has been corrected, that test first must be run against the current release to ensure that the problem is repeated.

Management responsibility and quality system

There must be a *statement of quality* policy that documents the authority for the implementation of a quality management system. The quality policy should be in the form of a letter signed by the chief executive officer or the person in charge of the organization implementing the quality management system. It should broadly describe the processes, products, and services covered by the quality management system. These are the capabilities for which the organization will be seeking certification. It should describe the intentions of the enterprise concerning the quality of the products it produces and services it supplies (for example, the supply of only those services whose quality will ensure end-user satisfaction and/or repeat business). It should define the attitude and overall commitment of the organization to quality and the standard(s) on which the system will be based. It should describe how to establish and maintain an effective quality management system as part of the overall management function and direct staff to conform to the system. It should describe the results the enterprise expects to get from the system. This may include competitive position and reputation in the market place. A copy of the letter should be sent to all staff as well as being prominently displayed in the workplace. Figure 6.1 is an example of a statement of quality policy.

Organization

There is a requirement to document a *quality-related organization.* it does not mean a full organization chart but rather a series of generic functions and how they interrelate. For example, we will need to specify the responsibility and authority of the person (function) who signed the quality policy statement, the responsibilities and authorities of the executive management level(s), and the responsibilities and authorities of the operational level(s). We use this section to let people know what we are expecting of them and what they are allowed to do. Within this structure the roles and responsibilities of all of our people involved with the quality management system are defined in terms of their participation in the quality process. Be careful that this section of your documentation does not swamp the rest of the documentation. It should only be a few pages and cover the broad issues addressed in the standard and how these are allocated to the different levels of management. If you want to use this section to refer to the detailed organization structure, then do so, but make sure people can see the major issues addressed succinctly and can clearly distinguish what they are empowered to do.

Empowerment is the art of making people responsible for their own actions and future. Management can empower or restrict staff as they see fit, but whatever they decide they must document for all to see and understand. Reading this section of an organization's documentation gives a picture of how much the staff are empowered, how much authority for quality is delegated down the organization structure, and how quality really happens rather than how management says it happens. This is particularly so when we see who has the freedom to take action on specific quality issues. If we examine these in more detail we see the requirement in ISO 9001 to give somebody the freedom and authority to "initiate action to prevent the occurrence of product nonconformity." In other words: Who is allowed to do something to stop us producing defective product or providing service that is not within specification? Similarly, who is empowered to identify and record any product (or service) quality problems? How about solving quality problems? Who is allowed to come up with ideas for making things better? and then verify that the ideas worked?

Finally, who is empowered to stop the process altogether? Who makes the decision to stop processing, stop the project, close the service down, and so on, until problems are solved and the process can be recommenced? This is a major issue covering the right to stop a production line, close down a restaurant, shut a hotel, or stop doing whatever it is the organization does.

There is a requirement to identify what resources are required to ensure our products and services meet requirements. It does not state that we need some form of quality assurance department or that we need separate inspectors and workers. The philosophy of peer review and team responsibility for quality is totally consistent with this requirement of ISO 9001. There is a requirement for people to be suitably trained in managing, doing work, and performing quality assurance activities. There is also a requirement to provide evidence of training in the form of training records.

There is a requirement to appoint a management representative who is responsible for ensuring that the quality management system is implemented and is kept up to date as well as reporting on the performance of the quality management system. The management representative must be a member of the executive of the organization unit developing the quality management system. There is no need for the management representative to be a full-time job.

The operation of the quality management system shall be the responsibility of the quality manager who shall be the management representative. Where the quality manager is also a project manager, then quality management issues relating to this project shall be the responsibility of the deputy quality manager (the technical manager). The project manager and professionals report to the development manager when performing project work. One or more quality inspectors are appointed for each project on the basis of skill and experience in verifying the work to be performed. The quality inspectors report to the quality manager.

The responsibilities, duties, and authorities of each of the positions, in relation to quality are described below. These examples detail the information to be provided with specific reference to the need to give somebody in the organization the responsibility and authority to take the ISO 9001-required actions with respect to quality,

Chief executive officer

The chief executive officer has delegated authority for operation of the software quality management system to the divisional manager,

Divisional manager

- Promulgates company policy on quality-related issues.
- Encourages the development of a center of excellence.
- Authorizes changes to the quality management system.
- Directs conformance to the quality management system.
- Other responsibilities appropriate to your organization.

Management representative

- Provides a center of excellence in the application of quality management.
- Develops and maintains the quality management system.
- Conducts internal quality system audits.
- Reports on the performance of the quality management system.
- Identifies problems or deficiencies in products or services.
- Resolves problems and implements solutions in the quality management system.
- Other responsibilities appropriate to your organization.

Manager

- Participates in internal quality management system audits within their area of responsibility.
- Ensures compliance with the quality management system.
- Undertakes corrective action for any nonconformance identified during quality management systems reviews.
- Analyzes trends relating to deficiencies and reviews effectiveness of corrective measures.
- Initiates action to prevent product or service nonconformance.
- Other responsibilities appropriate to your organization.

Project manager

- Participates in the preparation of development strategies.
- Prepares development plans.
- Implements development plans.
- Arranges and schedules required reviews and inspections.
- Reports on progress as compared against the development plan.
- Initiates action to prevent product nonconformance.
- Identifies problems or deficiencies in product or the quality management system.
- Resolves problems and implements solutions relating to the quality management system.
- Analyzes trends relating corrective measures.
- Authorizes the implementation of changes that do not scope or cost of the project.
- Authorizes rework to rectify nonconforming product.
- Other responsibilities appropriate to your organization.

Quality inspector

- Reports to the quality manager on quality-related issues.
- Participates in the inspect-and-approval process as requested by the project manager or as defined in the development plan.
- Identifies problems or deficiencies in product or the quality management system.

Professionals

- Ensure all work they do is performed in accordance with the development methodology.
- Participate in quality reviews and inspections as required.
- Attend scheduled training courses.
- Identify problems or deficiencies in products or the quality management system.
- Conform to the development plan.

Customer

- Participate in the definition of product requirements.
- Participate in quality reviews and inspections as defined in the contract.
- Prepare test plans according to the contract.

Management review

There is a requirement for management to regularly review the suitability and effectiveness of the quality management system. This calls for management to examine the organization's processes and decide if the system is still suitable for the organization's needs and determine if it is still operating effectively. The reviews are typically held every three, six, or twelve months and should examine business directions, changes planned in products and services, organizational plans, and other strategic planning issues. The review should examine the results of internal quality audits and external assessments as well as input from the management representative and other interested parties. The results of the review should be recorded and actions taken to update the system. This is where management leads the organization by use of the system.

As well as formal management review as required by ISO 9001, an excellent practice is to review quality within the organization by making it the first item on every meeting agenda. There may, in time, be little need for other items. After all, satisfying customers (meeting customers' needs) is why the organization exists.

A typical policy addressing the management review requirements of ISO 9001 is:

> Management shall regularly (approximately quarterly) conduct a formal review of the suitability and effectiveness of the quality management system.

This policy satisfies the requirement to review the quality management system on a regular basis for suitability and effectiveness. A procedure is required to specify how to implement this policy and the evidence to be produced. The procedure in this case would describe how to call and run a management review meeting and prepare the minutes and have them signed before filing them in a management review file.

Issues

When examining your quality management system documentation you should be asking yourself if the following issues have been addressed and whether you can produce evidence in the form of records or documents that they have been followed in practice:

- Is the quality policy distributed to all levels of the organization?
- Is an organization chart available? Is it up to date?
- Are roles and responsibilities recorded for functions/areas doing work affecting quality?
- Are relationships between functions/areas clearly defined and documented?
- Are job descriptions available for major functions in areas affecting quality?
- Is there a formalized system to ensure that trained personnel equipped with suitable resources are identified for managing, performing work, and quality assurance activities?
- Is a management representative appointed having defined authority and responsibility for ensuring the requirements of the quality management system are met?
- Is the management representative a member of the executive?

Quality system

Documenting the quality management system means that it must be written down so that people can see a consistent story about the way the organization is run. "Written down" does not have to be taken literally; an on-line computer system is satisfactory, as are photographs. The medium adopted must be one that is permanent, accessible, and understandable to the user. An on-line information retrieval system would be useful to knowledge workers who use a computer to do their work. They could call up policies, procedures, processes, practices, and standards at the touch of a button. For example, even if workers in the food and beverage industry were illiterate and could not understand complex descriptions, they could set up a table for dinner from a photograph of the end result. Similarly, in the footwear and garment industry quality standards could be presented in the form of samples showing acceptable and unacceptable work.

The quality management system defines the policies, procedures, methods, work instruction, and standards of the organization for the management of development including software product, documentation product, and product maintenance. The policies are designed to ensure that customer requirements, including quality, are met. Within this section the quality management system must be described in terms of what constitutes it and the basis on which it is built. A quality management system usually consists of:

- A quality manual containing company policies for meeting the requirements of the basis of the quality management system, for example ISO 9001, IEEE 1298.

- One or more procedures manuals containing the procedures necessary to implement the policies in the quality manual.
- A methodology describing what must be done to complete development tasks and describing the deliverables (both intermediate and final).
- Standards for deliverables, including on how to perform the work.
- Quality documentation should be prepared i accordance with ISO 10013-Guidelines for developing quality manuals.

Basis

Also required in the description of your documentation is the basis of *your quality management system.* This will minimally refer to ISO 9001 but may also refer to ISO 9000.3, ISO 9004.2, ISO 8402, IEEE 1298 and other national or international standards. When you list these as a component of your quality management system you must have the originals as part of your documentation. Don't have photocopies: illegal copies of standards are not the best way to start impressing an assessor with your credibility, especially if you are using the national body who owns the copyright of the local version of ISO 9001 as your certification agency.

Vocabulary

An important part of quality management is *vocabulary.* While ISO 8402 gives the meaning of some basic words such as *quality, quality management, quality assurance,* and *quality control,* national standards may exist that provide a significantly richer vocabulary. It is important to ensure that everyone uses the same words for the same thing, so a quality vocabulary section is highly advisable. When commencing implementation of your quality management system, let the first session cover the vocabulary; this will reduce arguments and misunderstandings later on. If you don't do this people will interpret the documentation of the quality management system through their own understanding of the words rather than according to the official definition. How many lawsuits have been fought over different understandings of *approved* and *accepted?* And how many internal wars have been fought over words we all know or understand? In this book the word *approved* means passed by quality assurance, *accepted* means being passed (accepted) by the customer, and *authorized* means that a record now exists that a product has been released for use or delivery.

Planning

When you work in a project-based mode, a subset of the quality management system is required for each project. This "quality management system for project X" is known as a *quality plan.* Plans for specific activities, such as design or production, are called for in the relevant sections of ISO 9001 but these do not cover the rich requirements of a full project quality plan. Obviously, we cannot produce a complete quality plan at the beginning of a project but we can prepare a plan that goes as far as we can see and ends with a requirement to produce an updated plan. One of the interesting points you will notice in a detailed plan is how closely it examines what should have been in the contract, and what should have been in the original proposal or tender. You will quickly find yourself using the planning process right up front. You will eventually find your customers accepting your proposals as a contract to execute the project. Think of the time and cost savings if you don't have to prepare a proposal, then a contract, and then a plan, and then spend the rest of the project arguing which of the three documents is applicable to what situation. Obviously, plans need to be treated the same as any other quality management system document and managed accordingly.

While the need for development methods, standards, and procedures would appear to be self-evident, few enterprises have these issues under control. A programming standards manual including naming conventions for design and some sample tables of contents for reports is not a satisfactory methodology for systems development. The methods, standards, and procedures must clearly address each requirement of software quality management. This means that there must be a defined process to follow and a set of standards to use for:

- Requirements specification.
- Design.
- Programming and user documentation.
- Inspection and testing (software product validation).
- Installation and implementation.

Quality system documentation

The quality management system is documented in the following:

- Quality manual.
- Quality plan for each project.
- Quality procedures manual.
- Development methodology.
- Standards, tools, and techniques.

It is managed in accordance with quality management system document control. Records are maintained in accordance with quality records to provide evidence of processes being followed. The quality management system and related records are audited on a regular basis according to internal quality audit to ensure they are understood, have been implemented, and are being maintained.

Basis

The quality management system is based on conformance to the following standards:

ISO 9001, Quality Systems-Model for quality assurance in design/ development, production, installation, and servicing.

Other standards and publications referenced and used are:

- ISO 8402, Quality-Vocabulary.
- ISO 9004.2, Quality Management and Quality System Elements-Guidelines for services.
- ISO 9000.3, Quality Management and Quality System Elements-Guidelines for development, supply, and maintenance of software.
- IEEE 1298, Software Quality Management System-Requirements.

Vocabulary definitions

Because of the varying usage of words (especially in the information industry), some specific definitions have been adopted. The following is a sample list of definitions:

Accepted The recorded decision that the product or part of the product has satisfied the requirements and may be delivered to the customer or used in the next part of the process.

Approved The recorded decision that the product or part of the product has satisfied the quality standards.

Authorized The recorded decision that the record or product has been cleared for use or action.

Quality plan

The quality plan should typically contain the following sections:

— Introduction
— Management Plan
— Quality Plan
— Purchasing Plan
— Development Plan
— Test Plan
— Installation, Implementation, and Delivery Plan
— Product (Configuration) Management Plan
— Maintenance Plan
— Project Plan (Cost & Schedule)

Policies

The policies for developing, implementing, and maintaining the quality management system are covered in the other sections of your quality management system.

Issues

When examining your quality management system documentation you should be asking yourself if the following issues have been addressed and whether you can produce evidence in the form of records or documents that they have been followed in practice:

- Are there documented policies?
- Are there documented procedures?
- Are there documented methods?
- Are there documented standards?
- Are there documented processes?
- Are there documented guidelines?
- Are there documented work instructions?
- Is the basis of the quality management system defined? Are definitions recorded?
- Is there a list of procedures, processes, methods, guidelines, and work instructions used to implement the policies?
- Are there clear references in the policies to the relevant procedures, processes, methods, guidelines, and work instructions required to implement the policies?
- Is referencing carried throughout the documentation as you are referred from policy to process to standard, etc.?
- For project-based work, is a quality plan generated for each project? Does the quality plan clearly reference the relevant procedures, processes, methods, guidelines, and work instructions required to implement the plan?
- Does the quality plan specify the roles and responsibilities ()fall parties, especially customers' responsibilities?
- Does the quality plan include:

  Organizational and technical interfaces?

  Quality issues, including:

  - Methods, procedures, work instructions, and standards?
  - Inspection and testing tools?
  - Development cycle?
  - Review, inspection, and test requirements?
  - Development environment?

  Development plan, including:

  - Phases?
  - Management?
  - Processes and tools?
  - Progress control?
  - Phase input?
    - Phase output?
    - Verification of phases?

- Test Plan?
- Installation and Implementation Plan?

- Product Management Plan?
- Postinstallation Maintenance Plan?
- Project Plan (resources, schedules, and costs)?

- Does the system require plans to be reviewed by qualified personnel?
- Does the system require plans to be authorized before issue?
- Does the system require plans to be updated as the project progresses?

Document and data control

This section addresses the requirements of ISO 9001-1994 Section 4.5. *Document and data control is* concerned with making sure that the documents that make up the quality management system are properly managed. The documents and data refer to the policies, quality plans, methods, procedures, work instructions, and standards. Requirements specifications and designs may either be considered also part of the documentation or may be treated as products. Programming and deliverable documents (user guides, reports, consulting studies, etc.) are products and subject to configuration control (referred to as product identification and traceability in ISO 9001) but the actual processes of control are usually the same as for quality management system documentation and data.

Document and data control has the objective of ensuring that people performing work have access to the correct versions of the process documentation. To this end it is essential that all process documentation is' available to the people who need it, all process documentation is authorized, and all changes are authorized by the same person (unless this is impractical). Changes should be made effective at an agreed time and the changed documentation should show what changes have been made. Obsolete documents must be removed from use although there may be a need to retain copies of them. Approximately 20 percent of all failures found in quality management systems by external assessors are due to poor document and data control.

Policies

Typical policies addressing the document and data control requirements of ISO 9001 include the following: The quality management system documentation is managed by the Management Representative who retains the master copies of documents, the distribution list for controlled copies of documents and a master list showing the current version of each document.

This lets us know who controls the quality management system documentation and what information they have available. No specific procedures are required to satisfy this policy although distribution control procedures are specifically identified later.

Project based documentation and data is managed by the project manager who retains the master copies of documents, the distribution list for controlled copies of documents and the master list showing the current versions of each of the documents. Control of project based documentation is addressed in the specific sections covering that documentation.

This policy identifies the responsibility for the control of project-based documentation including plans, requirements specification, and design documentation. While user documents are logically addressed in this policy, they are more correctly addressed under configuration control as deliverable products.

IF A DOCUMENT HAS A NUMBER ON THE COVER IT HAS BEEN ALLOCATED TO THE PERSON SHOWN ON THE DISTRIBUTION LIST FOR THAT DOCUMENT AND SHALL NOT BE LOANED OR TRANSFERRED TO ANY OTHER PERSON. THE PERSON TO WHOM IT IS ALLOCATED IS REQUIRED TO APPLY ALL CHANGES ISSUED. IF THERE IS NO NUMBER ON THE COVER IT IS AN UNCONTROLLED COPY OF THE MANUAL AND WILL NOT BE KEPT UP TO DATE.

This is a statement of policy on holding and updating of documentation. Update policies and procedures are addressed later.

PROCESS DOCUMENTATION SHALL BE PREPARED IN A STANDARD, CONSISTENT MANNER

This is a very bald and simple statement and exists so that the process for developing procedures, and so forth, is brought into the quality management system.

THE QUALITY MANAGEMENT SYSTEM DOCUMENTATION IS MAINTAINED AND CHANGED IN A CONTROLLED MANNER WITH EACH REVISION BEING MANAGED UNDER FORMAL CHANGE CONTROL PROCESSES. THE NATURE OF THE CHANGES SHALL BE IDENTIFIED IN THE RELEVANT RELEASE NOTICE.

This policy calls for a change procedure to be followed to initiate and manage changes and updates to the quality management system documentation. It also calls for a release notice to be produced for each update that identifies the nature of the changes released. This would point to a change request procedure. It is not necessary to have a variety of change requests; one form and procedure can be devised to cover all the different types of changes required under a quality management system.

AS EACH CHANGE OR GROUP OF CHANGES TO THE QUALITY MANAGEMENT SYSTEM DOCUMENTATION HAS BEEN COMPLETED TO THE STAGE WHERE IT CAN BE INSPECTED IT SHALL BE ISSUED FOR REVIEW. THE REVIEWER SHALL FORMALLY REVIEW THE DOCUMENTATION AND SHALL HAVE FREE ACCESS TO PERTINENT BACKGROUND INFORMATION UPON WHICH TO BASE THIS REVIEW. IF THE OUTPUT PASSES REVIEW THEN THE REVIEWER SHALL APPROVE IT.

This policy calls for all changes to be subject to a formal quality assurance review. A review procedure can be devised that caters for most or all of the reviews needed in a quality management system. These reviews should be modeled on the requirement of design reviews. The policy sentence on access to background information is there to enforce the requirements of ISO 9001. Note that the review should ensure that the documentation is understandable by its end use

WHEN THE CHANGED QUALITY MANAGEMENT SYSTEM DOCUMENTATION HAS BEEN COMPLETED, REVIEWED AND APPROVED IN ITS ENTIRETY THEN IT SHALL BE PROVIDED TO THE CHIEF EXECUTIVE OFFICER FOR AUTHORIZATION. IF THE QUALITY MANAGEMENT SYSTEM DOCUMENTATION IS NOT ACCEPTABLE TO THE CHIEF EXECUTIVE OFFICER THEN CORRECTIVE ACTION SHALL BE INITIATED.

This policy calls for all changes to be authorized. It may be that the CEO only authorizes the quality manual and each executive authorizes the documentation used in his or her area of responsibility. A procedure will be required to cover this signoff and, of course, a record kept of the signoff. The use of corrective action if the document is unacceptable is a demonstration of the improvement process. Obviously, if something is unacceptable it must be fixed, but what we are doing here is identifying our attitude to our work. We are saying that if we have produced something and processed it through our quality assurance and yet our customer (in this case our CEO) is not satisfied then we have wasted our efforts in producing it and we should find out why and fix the root cause.

THE QUALITY MANAGEMENT SYSTEM DOCUMENTATION SHALL BE DISTRIBUTED TO REGISTERED HOLDERS TO TAKE EFFECT ON A SPECIFIED DATE. ALL REPLACED DOCUMENTATION SHALL BE DESTROYED. A BACKUP SHALL BE RETAINED ON COMPUTER READABLE MEDIA.

This policy leads to a procedure for numbering copies of documentation and recording the holder of each numbered copy. The policy also identifies the requirement to destroy old material to prevent people using obsolete copies of documentation. A policy on backing up the word processing files containing the documentation is a good idea but is not mandated by ISO 9001.

CUSTOMERS SHALL BE GIVEN ALL REASONABLE OPPORTUNITY TO EXAMINE AND REVIEW THE QUALITY MANAGEMENT SYSTEM. NOTE THAT WHILE COPIES OF THE QUALITY POLICY DOCUMENT MAY BE PROVIDED TO PROSPECTS AND CUSTOMERS, THE PROCESS DOCUMENTATION IS CONFIDENTIAL AND IS ONLY TO BE MADE AVAILABLE FOR AUDITS AND ASSESSMENTS AS REQUIRED BY CONTRACT.

Obviously customers and prospective customers will want to see how we approach quality. This policy lets our staff know our views on the subject. It also identifies the sensitive nature of our procedures and processes. While initially these would be fairly broad, after a period of continuous improvement they are what we are, and would enable others to do what we do, and do it the same way we do it.

CUSTOMERS SHOULD BE NOTIFIED OF THE RELEASE OF ANY NEW DOCUMENTATION BEING USED TO PERFORM WORK FOR THEM AND ANY EFFECT THE NEW VERSION WILL HAVE ON THE WORK.

This policy is one of general courtesy for ISO 9001 users but is a requirement under IEEE 1298. No specific procedure is required and a copy of the release notice and a covering memorandum should suffice.

When required by contract or when deemed prudent to do so, a copy of the version of the documentation used to perform work for a specific customer shall be retained as part of the work records. For IEEE 1298 users this is a requirement but is not required under ISO 9001. It does, however, make good sense to keep a copy of the methods and standards used during a project so that maintenance staff can understand the programming and documentation for the system. There is no need for a specific procedure. All that is required is to remove the copy from the distribution list for updates *and clearly* mark the copy as uncontrolled ("not to be used for development") and as part of the XYZ project records.

Issues

Examine your quality management system and ask yourself if the following issues have been addressed and whether you can produce evidence in the form of records or documents that, they have been followed in practice:

- Is there a system to control the issue and updating of documentation relevant to the standards (quality management system documentation)?
- Does the system ensure approval before issue of the above?
- Does the system ensure effective distribution of documents?
- Does the system ensure obsolete documents are removed from all points of issue or use?
- Does the system ensure changes to documents are approved by the originating function?
- If changes are not approved by the origination function, does the system require that the designated change control function have access to pertinent background information?
- Does the system allow for the recording of changes to documentation?
- Does the system require a master list or similar mechanism to identify the status and version of documents?

Software environment

The computerization of America is reaching epidemic proportions. Demand for software to perform ever-expanding computer applications is outgrowing the industry's ability to produce it. This gloomy outlook stems from the fact that writing workable software to meet established requirements historically has proved to be costly and time-consuming. It has consistently resisted the kind of cost-saving breakthroughs that have characterized the hardware side of the computer business. Even though there has been significant progress in software methodologies and disciplines, software development remains substantially a labor-intensive and unpredictable effort. After years of attempts to harness the software problem, creating software is still more of an art than a science.

Much has been written about the creative process of computer programming, and various structured methodologies and procedures for converting algorithms into programs have been devised. This book has presented an important component of the equation, an effective management control methodology. Part of this software development methodology is the environment in which the technical teams and managers must work.

Software organization

The following figure shows a representative software functional organization similar to the matrix-type organization described by Daly. Such an organization can provide a concentrated and controlled environment for building, supporting, and safekeeping a growing base of software assets.

Software development

The software development function supplies the skill resources required to plan and execute software development projects and software product lifecycles. This includes defining the software problem, detailed planning, time and resource estimation, proposal writing, functional analysis and specification, environment analysis and specification, design, development, and prerelease testing. Managers of projects that are primarily software in nature fall into this group. Team leaders responsible for supporting projects managed from outside the software area may also fall within this function. Standards for documentation, programming, testing, and quality control of software that is to be applied to the software development effort may be generated within this function, with exceptions justified on a project or product basis.

Software product support

Two major differences between hardware and software warrant a modified organizational approach to software production and support efforts. First, each time software is "maintained," the design is changed. Software does not "wear out" as hardware does; there are no "replacement parts." Second, one would usually not build into hardware the complex systems built into software. Hardware is too difficult to change. Software is used because it is relatively easy to change. Statistics on successful software products indicate that 60 to 90% of the software maintenance support resources are spent on enhancements to the functional capability. This process can continue for 5 to 15 years for a given product. Personnel turnover is a major consideration, along with protection of the assets (embodied in the documentation, program, and test libraries) as they constantly undergo change.

A breakdown of the software product support function is briefly described in the following paragraphs. A more detailed discussion is given in Chapter 9.

Customer interface. One of the product support activities is a function for receiving customer or internal problem reports, resolving actions to be taken, and soliciting solution recommendations for the reported problems from the technical support functions. Problem reports are translated here into change orders to the software libraries and then are diligently tracked until finally solved. The interface function is also responsible for the distribution of new releases of software products to the existing customer base and the installation of new customers.

Responsibility for customer training on the use of the products may also reside within this functional area. Entry- or junior-level software and clerical skills normally are sufficient for this function, supported by ample knowledge of the application.

Software library. Another important software support activity is a facility protecting the basic software product assets (e.g., the document library, program library, test library, version and release control records, and configuration control). With proper procedures and standards in place, the library can be realized by a high-level clerical function supported by lower level software backup skills when necessary.

Technical support. This function maintains a pool of skill resources to provide technical support across software product lines. It provides the technical expertise needed to interpret difficult problems, recommend changes, implement approved changes and generally to support the previously discussed functions as needed. This function should be a core group of medium to high-level software technical persons responsible for doing but not controlling. Technical persons newly assigned to the software area may start in this function to gain familiarity with a software product before assignment to new development projects. Organizational flexibility should also exist between this function and the software development function so that skill resources can easily be allocated based on need priorities.

Software operations

This function is responsible for the maintenance and operation of the physical computer facilities required for development and support of software products. Planning, aquisition, maintanance, controlling, and scheduling of computer facilities are typical activities of this function. Knowledge of available computer vendoı hardware and support software, telecommunication facilities, and peripheral products are important attributes of this function's personnel. In addition to in-house computer facility management, this function may also supply rental of time-sharing services where they can be shown to be cost effective. Heirarchical library storage facilities and security interactive edit, compile and test, and symbolic debugging facilities provided by this function may cut manpower costs significantly, may speed up development, and may improve overall control of the software development process.

System software

This function often serves three purposes. First, it provides the special' software expertise when changes and interfaces to the standard operating system (OS) are required for a development project. Second, the selection or creation of OS-related development support tools (e.g., precompilers, librarians, self-test aids) may also require the same special expertise. Third, this function is a convenient consultation center for problems relating to the usage, performance, or service features of the standard software operating systems used by the software development projects. Although people with such specialized skills could be placed within the software development and operations support functional areas, there are personnel attraction and retention considerations that may warrant separate grouping.

Quality control

Quality control typically is a review and audit function. The only "doing" type of task normally found in this function involves participation in the modification of standards and procedures. This function is normally attached at the staff level of the software area, but should have a direct reporting channel to higher management to ensure its functional independence.

Software technical environments

The term "software" is an all-encompassing word covering a wide variety of programming products. Development and maintenance effectiveness for may types of software products largely depends on the software development environment provided for the technical staff. An efficient software development system improves productivity by liberating programmers from unnecessary routine work, by automatically coordinating the program development efforts of different persons on the same project, and by providing systematic means for producing high quality software and supporting documentation. The specific configuration of a software environment must be closely tied to the nature of the software products to be developed in order to be most cost effective and to afford maximum support to the technical staff. One important consideration in establishing an efficient software development environment is an emphasis on in-house support software to support the development and maintenance of the end product applications software.

A host computing system is one on which an application software product is developed and is necessarily fully equipped with a wide range of support and utility software. The host is also the system necessary to fix or modify an application's software product. A target system, on the other hand, is the system on which the application's software is to ultimately operate in the end user's environment. In some cases, such as commercial computing centers, schools, scientific research centers, or any large-scale mainframe installation, the host and the target systems may he the same. In other environments, such as commercial "turnkey" systems (point of sale systems, air line reservation systems, small accounting systems), process control systems, or military field computers, the host and the target systems are often considerably different. For environments in which the end user's target system configuration is compatible with the vendor's host system, a full range of support software can be provided at the end user's site that will permit software updating and maintenance in the field. Such environments also permit the end users to develop their own applications software if so desired. In a turnkey computer environment, it is usually not desirable nor economically feasible to provide facilities within the target system for field development or maintenance. Often the end user of such systems is not knowledgeable in computer usage or programming; the systems are deliberately designed to be used within the context of their intended applications in the same way that an automobile is designed for use by a driver rather than a mechanic. In fact, the support function can fix the software without going near the user's installation.

Software development tools and facilities

A host computing center should have all the sophistication with respect to system software capabilities, software development tools, peripheral hardware devices, and languages necessary to make the most efficient, highly productive use of the technical talent available. A typical modern, medium-scale development environment is shown in Figure 10.3. A centrally located host computing system is provided that can support a community of real-time, interactive terminals located at remote programmer work stations. The host also has the capability to communicate with and download programs to a target system. The host software is capable of simultaneously supporting the interactive terminals in the foreground and a batch job stream in the background. The conversational timesharing nature of the interactive terminals typically provides each development programmer with a problem-solving work station, complete with system control commands, a library of time-saving development and debugging tools, a word processing facility for program documentation, a selection of program language compilers, and a prompt-driven help system.

A comprehensive host system configuration is only part of the story. A software "craftsman" must have the proper tools to perform efficiently and effectively. The state of the art is currently far beyond the historical software development approach of manual debugging, wholly dependent on the wits and deductive skills of the programmer, with little use of the computer for debugging assistance. Today's "tools" permit extensive use of the host computer to carry out the clerical work necessary to build software properly and to eliminate the inherent guesswork. Some of the generic software "tools" available to today's software practitioners are:

- Structured program design languages (PDL) to clearly map a design. This is the latter-day successor to the classical flow chart
- Structured application-level languages to facilitate structured programming methodologies and to minimize the need for assembly coding
- Interface documenters to generate complete and clear cross-reference documentation at the object module level, thus minimizing interface errors and improving productivity
- Symbolic debuggers to provide interactive debugging facilities at the work station and to accelerate software testing
- Tracing, testing, and optimization tools that can allow management to establish, facilitate, and enforce methodologies and standards for software tracing, testing, and optimization and to provide an audit vehicle for quality assurance
- Word processor to expedite the uniform documentation of source programs and to provide an easy facility for keeping software documentation abreast of software code development
- Productivity library to facilitate the use of data structures in structured programming and to allow the use of prefabricated sections of code

- Memory management package to provide the software developer with a selection of dynamic memory managers that minimize the amount of data space required
- Library of preprocessors to facilitate the generation of portable programs between dissimilar machines
- Configuration control facilities to assist in the orderly and consistent management of software revisions and releases. This facility can also support automatic backup and archiving of software modules and programs

Conventional approaches to software development in the past generally have made little use of the computer to assist the programmer in developing quality software products. Today's software tools, on the other hand, make extensive use of the computer to carry out many of the clerical tasks inherent in the development process and, thereby, eliminate much of the guesswork and costly rework that have plagued the software industry in the past.

Data processing (DP) users are becoming more and more confused about the different approaches to producing and maintaining their software systems. Some talk of expensive methods within the framework of a strict phase concept, others of simple, friendly user languages which will satisfy users' requirements simply and cheaply. What is the case of this apparent contradiction? The answer is readily at hand. The field of data processing has become ever larger and, as with everything which grows, has split into subfields. Contradictory tendencies develop for the different application areas, and the user, depending on which area he is currently concerned with, things that the approach used there is the only correct one. One firm quite often has three different application areas, namely:

- technical and scientific processing
- process data processing
- commercial data processing.

Technical and scientific processing

Here great emphasis is placed on creating a prototype of the product. The developer and the user are often the same. There should be as few formalisms as possible, and a strict phase concept is not adopted. Most programming is done in FORTRAN. The most important factor is the static and dynamic analysis of programs. Osterweil's TOOLPACK" toolkit package is characteristic of developmental approaches in this area.

Process data processing

Here the emphasis is on a valid processing concept with accompanying quality control of the project. Here the specification and verification of programs should be as formal as possible, and so specification languages and test techniques are very important, as critical control processes must be correct and reliable. This need not be overly expensive, as such process control usually has only limited amounts of data and functionality. Programs are written in languages such as PASCAL, PEARL and ADA. Lauber's 'EPOS' system and Alford's 'REVS' system are characteristic of the developmental approaches in this area.

Commercial data processing

There are two different approaches to commercial data processing. On the one hand, increasingly high-level languages are becoming available which allow the user or the developer to program, test and get applications running quickly and easily without too many formalities. This tendency goes alongside decentralization of corporate data processing. It is supported by PC systems such as DBase-III and Open Access as well as by 4th generation languages such as NATURAL, RAMIS, FOCUS, IDEAL and MANTIS. What all these systems have in common is that they offer users a relatively simple interface for defining their ideas. The developer can therefore be a layman. These widely varying approaches come within the framework of individual data processing. On the other hand, there is much discussion of software engineering and the software life cycle. Here expensive methods such as HIPO, MJSD, SADT and Structured Analysis are used and programming is done in languages such as COBOL or PL/1. The development process is divided into phases and is subject to strict control. Developers are professional programmers and analysts.

The nature of software engineering work is subject to numerous conditions. Almost half the cost goes on documentation. The other half is taken up mainly by systematic testing. The actual programming is the smallest part. The basic difference between these two subfields of commercial data processing consists in their opposing objectives. In individual data processing the system is simply a willing and more-or-less intelligent 'slave' of the individual person. The user can do with it what he wants. He can input data in various forms, store it, and view it on demand. The user is self-sufficient, that is, he can solve his problems quickly and cheaply, independently of anyone else.

There are, however, complex applications which cannot be implemented in terms of a short dialogue between the user and the computer. These are mainly applications involving a number of people, primarily automated processes such as stock control, job processing and payrole management, which have to be planned and specified just as carefully as process data processing and programming, which must maximise their use of available resources.

Individual data processing programs are thrown away once they are obsolete. They are designed to be disposable from the start. Automated processes are different. They are maintained and developed over many years., Maintenance represents more than two-thirds of their costs. This leads to the emphasis on the systems' maintainability and extensibility, highlighting such characteristics as modularity, flexibility and ease of maintenance. It should not, therefore, be surprising that the development costs of such a system are many times higher than those of individual programs. It is in the nature of the beast. Management of corporate software development must therefore include, as a prime requisite, a typology of software systems in the company. On the one hand we have the classical division into:

- technical and scientific systems
- production control systems
- commercial systems.

We should note that these systems may overlap considerably. On the other hand we have the newer division into:

- individual, short-lived programs
- complex, long-lived systems.

Different methods and tools are necessary for each of these types of system. The dream of a uniform procedural model for all software development in a company is just as unattainable as the dream of a single model of society. This is the first lesson that a software manager must learn. He must also, like a good politician, be in a position to make compromises between, and even coordinate, conflicting interests and working practices. That is the true art of software management.

Software system types

The typology of software systems gives us three types of software system in all application areas:

- throw-away systems
- static systems
- evolutionary systems.

Throw-away systems

Throwaway systems are the result of individual data processing. In general, they are implemented by one person at the site of their application for one quite specific purpose. They are of only local importance and can be written inside six months are minimal costs. According to Gumaraes, their average lifetime is less than two years. They are neither maintained nor developed further. When they are obsolete, they are thrown away. Such systems can be likened to daily newspapers, which are of only transitory value.

Static systems

Static systems are integrated operational applications in a well-defined area of application. While they are of universal importance, they can be written within two years. After that they are maintained and developed to only a limited extent. Their annual rate of change is less than 10%; in other words, they are relatively static. Once developed, they remain in use until they become obsolete on technical grounds.

Evolutionary systems

Evolutionary systems are systems which come into being step by step through iterative repetitions of the software life cycle. Each passage through the life cycle expands the available system and makes it more complete, so that the development of such a system can last many years. The system will pass through several intermediate states or versions during its development. Applications for such systems are not sufficiently precisely defined and/or they are constantly changing, so that the development process is never completely finished. Maintenance and further development can hardly be distinguished from one another. The cost of the first version is of course only a fraction of the total cost of the system. It is therefore very important to plan and document these systems carefully.

The software life cycle

The 'software life cycle' is a central concept in software engineering. This encompasses the view of the software development as an iterative process or as a loop, in which each iteration builds on the results of the previous iteration. There is no final result, as the applications that the software represents are themselves always in a state of flux and the technical environment in which the software exists is also changing. A software system is therefore maintained as long as it is needed and is not obsolete. Software becomes obsolete to the extent that it can no longer be adapted to the changes in the application. Software systems are similar to biological systems in this respect. They arise out of a painful birth, require intensive care at the beginning, slowly mature, reach their state of maximum benefit after several years, become increasingly inflexible and difficult to suport, die, and leave behind experience from which grows a new generation of systems. This birds-eye view of software development is one of the most important prerequisites for successful software management. The project manager must always be aware that his project is only one iteration in a series and that his results are the starting point for the next project. Each software element should therefore be constructed such that it can be changed or extended at any time with minimal effects on other elements. For the purposes of project management it is worthwhile dividing the development of complex systems into three stages:

- primary development
- further development
- maintenance.

Initial development

Initial development is the first iteration of the software life cycle. It derive from a limited system, perhaps a prototype developed beforehand to serve as a model of the production system. On the other hand, the system might, first be formally specified by modelling the application which is to be automated. In any case, the system passes through several phases in which the operational requirement is translated into an executable and reliable product. Finally the product is introduced into the company according to the agreed delivery criteria.

Further development

Further development represents those iterations of the software life cycle which follow the operational introduction of the first version and where the system is extended and made more comprehensive. Static systems undergo no further development, only maintenance.

Evolutionary systems may however pass through numerous cycles of further development until the system is fully mature. Each passage through the phases of the life cycle gives rise to a new version of the software. Each version enhances and completes the previous version. The rate of change can be as high as 5% to 25% from one version to the next. This change entails the simultaneous updating of all the software elements, the specification and documentation as well as the programs and test suites. A software system quickly becomes obsolete if all its components are not compatible with each other. This step-by-step further development of a complex software system makes considerable demands on both the software developer and the software manager. Discipline and systematic ways of working are essential here.

Maintenance

Maintenance denotes keeping a system in a functioning form. This includes correcting faults and, in addition, adapting the software to changes in the technical environment. Changes in component systems, such as database systems, graphics terminals and operating systems must be catered for immediately. Critical errors must be corrected or avoided. Functional changes are only undertaken where previous performance has to be maintained. For this reason, the cost of maintenance is sporadic and so difficult to plan. It is therefore ad hoc in nature and should not be confused with the planned phases of further development.

Software development phases

A project is a passage through the software development cycle. In consequence, a software product is a version of a system, one stage in the automation of an area of application. As projects can take up to two years, they last too long to allow effective project control. Management, however, needs to be able to measure the progress of a project. In addition, many individual activities in a project must be structured, and to this end projects are divided into phases.

There are many different phase concepts, typified by those of the DoD, ACM, IEEE and IBM-FSD. Almost every company that produces software has its own phase concept with its own terminology for the phases. One of the best-known phase concepts in Germany is ADV-Orga's ORGWARE concept.

What almost all phase concepts have in common is that they differentiate between implementation and planning. Implementation involves producing the kernel of the software the programs themselves. Planning involves designing the system as a whole. A distinction is also usually drawn between application-oriented and technical planning. Application-oriented planning leads to an application concept, whereas technical planning leads to the technical DP concept. There is often a difference, too, between programming and testing in the implementation stages. Finally, there is a phase at the end of the project to allow for delivery and introduction of the new product. Hence we have the following five project phases:

- application specification
- system design
- programming
- testing
- delivery.

Application specification

In the application specification phase, the requirements of automating an application are established, analysed and assigned priorities. They then serve as a starting point for the rough specification using a function model and a data model. The external users' view and the internal data structures are drawn up from the data model, and program structure and decision logic are drawn up on the basis of the function model. Finally, all the data and function elements relevant to the application are catalogued. This phase should result in a comprehensive, formal, consistent and plausible concept for the application.

System design

During the design phase the application concept is translated into a technical DP concept for the particular target environment. This involves converting the logical data model into a physical database schema, the logical function model into a program outline and the user views into physical masks, reports and so on. A test environment is designed at the same time. In this phase developers use data description languages for the relevant database systems and use program specification languages to design the programs. The aim is to standardize the data structures and to ensure that the programs are modular and structured. This phase should result in a system design that is ready to be implemented.

Programming

In the programming phase the design elements are coded into a particular compiled programming language and/or a database language. This should bee the least problematical phase of all, as program coding has recently become highly automated. This phase should result in executable programs and accessible databases.

Testing

The first part of the test phase is to run the individual program modules in a test framework, checking their logical correctness. This involves testing each branch of a module, validating all results and confirming that all the parts of the module work together as they should. Here the programs are being checked against their specification. Next the databases are fed test data, terminal interfaces are simulated with test masks and the programs are tested in combination with one another and with the databases. Here the interfaces are being checked. Finally the programs are tested in this latter environment with actual users and under real production conditions. Here the system's interaction with the user and with the technical environment are being validated. This phase should result in a fully tested program system.

Delivery

In the last phase, the fully tested system, complete with the application's documentation, is handed over to the end user or installed at the end user's site. At this point the programs may be checked again to ensure that they conform to their guidelines and to the application documentation. This phase results in an automated or semi-automated application.

Aims of Software management

In a narrow definition, software management has two main aims:

- to increase software productivity
- to improve software quality.

In addition to these purely technical aims, the software should serve the following corporate financial aims:

- the automation of all corporate application
- machine storage of all corporate data.

These four aims are of course interconnected, and so it is not possible to pursue one aim without affecting the others. In the final analysis, everything is related to everything else.

Increasing software productivity

Software productivity is measured in units produced, be they statements, function points, components, data elements, decisions or a combination of these elements. What is important is quantifiability of productivity. Without being able to quantify productivity, we cannot measure it. Without being able to measure productivity, we cannot measure the extent to which we have achieved our aim. Software is, of course, a multidimensional product. Individual phase results — the application concept, the system design, the programs, the test environment, the user documentation are in one dimension. In the other dimension we have the measures of the phase results, such as the number of:

- objects, procedures, functions, data, decisions and relationships in the application concept
- databases, DC-interfaces, data records, data fields, processes, programs, modules and pseudo-code statements in the system design
- database descriptions (DBDs), maps, modules, branches, paths, arguments, results, predicates and statements in the programs
- test cases, test data, test procedures, test drivers and test stubs in the test environments

- pages of text and diagrams in the user documentation.

Improving software quality

Software quality is measured by a variety of characteristics, such as:

- reliability
- security
- efficiency
- user friendliness
- maintainability
- adaptability
- portability.

Here, too, we must quantify quality. For example, reliability can be measured by the relationship between the number of errors and the number of test cases, or maintainability by the relationship between the cost of maintenance and the cost of development. Quality is of course relative to the user's expectations. For some users, security is everything, while for others it is efficiency, and for yet others user friendliness is the most important factor. Quality characteristics must therefore be weighted according to the user's criteria.

Automating corporate applications

The degree to which corpoarte applications are automated is measured by the extent to which the firm's functions are supported by machines. I measure this of course implies that we need to know the firm's function Only then can we determine which of these function are automated.

Functions requireing physical energy should be carried out by robots and functions requiring mental energy should be carried out by programs. This means that the application is completely automated once no-one working in the pure application area.

Automating corporate data

Automation of corporate data is measured by the percentage of the firm' data which is stored on a machine and can be processed by machine. Her too we must of course know what data the firm needs. We can determine this from an analysis of corporate data, and at the same time we can establish which of these data items are stored on machines. Stored on machines mean that the data exists in a codified, machine readable form which programs can access without human interaction. The aim of data automation is therefore to store as much data as possible on machines.

Software management tasks

With regard to the aims stated above, software management is responsible for a series of related tasks ranging from analysis of the firm's operation through to management of existing software systems. In particular, this includes:

- establishing and documenting corporate applications (both actual an target)
- establishing and documenting corporate information requirement (both actual and target)
- defining and costing DP projects to meet requirements
- planning and managing DP projects
- managing DP systems in operation
- advising users on the use of the DP systems on offer.

It should of course be borne in mind that, alongside these mainstream activities, software management has numerous peripheral activities such as looking after corporate users, advising corporate managers and extending the actual production environment. The introduction of modern software technology is in itself a far-reaching project which demands many resources without, bringing immediate benefits. Benefits are only gained in the medium term from the firm's own software production and improved quality. Nevertheless such support tasks are indispensable for the achievement of the main aims.

Establishing and documenting corporate applications

To achieve the aims of automating corporate applications, the software manager must know to what extent current applications are automated and to what extent they should be automated in the immediate future. He must therefore examine the firm's procedures and data flows, identify individual processes and determine the level of automation. This actual situation must be documented and at the same time a projected target situation must be modelled incorporating a higher degree of automation of existing applications. This should be done by using procedural analysis methods.

We should mention at this point that on-line data processing is only a temporary state of automation, a state of semi-automation. What many proclaim as progress, namely tying the user to a terminal screen, is for others a new form of salvery. The user is forced to react to the machine and to serve it as part of the on-line access to a system, be it a PC or a host.

Establishing and documenting corporate information requirements

An analysis of information requirements goes hand in hand with the analysis of corporate applications. here we have to establish which data is used from existing applications, how it is used and in what form it is stored. Once this is done, the next task is to establish future information requirements on the basis of the applications planned, i.e. how the corporate data is to be structured, stored and used. Here information analysis methods should be used. It ought to be obvious that total automation of a firm's operations presupposes machine capture of all corporate data.

Analysing corporate requirements

The demands made on data processing arise out of the difference between the actual and the target state of affairs, both in automating functions an storing data on machines. It is incumbent on the software manage measure this difference and to define various levels of automation. E level should be achievable within two years. In addition, the demands should be categorized by subject area. The demands can then be divided their respective subject areas and time units.

Evolutionary software implies hauling oneself up from subject are subject area and from level to level. Automation is therefore implemented in many small steps instead of in one large jump. The demands are dealt one after another.

This of course presupposes that all the data processing demands can precisely formulated, identified and recorded. That is the task of demand analysis.

Defining and costing DP projects

A DP project is a bundle of tasks having a time limit. The aim of the tasks to achieve a higher level of automation. A project may encompass on more demands. Defining a software project involves determining the scope of the target software system which is to be produced or altered. Software systems defined in terms of their quantity and quality. The quantity of a system i sum of all the affected elements in the system plus the sum of their relationships. The quality of a system is the product of its quality characteristics.

Costing a software project involves calculating the expense and duration of a project. The quantity and quality factors are accompanied by productivity factor. To be able to cost the project, the software man must be able to establish the productivity of his software developers and to compare quantitative and qualitative demands with the time and cost constraints. The result is what is feasible for the project.

Planning and managing DP projects

Once a project has been evaluated and authorized, the software man has to plan and manage the implementation of the project. Planning a software project involves dividing it into phases and phases into tasks. At the same time the product is divided into p products and the partial products into individual resuls. Then a time-scale for the tasks must be drawn up and their interdependencies must be explicit. Finally, corporate resources must be allocated to the tasks.

Managing a software project involves monitoring deadlines and cost as well as progress and quality and, if necessary, making corrections or altering plans. Deadlines and costs can be derived from an acounting system. The project's progress can be measured form the number of tasks completed. Product quality can be determined with appropriate machine aids as well as from reviews and inspections. Planned deadlines, tasks, progress and quality are regularly compared with their actual counterparts to establish any variances from the plan.

Introducing and managing finished systems

Developing a complex DP system is one thing, introducing and managing it is another.

Introducing the system entails allocation of necessary corporate resources, training users and often reorganizing the areas affected. It is obvious that this is not a painless operation. It is not only staff that have to be systematically prepared from a new system; the corporate organization must also be adapted, particularly as far as communication with neighbouring systems is concerned. This is a difficult corporate economic, sociological and technical task.

Once a new system is in use, the software manager has to maintain the software components of the system. To do this, he must use the techniques of configuration management. ALl the software components and documentation in use must be identified and recorded. The state and location of the software must be tracked and responsibility must be regulated. In addition, error reporting and changes must be kept up to date. The software manager is responsible for recording all reported errors and changes and for ensuring that they are included as new demands. This requires a certain software 'bureaucracy'.

Looking after software users

A final, but no less important, task of the software manager is to look after software users. As long as there are people who have to interact with systems, there will be problems with man-machine communication. It is therefore incumbent on the software manager to make staff available in a user support centre —who can advise and help users in carrying out their daily tasks. This is just as true for systems developed in house as for systems acquired from outside.

The support staff must, of course, themselves have been trained in the use of the new systems as well as in dealing with users. This support task is becoming more and more important as automation increases.

Quality assessment

The role of *internal quality management system audit is* different from that of an external assessment. Internal quality system auditing is concerned with verifying that the work being performed in an organization is in accordance *with planned arrangements;* that is, in accordance with the organization's quality management system and quality plans. If the quality management system is being complied with, then it will be acceptable to internal audit even if it does not conform to ISO 9001. Internal audit is also concerned with the effectiveness of the organization's quality management system, to make sure it gives the organization the maximum benefits. Internal audit should add value, not increase costs.

External assessors have the responsibility of determining if an organization's quality management system complies with a selected quality management system standard. While this will obviously include some observations on effectiveness and suitability of the system, it is more concerned with conformance to ISO 9001.

Internal audit can be seen as a form of management by walking around. Internal audit is finding out if the organization is running the way management want it run. In many cases, management would be better off finding out for themselves than sending somebody around to do it for them. If you use an internal auditor, remember that they are management's representative and have a contribution to make to the efficiency and effectiveness of the organization. The auditor should add value and be quick to identify opportunities for improvement as well as to condemn inefficiency, over control, and overly complex processes. All of these are related to the need specified in ISO 9001 for the system to be effective and suitable. If the auditor does not add value then this is unnecessary overhead.

To assist with the conduct of an audit, checklists should be prepared. These checklists will guide the auditor to points that need to be covered during the audit. They may be used prior to the audit or during it, at the auditor's discretion. However, care must be taken to ensure that the checklists do not become confining. The auditor must always be prepared to follow up any line of inquiry that could yield information, Forms and other working records may also be used for reporting observations and documenting supporting evidence for conclusions reached by the auditor. Working records should be designed so that they do not restrict additional audit activities or investigations that may become necessary as a result of information gathered during the audit. Working records involving confidential or proprietary information should be suitably safeguarded by the auditor.

An auditor should be formally appointed to conduct the audit to ensure the people being audited are aware of the source of the auditor's right to question and investigate. The auditor must be independent and ;must not have direct responsibility for the work being audited. The auditor should review previous audits relevant to the one being conducted, review the requirements of the quality management system, and prepare a plan for the audit that addresses each procedure to be audited. The plan for each audit within the program should be designed to be flexible in order to permit changes in emphasis based on information gathered during the audit, and to permit effective use of resources. The auditor should prepare a written audit report based on the audit plan. The auditor is only responsible for identifying nonconformance. The auditee is responsible for determining and initiating the action needed to correct nonconformances and to correct the root causes of nonconformances. A copy of the audit report should be made available for the next management review meeting.

Policies

Typical policies addressing internal quality system audit requirements of ISO 9001 include the following:

> THE MANAGEMENT REPRESENTATIVE SHALL APPOINT AN AUDITOR WHO SHALL BE INDEPENDENT OF THE WORK BEING AUDITED. THE AUDITOR SHALL HAVE BEEN TRAINED IN THE RELEVANT AUDIT PROCEDURES AS WELL AS IN THE CONCEPTS OF AUDITING.

This policy identifies who is responsible for appointing the auditor. It also gives the auditor the authority necessary to perform the audit. Auditor training is always a topic of great interest to assessors, so you will need to lay down training requirements for auditors. These may be as simple as on-the-job training by participating in two or three audits with your consultant or another trained auditor or may involve attendance in a training course. It is your quality management system; you decide what is needed.

Audit scheduling is the responsibility of the management representative. The audit schedule shall be revised and updated regularly. One full audit of the quality management system shall be performed each year. Audits in addition to those scheduled shall be performed as deemed necessary.

AUDIT SCHEDULING IS USED TO GIVE A BROAD VIEW OF THE AUDIT ACTIVITIES FOR A YEAR AND IS DESIGNED TO ENSURE ALL PROCESSES AND PROCEDURES AND ALL PARTS OF THE ORGANIZATION ARE AUDITED. DON'T FORGET TO AUDIT THE AUDIT PROCESS ITSELF (AUDIT THE AUDITORS). PROJECT AUDITS MAY BE SUBJECT TO A SEPARATE SCHEDULE. PROJECTS SHOULD BE AUDITED EARLY BEFORE THEY HAVE A CHANCE TO HEAD IN THE WRONG DIRECTION, AND LATE WHEN SHORTCUTS START TO HAPPEN TO MEET DEADLINES. MAKE SURE YOU AUDIT IMPORTANT THINGS MORE OFTEN THAN TRIVIAL ONES. THERE IS A TENDENCY TO KEEP AUDITING THE EASY PARTS AND AVOID THE DIFFICULT AREAS WHERE REAL CONTRIBUTIONS CAN BE MADE.

The Auditor shall conduct the audit in accordance with the defined procedure. Nonconformances to the quality management system shall be classified as major (significant nonconformance requiring major corrective action) or minor (minor nonconformance that can be readily corrected). On completion of the audit, the Auditor shall prepare an audit report describing the audit findings, summarizing the nonconformances and listing any proposed corrective actions. This policy points to the appropriate audit procedure. You should choose a classification scheme (e.g., major and minor) suitable to your business. Nonconformances should be documented and the manager of the group being audited should commit to rectifying the nonconformances in an acceptable time. A basic rule is that the auditor finds the nonconformances and the manger fixes them. This does not mean that the auditor cannot support the manager in identifying possible causes and fixes. You need to be careful to maintain auditor independence but keep in mind that auditing should mean adding value, not picking on every little detail.

When a nonconformance has been recorded and agreed to by the relevant manager then corrective action shall be initiated by the manager. Dates for implementation of corrective action shall be agreed between the manager and the auditor and these shall be recorded. This should point to the standard problem reporting procedure. The manager should commit to a date for clearing the nonconformance and this must be monitored. The management representative should have a record of the status of all nonconformances to the quality management system and the executive should take action on nonconformances that have not been cleared by the agreed date. Failure by the executive to take action on late clearance of nonconformances is a symptom of lack of management commitment.

Issues

Examine your quality management system and ask yourself if the following issues have been addressed and whether you can produce evidence. in the form of records or documents that they have been followed in practice:

- Does the system for internal quality audits operate against a planned schedule?
- Does the system require the scope of each audit to be clearly defined?
- Does the internal system extend to on-site/remote site activities? Does the system require the audit results to be documented?
- Does the system require necessary corrective actions to be initiated, reviewed, and closed out positively within a reasonable time scale?
- Does the system require audits to be performed by qualified personnel having sufficient independence and authority?

Corrective and preventive action

The techniques used to identify and correct the cause of problems will be those used by TQM practitioners and include those defined in ISO 9004.4.

Corrective action

Corrective action is the process of determining the *cause* of problems, defects, and deficiencies, and rectifying that cause. This means that there must be a mechanism to record *everything* that goes wrong. A common concern with this need to record is the fear of being inundated with problem reports. A much more common problem is the failure of people to record problems for fear of repercussions or delaying the work. A significant part of the implementation program must be to drive out this fear and encourage input.

Preventive action

Preventive action analyzes the way things are done to identify and eliminate potential causes of problems. This includes an ongoing process of review of the way work is done as well as examining customer complaints and feedback to identify ways of working better. This is often called process improvement and is a significant part of TQM programs. It is important, however, not to be sidetracked from quality management into a full TQM program at this stage. The formalization of the management system (quality management) is a precursor to TQM. The development and implementation of a quality management system usually brings significant benefits in its own right. Once the initial benefits are being obtained and staff develop an acceptance of quality as a way of life then a more formalized improvement process or TQM program can be initiated and documented as an update to the quality management system.

Policies

Typical policies addressing the corrective action requirements of ISO 9001 include the following:

> WHEN ANY NONCONFORMANCE, DEFECT OR DEFICIENCY IS IDENTIFIED IN A SERVICE OR RELEASED PRODUCT THEN IT SHALL BE RECORDED AND DOCUMENTED IN SUFFICIENT DETAIL TO ENABLE IT TO BE RESOLVED. WHERE THE PROBLEM RELATES TO A DEFECTIVE PRODUCT THEN CONTROL OF NONCONFORMING PRODUCT SHALL BE INITIATED TO RECTIFY THE DEFECT.

This policy identifies the need to record quality problems and should point to the problem reporting procedure. The policy also identifies what a problem is. In software development we need to decide at what point we should start recording and analyzing problems, otherwise we may find ourselves raising a problem report for each compilation error. A good starting point is to apply problem reporting when something is released outside the development team. As the quality improves you may decide to initiate problem reporting earlier in the development process. Finally, it is useful to point people to the other part of problem management, which is rectifying the defect (fixing the problem), by using "control of nonconforming product procedures."

> THE CAUSE OF THE PROBLEM SHALL BE IDENTIFIED AND ANY CORRECTIVE ACTIONS REQUIRED SHALL BE INITIATED. THESE CORRECTIVE ACTIONS SHALL BE VERIFIED AND THE SITUATION MONITORED TO ENSURE THE CORRECTIVE ACTION HAS BEEN EF

This policy identifies the need to find the cause of the problem. This is not some trivial exercise in allocating blame or identifying superficial causes. It should be aimed at identifying root causes and taking action to remove them. Root causes are usually resolved only by management as they are often part of the way we work (part of the management system). A whole industry has been built up that offers approaches to identifying and removing the root causes of problems. You may wish to implement such a TQM program or adopt some of the problem analysis techniques proposed; ISO 9004.4 contains some excellent techniques. This policy should reference the approach to be adopted.

> ON A REGULAR BASIS (APPROXIMATELY MONTHLY) REVIEW SERVICE REQUESTS; PROJECT, PRODUCT AND DESIGN REVIEWS; INSPECTION AND TEST RESULTS; PROBLEM REPORTS AND CHANGE REQUESTS TO IDENTIFY ANY TRENDS THAT MAY REQUIRE CORRECTIVE ACTION. CONCESSIONS, MAINTENANCE AND SERVICE REQUESTS, TRAINING EVALUATIONS AND CUSTOMER COMPLAINTS SHALL BE INCLUDED IN THESE ANALYSES.

Despite having a formal problem reporting procedure there are significant benefits in examining everything we do and seeing if there are any improvement opportunities or patterns developing that point to potential problems. As with problem reporting we should be looking closely at root causes and not just local, simple fixes.

ANY CHANGES TO THE QUALITY MANAGEMENT SYSTEM DOCUMENTATION SHALL BE MANAGED UNDER FORMAL CHANGE CONTROL PROCESSES. CHANGES REQUESTED DURING CORRECTIVE ACTION SHALL BE APPLIED TO THE QUALITY MANAGEMENT SYSTEM IN ACCORDANCE WITH QUALITY MANAGEMENT SYSTEM DOCUMENTATION CONTROL. THE NORMAL REVIEW AND ACCEPTANCE PROCESS WILL ENSURE THAT ALL OUTSTANDING CHANGES HAVE BEEN PROCESSED IN THE NEW RELEASE OF THE QUALITY MANAGEMENT SYSTEM.

As mentioned earlier, most problems are due to the management system and, therefore, correction of the root causes would require changes to the quality management system. These changes must be properly managed and this is done by referencing the change request procedure with its associated reviews and signoff.

Any skills deficiencies and/or training required as part of corrective action shall be included in the training plan.

Problems are often caused by people not following processes or not knowing that there are processes to be followed. The action to be taken is to train the people in the existence and use of the processes. This training may be provided on-the-job, or the need for longer-term or more intensive training recorded in the training plan.

Where work is being undertaken as a project then the project manager shall prepare regular reports on the status of, and progress made on, each project. These reports shall include the achievement of targets, compliance with the quality plan and the status of internal management milestones.

Status reporting only provides information unless there are problems or potential problems. For this reason it is logical to put a policy calling for status reporting in this section. Status reporting may also be used to provide evidence of process control.

A monthly status report shall be provided to the executive which includes a summary of each corrective action raised within the organization, actions taken and an analysis of the effectiveness of the corrective action.

This status report records the corrective actions being taken to clear nonconformances identified by audit as well as the actions being taken to remove the root causes of all problems identified. This report should be presented to the executive as evidence of control of corrective actions. Management of this report is one of the most important tasks undertaken by the executive. If they are not managing what is going wrong and driving the organization to improve, then what are they doing?

Control of quality records

Quality records are the evidence that the quality management system is operating in accordance with defined processes and plans "in accordance with planned arrangements" as well as in accordance with ISO 9001; these records are used by external assessors, customers, internal auditors, and management.

Each process should generate evidence that it has been performed properly.

However there is no need to go overboard with records. Trees look much nicer growing than they do as pieces of paper in a filing cabinet. The extent of recordkeeping should be consistent with the need to demonstrate that you have done the right thing or followed due process. A rule of thumb to apply if you are concerned about records is to ask yourself if you would look foolish if you were required to prove your competence and you had forgotten to keep the records.

Quality records is where the bureaucrat comes to the fore. Bureaucrats generate mountains of useless paper and justify it, and its management, as being required. Unless you are a totally paperless organization there should not be a quantum increase in records. Hopefully, by thinking about your processes you will experience a quantum decrease in records. (If you subcontract work, then copies of quality records produced by your subcontractor should be kept as part of your quality records for your contract with your customer.)

Records may be kept on computer providing you can attest to the authority under which a product was released as passing inspection. This can be done by signing, when required, that the attached computer printout is a true record of inspection. Be careful; the records and evidence we talk about in quality management are not necessarily legally acceptable records. Consult your legal advisers regarding legality of records. The acceptability of records referred to here is acceptability to a quality system assessor.

Quality records management is a straightforward exercise. There is a need to make sure that records are identifiable to the thing that they record; the project, product, batch, version, and type of record should be easily ascertained. People need to know how to collect records and where to send them. If a computer is used to collect records then its use needs to be described. There must be a catalogue (index) of records so that authorized people can find quality records even if the person we normally ask is unavailable. Records must be filed on some media that has to be stored somewhere. For example, records may be filed in manila folders and stored in a filing cabinet. Records may need to be updated by new information being appended. They need to be retrieved for examination and processing. They need to be culled when superseded, archived when no longer required for current processing, and have other maintenance tasks performed on them. Finally, records need to be disposed of when no longer useful. This is always of concern because of the varying legal and contractual conditions for retaining records. Consult your legal adviser on the issue of records disposal.

Quality management system records

Records must be kept for all activities connected with the quality management system. These records include the configuration management records for the quality management system documentation itself, problem reports and change requests relating to the quality management system, and other records relating to the development and review of the quality management system, including the following:

Quality system audits.

Software development environments.

Management reviews.

Training.

Project records

Records must be kept for each project. These provide the evidence that the project was executed in conformance with the quality management system, including the quality plan for the project. These records must be retained:

- For legal reasons; based on both the contract for the project and the need for the enterprise to protect itself from future actions.
- For the team; to provide evidence for future inquiries, audits, and routine system reviews that correct procedures were followed. This material also assists future reviews of functionality.

Project quality records are retained by the project manager until completion of the project when they are handed to the quality manager. They include the following:

- Project quality records file.
- Project deliverable documents.
- Standards and procedures used (optional).

Retention periods of five to ten years are not uncommon.

Polices

Typical policies addressing records management requirements of ISO 9001 include the following:

THE MANAGEMENT REPRESENTATIVE MAINTAINS A CATALOGUE OF ALL FILES CONTAINING QUALITY RECORDS.

ISO 9001 requires records to be indexed. This is best done by having an index or catalogue of files, particularly those relating to quality management. The catalogue should identify what the file is, what it contains, how the records are filed, and who has custody of it.

For work performed as a project the project manager retains the records until the project is completed. At this time the records are handed into the care of the management representative.

Project records should logically be managed by the project manager. After completion of the project the new custodian should be identified. This may be the management representative, the company archives, or the maintenance/support manager.

FOR WORK PERFORMED AS A CONTINUOUS PROCESS OR PROCESSES THE RECORDS SHALL BE RETAINED BY THE PROCESS SUPERVISOR.

This policy would be useful for help/support desk records and computer operations records.

Records no longer required for reference or internal quality audits shall be archived with the organization's archives

Specify the policy with respect to archiving records. You will need to refer to an archive procedure that will show how records are indexed and stored as well as how to retrieve records from the archives.

As each process, review, inspection or test which generates a record is completed then the original or copy of the record produced shall be filed in the relevant file.

This is one of a number of policies you will specify that appear so self-evident that you wonder why you need to write them. There are two reasons: First, they need to be written down somewhere. Second, while you may believe everybody knows your policies it is very often not the case. Many people have no idea how even the most basic things are done in an organization.

Records shall be legible and kept in accordance with normally accepted office practices and shall be protected from loss or damage. Records shall be available within one day of being requested.

This is an apparently self-evident statement. You must be able to read the records; in a multi-language culture you may need to specify what languages are acceptable. Records should be put away where they won't be damaged by coffee or engine oil or thrown out by the cleaners as rubbish.

Records shall contain identification of the project (if a project record), the work being done and the product to which it refers (including versions and release, as applicable).

Records should show what they apply to. This may include a version number of some sort or the date and time stamp on a computer file. After all, you do not review a document, you review a version of a document.

Where copies of the quality management system documentation are to be kept as records then they shall be removed from their distribution list, marked as not to be used or updated and filed with the relevant records.

It is often useful, or even necessary, to keep an old copy of documentation (such as a standards manual), and yet we have to make sure old versions of documentation are not used during development. We can do this by converting the document to a record by making it unchangeable.

Pertinent subcontractor records shall form part of the records. These will be defined in the subcontract.

One of the important points about using subcontractors is that it in no way relieves us of the need to meet requirements. This means that any records we are required to produce or retain for our customer will have to be produced by our subcontractor. Consequently, we must make sure we get copies of relevant subcontractor records and keep these as part of our records.

Records shall be kept for a minimum period of five years from the date of final inspection unless a longer period is required by contract or legislation. A written request to dispose of project quality records shall be signed by the management representative and other appropriate authorities.

We need to define policies with respect to the retention of records. This is a difficult task in most societies where we may be subject to many legislative requirements for recordkeeping. Check with your legal advisers before you commit to a disposition policy.

Customers shall be given access to all records related to work done for them. The customer shall undertake to protect the confidentiality of all information provided. If a confidentiality agreement is not in force then one shall be executed.

We should be happy to let our customers see records relating to work we have done for them. In some cases the records may relate to some proprietary processes, so we may need to ask the customer to sign a confidentiality agreement.

Third parties, other than our certification agency, shall not be given access to, or information about, records relating to customers without the written permission of the customer for whom the work was performed.

We should look after the confidentiality of our customers and this can be accomplished by refusing to divulge either records or even the existence of records. Obviously, the laws of your country will contain situations, such as court orders where you will have to breach this requirement but it is not really necessary to specify these in your policy. The identification of your certification body as a third party able to look at customer records is there so that assessments can be made without having a nonconformance raised for breach of this policy.

Issues

Examine your quality management system and ask yourself if the following issues have been addressed and whether you can produce evidence in the form of records or documents that they have been followed in practice:

- Is a system established for the identification, collection, indexing, filing, storage, maintenance, and disposition of quality records?
- Does the system require records to be readily retrievable?
- Does the system require inspection results to show if specified requirements have been achieved or the nature of nonconformance?

- Does the system extend to subcontractor records?
- Does the system require retention times for records to be established and recorded?
- Does the system require records to be stored in an environment that will minimize deterioration or damage and prevent loss?
- Does the system allow for customer evaluation of the records?

Training

Training is a significant part of our drive for quality. We should be training people all the time as we diversify their abilities, enrich their jobs, build a more flexible work force, and improve our processes. It is important to identify the training needs of our people and make sure that all staff have the education, training, and experience necessary to do their jobs. Any training required to satisfy customer, regulatory, or contract requirements should be identified during the contract review process and included in the quality plan.

There is a need to have records that people have been trained in specific processes as well as records of their previous skills, training, education, and experience. These records should then be used to allocate our people to the work that has to be performed. Most of us are poor at keeping training records and it can be surprising to discover that we really do a lot of training, from on-the-job right through to formal external training. We usually only record the external training or special internal training that costs us direct money paid out to some trainer or training organization. We must now collect and verify (as best we can) the skills and experience of our people and then supplement this with records of which processes they have been trained in. Each time somebody receives some training, including counseling on how to follow processes properly, an informal walkthrough of a process, or an on-the-job coaching session, this should be recorded.

If you deliver training as a product or service, your quality management system will need to address the design of training courses and materials, the processes of delivering training, and the evaluation of training delivery. In other words, training is one of your products or services. This section of ISO 9001 would then apply to ensuring your staff are trained in the preparation and delivery of training.

Policies

Training needs shall be identified and recorded as part of management review, performance appraisal, quality planning, corrective action, and input from employees, supervisors, and management. All new employees have a need for initial training in the quality management system. Auditors shall be specifically trained in audit procedures and in the concepts of quality system auditing.

Identify what processes and/or situations will identify the need for training. This includes the introduction of new processes, procedures, and technology. Make sure all staff are trained in the quality management system. Note that training includes what is often referred to as counseling, guidance, admonishing, and possibly disciplinary action. It is useful to specifically mention the training needs of internal quality auditors.

When a member of our staff has received any training this shall be recoraed and management shall make an assessment of the effectiveness of the training and its contribution toward proficiency. Training includes in-house and on-the-job training as well as external training and education.

All training provided should be recorded. This is especially important for training in internal audit and initial training in the quality management system. You should be able to provide evidence that your people are qualified to perform the work assigned to them. Make sure you have a record of the skills your people brought with them when they started working with you. A copy of their resume annotated as accepted by the selection team is a good record of these skills. IEEE 1298 also calls for an assessment of training effectiveness that may be as simple as management signing off the training.

Our people shall be assigned to tasks on the basis of their skills, education, training and experience in performing the work required. This shall be done with reference to the training records.

This again refers to the need for our people to be properly trained. We often assign people to tasks without analyzing their capability to do the job, or worse, fail to assign somebody because we forgot that they had the skills we needed.

Issues

Examine your quality management system and ask yourself if the following issues have been addressed and whether you can produce evidence in the form of records or documents that they have been followed in practice:

- Is there a system for the identification of training needs of all personnel?
- Does the system require education/training to be provided where required?
- Does the system require training records to be maintained?
- Does the system require records containing details of education, training, and skills to be maintained for all personnel performing activities affecting quality?

Product identification and traceability

Product identification and traceability is also known as configuration management. It addresses the requirement to be able to trace a product (or component) back through the various specification documents to its original specification.

The point in the process at which products are subject to formal configuration control should be carefully chosen to optimize the benefits of flexibility of development against control over inspected products. As a general rule, configuration management should be initiated once we start spending money on inspection and test.

This prevents people from continuing to work on products that have already been through an inspection and approval process thus negating the inspection and incurring additional reinspection costs. In certain cases the product is documentation. Sometimes it is not even clear whether that documentation is quality system documentation as managed in accordance with Document and Data Control or a real product. For instance, we may consider plans, requirements specifications, and design output to be documentation products or quality management system documentation. It really does not matter as there should be adequate control over these and the mechanisms for control should be the same. That is, they will include proper authorization, version control, change control, and distribution control. For the purposes of drawing a line between quality management system documentation and documentation product, you might look on quality management system documentation as anything contributing to the quality of what we deliver to the customer and documentation product as any document we deliver to the customer to satisfy their requirement. To this end quality management system documentation would include plans, requirements specifications, and design output, as these are all part of the definition of what we have to produce in terms of user guides, operations manuals, and computer programming. We also deliver the requirements specification and design documentation, but this is to enable customers to take over the ongoing maintenance of the product we have developed.

Policies

Typical policies addressing product identification and traceability requirements of ISO 9001 include the following:

> WHEN A PRODUCT OR MANAGEABLE PART OF A PRODUCT IS TO BE PRODUCED THEN ALL RELEVANT IDENTIFICATION INFORMATION SHALL BE RECORDED INCLUDING THE SOURCE OF SPECIFICATION AND DESIGN. THE IDENTIFICATION OF VERSIONS SHALL BE AS DEFINED IN THE CONTRACT OR IN THE PRODUCT IDENTIFICATION PROCEDURE. THE IDENTIFICATION OF DOCUMENTATION PRODUCT IS NORMALLY BY VERSION NUMBER WITH REVISIONS BEING IDENTIFIED BY REVISION LETTER.

We need to identify our products with an ability to trace back to the original specification. In software development we usually have very clear traceability from the requirements specification to the design/programming specification through to the programming. This may prove more difficult with some techniques than with others. This is particularly so where we may have difficulty relating objects back to user requirements. The IEEE software engineering standards have some good informatior on the procedures necessary, but do not fall into the trap of meeting excessive DoD type configuration control if it adds no value. to the work you are doing for your customer. A product register identifying file number, version number (e.g., date and time stamp), and source of requirement is a reasonable starting point.

> WHEN A PRODUCT HAS BEEN APPROVED AND ACCEPTED THEN IT SHALL BE IDENTIFIED AS RELEASED BY AN AUTHORIZED RECORD SHOWING THE CURRENT VERSION.

This can be as simple as adding a status field to the product register and recording the status as released along with the identifier of the person (e.g., from logon authentication) who set the status to released.

WHERE RELEVANT, A MASTER LIST OF PERSONS OR ORGANIZATIONS HOLDING CONTROLLED COPIES OF PRODUCTS SHALL BE MAINTAINED.

Distribution lists are already being maintained for quality management system documentation. These could be extended to cover distribution of product. Note that you may not need (or be able) to have full distribution control. In the case of off the shelf software you must rely on people registering as users to provide partial distribution control. In other cases there is no value in maintaining any form of distribution control (for example, training course handouts).

When a product is to be changed the effect of the change(s) shall be reviewed through all possible affected items, both done before the change (e.g., product requirements and design) and applicable after the change (e.g., test plans, test specifications and testing) to ensure the change is properly integrated. Where the review shows that changes have effects on other products then these effects shall be identified and any necessary retesting defined. All affected products shall have the changes applied with the same date of effect. When the product has been changed a new version shall be created and released after all reviews, inspections and tests have been satisfactorily completed. This calls for proper control of changes to products after release. In the case of software it is very important to have full change control and accountability through the various releases of software. Once a unit of software has been placed under configuration control formal change management procedures will need to be followed. This indicates the need for careful control over the point at which product is subject to formal control. As with corrective action it is probably best to start off with controlling the programming when it is released outside the team, for example, when it is released for user testing. In some development environments, such as the clean room, concept configuration control is initiated as soon as coding is completed.

Issues

Examine your quality management system and ask yourself if the following issues have been addressed and whether you can produce evidence in the form of records or d t th t th have been followed in practice:

- Are there procedures for identifying the product from specifications during development, delivery, and installation?
- Is there a system to uniquely identify and record product for traceability?
- Do configuration management procedures include: Version identification, issue, and control? Obtaining approval to implement modifications?

Control of customer-supplied product

Customer-supplied product addresses the need to control and secure all Customer-supplied information and material and to ensure only suitable information and material is supplied by the customer and used in the process. If your business does not require you to make use of Customer-supplied product then you need only address this requirement of ISO 9001 by a statement of this form:

> THE NATURE OF OUR BUSINESS IS SUCH THAT THERE IS NO REQUIREMENT TO MAKE USE OF CUSTOMER SUPPLIED PRODUCT FOR INCORPORATION INTO THE GOODS OR SERVICES WE SUPPLY TO OUR CUSTOMERS.

Omitting such a statement may be construed by an assessor as an oversight or a failure to address this section of ISO 9001. Customer-supplied product may appear in many imaginative forms, such as hat-check services, safety-deposit services, goods left for repair, dry cleaning, papers submitted for passport applications, or fixed plant or machinery that you have to go to, such as service computers, elevators, and escalators. Customer-supplied product should be properly managed, stored, secured, and maintained. Disposition of Customer-supplied product should be defined. While we may initially accept the Customer-supplied product, we may subsequently reject it if it is found to be unsuitable for use.

Policies

Typical policies addressing Customer-supplied product requirements of ISO 9001 include the following:

> ALL PRODUCT RECEIVED FROM A CUSTOMER SHALL BE EXAMINED FOR SUITABILITY. THE VERIFICATION PROCESS SHALL BE BASED ON THE QUALITY MANAGEMENT SYSTEM AND SHALL FOLLOW RELEVANT REVIEW, INSPECTION AND TESTING PROCEDURES. IF THE CUSTOMER SUPPLIED PRODUCT IS ACCEPTABLE THEN IT SHALL BE RECORDED. WHERE THE PRODUCT IS DOCUMENTATION FOR ISSUE TO MORE THAN ONE PERSON, THEN PERMISSION TO COPY SHALL BE OBTAINED IN WRITING, COPIES PREPARED, AND DISTRIBUTED. WHILE WE MAY INITIALLY ACCEPT THE CUSTOMER SUPPLIED PRODUCT WE MAY SUBSEQUENTLY REJECT IT IF IT IS FOUND TO BE UNSUITABLE FOR USE.

This calls for the examination of customer supplied product to ensure it is suitable for use or for incorporation into the products we are going to deliver to them. To preclude failure to accept because "it may not work when we get further along in the project" you should reserve the right to reject it later if it is found to be unacceptable. While Customer-supplied product under ISO 9001 specifically refers to material provided for incorporation into the deliverables you should extend its coverage to all customer supplied product including office facilities, computers, software, and operating systems and documents. Where the customer supplies documents or software there may be a need to make copies for each team member; in this case make sure you protect yourself from copyright infringement by obtaining permission in writing from the customer to make copies.

> ACCEPTED CUSTOMER SUPPLIED PRODUCT SHALL BE KEPT IN A SAFE AND SECURE MANNER SUITABLE TO THE TYPE OF PRODUCT. OUR NORMAL PRACTICES SHOULD BE ADEQUATE BUT EXTRA REQUIREMENTS MAY BE DEFINED IN THE CONTRACT.

ANY LOSSES OR DAMAGE TO CUSTOMER SUPPLIED PRODUCT SHALL BE RECORDED AND THE CUSTOMER NOTIFIED IN WRITING. ANY EQUIPMENT SUPPLIED BY THE CUSTOMER SHALL BE MAINTAINED IN ACCORDANCE WITH CUSTOMER REQUIREMENTS OR MANUFACTURER'S RECOMMENDED PRACTICES.

Look after things the customer gives to you and let the customer know if anything gets broken, damaged, or lost. If changes are received to customer supplied product, then the new or changed product shall be reviewed and accepted and the full ramifications of the receipt shall be evaluated before the product is used.

This rarely happens in most industries but frequently happens in software development. No sooner are we given some software or equipment than we are given an updated version. The requirement to manage change also extends to changes to requirements and changes to the development environment.

Purchasing

Purchasing applies to the acquisition of services, material, equipment, or subcontract products or services for incorporation into what we are going to deliver to our customer. There is no requirement to bring all general purchasing, office supplies, or equipment purchasing into the system although it would obviously make sense to do so. If your business does not require you to purchase on behalf of your customer then you need only address this requirement of ISO 9001 by a statement of this form:

THE NATURE OF OUR BUSINESS IS SUCH THAT THERE IS NO REQUIREMENT TO PURCHASE GOODS OR SERVICES FOR DELIVERY TO OUR CUSTOMERS OR FOR INCORPORATION INTO THE GOODS OR SERVICES WE SUPPLY TO OUR CUSTOMERS.

Omitting such a statement may be construed by an assessor as an oversight or a failure to address this section of ISO 9001. A prime point of this section is that you cannot use vendors or subcontractors as an excuse for failing to satisfy your customer's needs. You are always totally responsible for quality and totally responsible for the goods or services you acquire from other sources. There is, therefore, the need to control the selection of suppliers of goods and services and a requirement to clearly and unambiguously specify what you want to purchase. There is also the need to carefully manage any subcontractors to make sure they do not cause a failure in the quality of goods or services you deliver to your customer.

You must also be sure that you are satisfied that the goods and services you have purchased meet specification. You can do this by inspecting and testing them yourself, by witnessing inspections and tests done by your supplier, or by accepting evidence that it has passed inspection and test. The acceptance of evidence should be used only where you have complete confidence in your supplier and would usually be only from suppliers who have a certificated quality management system covering the goods or services you are acquiring from them.

Your customers may want to inspect, test, or otherwise verify that goods or services you are purchasing on their behalf meet specification. When this occurs they should make all arrangements to meet with your supplier through you. You should always participate in these inspections, first to fully serve your customers and second to make sure your customers and your supplier don't end up working directly together to your disadvantage. Be aware that you cannot use your customers' visits to your supplier as evidence that you have control of the quality of the goods or services from that supplier. Your customers cannot be held accountable if, after verifying the goods or services at your supplier's premises, they subsequently reject them. Such are the joys of doing business. If we establish all the right relationships with our suppliers, enter into long-term agreements where possible, and totally service our customers, such problems should not arise.

If you are dealing with a new supplier who has a quality management system you should review their registration certificate to make sure they are certificated to perform the work you want. You should review the supplier's quality manual and perhaps review or audit the supplier's quality management system as it applies to the work you want them to perform.

Policies

Typical policies addressing the purchasing requirements of ISO 9001 include the following:

> VENDORS OF "OFF THE SHELF' GOODS AND SERVICES SHALL BE SELECTED ON THEIR ABILITY TO DELIVER THE GOODS OR SERVICES IN A TIMELY AND EFFICIENT MANNER. EVIDENCE OF QUALITY MANAGEMENT SYSTEMS SHOULD BE SOUGHT. A RECORD SHALL BE KEPT OF THE PERFORMANCE OF EACH VENDOR IN THE VENDOR FILE. VENDOR SELECTION SHOULD BE MADE ON THE BASIS OF THEIR HISTORICAL PERFORMANCE AT ACCEPTABLE PRICE FOR THE GRADE REQUIRED.

Although the first sentence appears totally self-evident, it is not what most of us do. Most purchasing concentrates solely on price, with quality and delivery almost universally ignored. It comes as no surprise to find that companies that purchase carefully have far fewer problems than the majority who buy with the motto "Cheap is best, free is better." It is good practice to encourage others to follow the quality path, so always ask potential suppliers if they are certificated to deliver what you want to buy, and if they are not certificated, when they intend to gain certification. The need to keep records means that you start your buying activities from a knowledge base rather than by relying on memory. This is especially important when many people may have the right to make purchasing decisions and we need to communicate our experiences with suppliers. Vendor selection policies may be as simple as "acceptable grade, on time at acceptable price" or may be only on the basis of established long-term relationships.

> TO ENSURE THAT PURCHASED GOODS AND SERVICES CONFORM TO CONTRACTUAL REQUIREMENTS ALL ITEMS TO BE PURCHASED OR DEVELOPED FOR A PROJECT SHALL BE DEFINED IN UNAMBIGUOUS TERMS AND SHALL BE IDENTIFIED BY SUITABLE MEANS TO ENSURE THAT THE VENDOR IS IN NO DOUBT AS TO WHAT IS

REQUIRED. DETAILED INSPECTION AND TESTING REQUIREMENTS AS WELL AS THE NEED FOR SPECIAL PACKAGING, TRANSPORT ARRANGEMENTS AND DELIVERY SHALL BE CONSIDERED. WARRANTY REQUIREMENTS SHALL BE DEFINED AS SHALL THE LIABILITIES OF THE PARTIES. THE PURCHASE SPECIFICATION SHALL BE REVIEWED AND APPROVED BEFORE BEING ISSUED.

The need for careful specification of purchasing becomes clear when we think of the multimillion-dollar disasters in any industry and see them being caused by suppliers who "didn't do what we wanted." The more time spent on specification the less time spent in litigation. For software developers this is especially true and applies to specification for in-house development as well as for subcontract development. IEEE 1298 has a section on the control of requirements specification and this should be carefully considered when preparing the specification for subcontract software development. The requirement to approve the purchase specification is one of only two requirements for approval (signoff) in ISO 9001 (the other is in document and data control), Subcontractors should be certificated to relevant quality management system standards with registered capability to perform the type of work we wish to subcontract. The subcontractor's quality management system should be reviewed or audited to ensure that procedures are acceptable and being followed.

Where subcontractors are not certificated then their quality management system shall be audited to identify the degree of conformance with the specified requirements. An estimate shall be made of the extra costs likely to be incurred to ensure quality is provided to the required standard and to put a cost on the risk of using them instead of a certificated subcontractor. These additional costs shall be added to the subcontractor's bid in order to compare subcontractor proposals.

Where the subcontractor's quality management system is unacceptable then it will be necessary to either manage the subcontractor personnel who shall work to our quality management system or to provide full-time inspection at the subcontractor's premises. The cost of managing and training the subcontractor shall be added to their bid in order to compare subcontractor proposals.

A record of all subcontractor assessments shall be kept in the subcontractor's (vendor) file.

What this complicated statement says is that we want to use subcontractors who are certificated. If potential subcontractors are not certificated we should increase the allowance we make for risk (scale their bid upward) or add in the cost of totally managing their staff.

Subcontractors shall be controlled on the basis of an accepted quality plan prepared by the subcontractor and showing deliverables, review points and records to be generated. Copies of relevant subcontractor quality records shall be obtained and shall form part of our quality records. We shall require the right to review products, participate in joint reviews, witness tests and audit the subcontractor and the work on a regular basis. The detail of subcontractor control shall be defined in our quality plan for the work.

This is a very important point. One of the major benefits of ISO 9000 management systems is communication. If we and our subcontractor both run ISO 9000 based quality management systems, then the two systems should mesh together to meet the needs of the subcontract. Both parties will understand each other, and the need for quality planning, records, inspections and tests, and so forth will be understood and built into the subcontract management processes.

Detailed inspection and testing requirements for acceptance of purchased products, goods and services shall be defined in the purchasing specification, the quality plan or the main contract and shall form part of the purchase specification. Acceptance inspection and testing shall be performed as specified.

When we buy things we must let our supplier know when it has produced what we want. This is partially done with clear purchasing specifications but may be made even more clear by providing acceptance criteria in the form of inspections and tests to be performed. You may find that the supplier already performs these inspections and tests and you may be willing to merely witness their tests or accept their inspection certificates thus significantly reducing your inward inspection costs.

The customer has the right (if specified in the contract) to verify at our supplier's premises that purchased product conforms to requirements. This verification in no way absolves us from conformance to all the requirements of the contract or our quality management system. Despite verification the customer may subsequently reject the product. Customer verification at a subcontractor's premises shall not be used by us as evidence that the subcontractor has effective control of quality.

This clarifies the role of our customer's inspection and testing at our supplier's premises.

Handling, storage, packaging, preservation and delivery

This section addresses the requirements of ISO 9001-1994 Section 4.15. *Handling, storage, packaging, preservation, and delivery* addresses the areas of stock management and delivery of a product to the customer. While the wording is based on traditional physical stock control it does not take significant leaps of imagination to see how this section may be used for other issues. Some examples may be the delivery of product by electronically downloading data or programming, electronic funds transfer services, faxed messages, and airline reservations.

The objective of careful handling is to make sure that products are handled in such a way that the risk of damage is minimized. This could, therefore, include issues relating to safety in materials handling. We can even extend this to minimizing the risk of environmental damage by controlling handling of material with processes to reduce the risks of toxic spills and leaks. The objective of careful storage is to prevent damage to or deterioration of products during storage, to make sure stored stock is regularly inspected for damage or deterioration, and to rotate stock. Obviously this can also be used to control the risk of environmental accidents by verifying that stored materials are still safe.

The objective of proper packaging and preservation is to make sure that products do not deteriorate and are not damaged in storage or transit due to inadequate or unsafe packaging. A further objective is to make certain products and packaging are properly marked so that there are no mistakes in identification. This obviously extends to markings relating to hazards and handling ranging from labels such as the international "radiation hazard" symbol to the "keep dry," "this way up," and "fragile" symbols. The objective of the delivery requirement is to make sure you identify exactly when title and responsibility passes from you to your customer and that you have suitable processes to protect the products until your responsibility for the product ends.

Policies

Typical policies addressing the handling, storage, packaging, preservation, and delivery requirements of ISO 9001 include the following:

> ALL EQUIPMENT AND MEDIA SHALL BE HANDLED AND STORED IN ACCORDANCE WITH THE CONTRACT OR THE MANUFACTURER'S INSTRUCTIONS. WHERE NEITHER OF THESE IS AVAILABLE THEN DUE CARE SHALL BE TAKEN CONSISTENT WITH THE NATURE OF THE PRODUCT.

State the policy, and where necessary, point to the procedure to be followed for handling. If you run a computer network this section will, for example, address the processes used for message handling and accounting for transactions. Exercise your imagination to apply this part of ISO 9001 to problems you may be having with your operations. Product developed for a specific customer shall be stored and secured as defined in the contract or in a secure area with a process to control receipt and dispatch of the product from the secure area.

Specify the storage and preservation needs for custombuilt products. Consider backup and restoration of soft products.

> STOCK PRODUCT SHALL BE STORED IN A SECURED AREA. STOCK MOVEMENTS (RECEIPTS FROM SUPPLIERS AND ISSUES TO CUSTOMERS) SHALL BE RECORDED.

Specify the control mechanisms for general stock. Consider the need for controlling user manuals and other documentation you may distribute to your end users (customers). Product shall be packaged for stock or delivery in a controlled manner to ensure the customer receives the correct product in good condition.

Specify packaging needs

> COMPUTER SOFTWARE PRODUCT TO BE DELIVERED TO A CUSTOMER SHALL BE

ASSEMBLED ONTO THE APPROPRIATE MEDIA. MEDIA THAT CONTAINS SOFTWARE PRODUCT SHALL BE LABELED WITH THE NAME OF THE SOFTWARE PRODUCT AND ITS VERSION.

We need to make sure we give the customer the software they order and verify that we have recorded it properly. Be careful that the customer cannot unformat a previously used disk and find something they shouldn't. Make sure you do not deliver a computer virus to your customer; this is not appreciated.

Product shall be securely packaged for delivery and clearly marked with the customer's name and address and our name and address. The contents shall be clearly marked for identification by the recipient.

Pack and wrap properly; goods arriving in poor packaging or damaged condition project a bad image.

Control of nonconforming product

Control of nonconforming product addresses the need to isolate product that does not conform to specification and the actions to be taken to address the nonconformity. Nonconforming product is any product that, having been released for integration or end use, is subsequently found not to conform to requirements. Nonconforming product may be reworked, scrapped, or a concession sought from the customer. Nonconforming product may also be regraded for another use. An example would be a watch chip that was supposed to support ten functions being regraded to go into a watch that only has five functions. Product found to be defective after installation should be reworked or replaced.

Consideration should be given to the need to identify and advise holders of nonconforming product that their product is (or could be) nonconforming. This includes such processes as national vehicle recalls for possible defect rectification.

Almost without exception, nonconforming computer software is reworked. It is, however, a characteristic of software that it can also be changed to provide different functionality. The process of changing software and reworking software is identical; because of this a single change management process should be used to accomplish both results. This provides consistency of approach to rework/change and the subsequent reviews, inspection, and testing.

There is often confusion about the difference between control of nonconforming product and corrective action. Control of nonconforming product is used for managing and rectifying product defects while corrective action analyzes the causes of defects and corrects the causes. In other words, corrective action is aimed at constantly improving our software development processes.

Policies

Typical policies addressing the control of nonconforming product requirements of ISO 9001 include the following:

WHEN ANY NONCONFORMANCE OR DEFICIENCY IS IDENTIFIED IN A PRODUCT WHICH HAS BEEN RELEASED THEN IT SHALL BE RECORDED AND DOCUMENTED IN SUFFICIENT DETAIL TO ENABLE IT TO BE RESOLVED.

This typically addresses the need to raise problem reports when something goes wrong. This does not mean that a complex multipage form is required. The procedure could be as simple as logging the defect onto a multiline register. Most organizations already have some form of problem/defect reporting and this should be continued. Do not redesign the process for ISO; rather use the corrective action process to drive the need for any change or improvement.

WHERE PHYSICAL PRODUCT IS NONCONFORMING THEN A COPY OF THE NONCONFORMANCE NOTIFICATION SHALL BE ATTACHED TO THE PRODUCT AND THE PRODUCT SHALL BE PHYSICALLY SEPARATED FROM CONFORMING PRODUCT.

Most software organizations have little to do with physical products so there is no need for special procedures to cover identification and isolation (quarantining) of defective product. Sometimes we may find ourselves buying a computer on which we will load our software and deliver the package to the customer. In these situations physically attaching a copy of the problem report to the offending article is sufficient to identify its nonconforming status and prevent its use.

WHERE THE PRODUCT IS REGISTERED ON A SUITABLE REGISTER THEN THE INSPECTION AND TEST STATUS OF THE NONCONFORMING PRODUCT SHALL BE UPDATED TO IDENTIFY THE PRODUCT AS NONCONFORMING.

Earlier we looked at the use of a product register for configuration management. Here we see a further use for the register. In the case of software we may well view nonconforming product as another state in which the product can exist and assign nonconformance as a status code.

WHERE APPROPRIATE, PERSONS OR ORGANIZATIONS ON THE DISTRIBUTION LIST FOR THE PRODUCT WHICH IS NONCONFORMING SHALL BE INFORMED THAT THE PRODUCT IS NONCONFORMING.

Where we choose to control the distribution of documentation or products then we can easily inform holders of the product that a nonconformance has arisen. Initially allow your people to exercise judgment on when to inform holders of the product, If this proves unsatisfactory, corrective action should look at providing more guidance and direction than the "where appropriate" statement above.

THE NONCONFORMING PRODUCT SHALL BE REWORKED, SCRAPPED, REGRADED OR A CONCESSION OBTAINED FROM THE CUSTOMER.

This is another statement of the obvious. You may need to replace this policy with some specific directions as to when each applies, but in the software sphere we traditionally rework the product (fix the bug).

WHERE THE NONCONFORMING PRODUCT IS TO BE REWORKED THEN THIS SHALL BE PERFORMED UNDER FORMAL CHANGE MANAGEMENT PROCESSES. THE NEED FOR ANY REVIEWS, INSPECTIONS AND TESTS SHALL BE INCLUDED IN THE REWORK AND SHALL ENSURE THAT ALL RELATED WORK IS ALSO REVIEWED. THE

REWORKED PRODUCT SHALL NOT BE FORMALLY RELEASED UNTIL ALL REQUIRED RETESTING OR REINSPECTIONS HAVE BEEN COMPLETED SATISFACTORILY AND AUTHORIZED.

If we have invested in a system for developing product then we should apply the same controls to rework (bug fixing) as we did to the original development. Obviously, we should also be using corrective action to fix the weakness in the quality management system that allowed the nonconforming product to be produced in the first place.

WHERE A MANAGED PRODUCT REGISTER IS USED FOR PRODUCT IT SHALL BE UPDATED TO RECORD CHANGES TO THE INSPECTION AND TEST STATUS OF THE PRODUCT AS THE REWORKED PRODUCT IS REVIEWED, INSPECTED AND TESTED.

The need to track the nonconforming product through rework and back to a released product may be achieved by use of a product register.

Contract reviews

This section addresses the requirements of ISO 9001-1994 Section 4.3. This calls for us to make sure that we review any offers (proposals and tenders) we present to prospective customers, understand the contract and the requirements, and have the capacity and capability to satisfy the contract requirements. It is important to remember that a contract may be a simple order for a product or service. An example is an offer to sell you an item in a shop and your agreeing to buy it.

In its simplest sense contract review means that you must examine whether you have the product or service available and whether you can deliver it. If a customer wants to buy a cabbage you must ensure that you have the cabbage and can execute the sales transaction from calculating the price to packaging the product, taking the money, and issuing a receipt. At the other end of the scale we have the situation where teams of lawyers review, probe, and examine the supplier's capability to deliver and customer's capability to accept the product and/or service.

Proposals

If the proposal/tender is not prepared with the detailed consideration of the quality management system that will be used to implement it, then we stand a good chance of seriously damaging the result before we even win the work. To this end, those of us who are required to present our offer to sell in writing must do so in accordance with the requirements of our quality management system. This means that proposal/tender preparation must be included in our quality management system so that we start the work the way we mean to finish it. We find our proposals/tenders should be prepared in accordance with our planning processes so that whatever is sold can be delivered.

Your sales and marketing people may vigorously oppose this policy and suggest that it will drive you out of business. Which is more likely to drive you out of business: being honest and open with your prospective customers, or promising the moon and then passing the unachievable promises to the delivery people? You will find your customers will be delighted at knowing exactly what you are trying to sell them and your delivery people will be ecstatic at being able to satisfy the customer. This is a very important part of the underpromise-and-overdeliver cycle.

Your policies should, therefore, address proposal preparation/tender response, including the formal preparation of documents in accordance with defined processes, the review and approval of the documents, placing the documents under formal control, and issuing copies of the documents in a controlled manner. Policies and processes are also required for updating and changing the documents. Everyone should know what the latest version is and who holds copies of which version so that we can avoid confusion and argument about which document is the right one. This process of formal preparation, review and approval, formal signoff and issue, and formal change control is required for all documents produced. Contrary to what might be your initial belief that this will stifle the system, slow everything down, and let your competitor gain an advantage, this process will reduce wasted time, increase the likelihood of a document being produced properly the first time, increase your credibility with your customer, and generally give you a significant edge.

Once the proposal has been presented to the customer there must be processes to monitor its selling to the customer and the preparation of revisions. Should the proposal not be accepted you should declare this to be a problem and initiate corrective action to determine its cause (why did we waste time and money on a proposal/tender that the customer did not accept?) and increase our chances of getting more accepted proposals/tenders.

When the proposal is accepted there is the need to formally review its acceptance and ensure that what is accepted was what was proposed and that any variations between a contract and the tender are reviewed and that we can deliver what we are being asked to deliver. The results of this review must be written down as evidence that the processes of contract review were followed.

Requirements specification

Part of the contract review process is a need to ensure the requirements of the contract are clearly understood and documented. What about contracts where one of the things we are called upon to do is specify the requirements? This is especially common in the computer systems development business where the requirements specification is the first part of the contract. This is a weakness of ISO 9001, which assumes the contract is the specification. The definition of requirements is discussed i. detail under design and uses IEEE 1298 for guidance on controlling requirements specification.

Policies

Typical policies addressing the requirements of ISO 9001 are as follows:

Proposals

Proposals should be prepared following the general principles of quality planning.

This is to enable a smooth transition from the accepted proposal to the execution of the contract. This is so obvious and happens so rarely that it often becomes one of the first major benefits of implementing a quality management system. It means that we start off planning to satisfy the customer by dealing with the customer and the customer's expectations in a manner that flows smoothly from the sale to the delivery.

PROPOSALS SHALL BE REVIEWED AND, IF ACCEPTABLE, AUTHORIZED FOR ISSUE BY THE CHIEF EXECUTIVE OFFICER.

You may change who authorizes proposals, but remember that they may be betting the business. A proposal may be accepted by the customer as a contract by the customer making it an addendum to their standard terms and conditions of contract.

PROPOSALS ARE TO BE SUBJECT TO FORMAL DISTRIBUTION CONTROL. A BACKUP SHALL BE RETAINED ON COMPUTER READABLE MEDIA.

If the customer is asking for changes to a proposal it must be assumed that some form of negotiation is now taking place and the control over this should be part of contract review.

Proposals are like any other document. They may go through many versions and it is vital that control is maintained over the copies. This will minimize the risk of copies getting to competitors and enable negotiations to take place without the confusion of people referring to different versions of the proposal.

Changes to the proposal are initiated as part of contract review.

Contract reviews

FORMAL WRITTEN CONTRACTS ARE TO BE REVIEWED TO ENSURE THAT THEY ARE FULLY UNDERSTOOD AND IN ACCORDANCE WITH THE PROPOSAL OR TENDER AND THAT WE HAVE THE FACILITIES, CAPABILITIES AND TECHNICAL SKILLS NECESSARY TO MEET THE REQUIREMENTS OF THE CONTRACT.

Contract review includes evaluating the contract, identifying areas of negotiation (including revisions to proposals), and ensuring that all issues are resolved before committing to signing the contract. Reference should be made to appropriate procedures.

WHERE A FORMAL CONTRACT DOES NOT EXIST THEN WE MUST ENSURE WE HAVE THE CAPACITY AND CAPABILITY TO MEET THE PERCEIVED REQUIREMENTS. THE DETAILED REQUIREMENTS AND CUSTOMER RESPONSIBILITIES SHALL BE DOCUMENTED IN THE QUALITY PLAN.

In many cases work is undertaken based on a letter of intent or a request from the boss, but it is still necessary for you to know that you can do the job. An amazing number of people are occupied with these kinds of special jobs and the impact on resources is significant. Applying some controls should reduce wastage and lessen overload by thinking before we throw odd jobs around.

ORDERS FOR STOCK PRODUCTS SHALL BE CHECKED, STOCK VERIFIED AND DELIVERY MECHANISMS VERIFIED TO ENSURE WE CAN SATISFY THE ORDER.

In a simple order-taking situation procedures must be in place to take the order, verify product (stock) availability, and verify delivery capability. Reference should be made to order-taking procedures.

> REQUESTS FOR SERVICE OR SUPPORT SHALL BE IMMEDIATELY ACTIONED TO RESOLVE THE REQUEST OR THE REQUEST SHOULD BE HANDED TO AN APPROPRIATE PERSON FOR ACTION. UNDER NO CIRCUMSTANCES IS A REQUEST FOR SERVICE TO REMAIN UNACTIONED FOR MORE THAN ONE WORKING DAY.

Servicing as a subject under ISO 9001 is usually taken to cover servicing and support of products we have delivered to our customers (maintenance). Servicing in the form of help desks, network support, and other support activities may be a business in its own right or may even be the business you wish to have certificated. In this case a request for service is a contract or an order.

Project initiation

When a project has been accepted then the relevant manager shall be notified of the full details of the project. This notification shall include originals or copies of all relevant tenders, proposals, contracts, work papers and correspondence. A verbal briefing should also be provided.

Within software development we often find that projects are not clearly assigned and therefore not clearly managed. To resolve this issue it is useful to include a transition mechanism to let the delivery people know that a project has started and that they are now responsible for its execution. To this end a procedure is needed to formally notify the relevant delivery or development manager of the job and hand over responsibility for its delivery.

> ON BEING NOTIFIED OF A PROJECT THE MANAGER SHALL ASSIGN A PROJECT MANAGER AND A QUALITY MANAGEMENT REPRESENTATIVE. OTHER PRINCIPALS INVOLVED SHALL ALSO BE ASSIGNED. ALL PARTICIPANTS AND INTERESTED PARTIES SHALL BE NOTIFIED IN WRITING OF THE PROJECT AND THE PRINCIPAL PARTICIPANTS.

The next step in initiation is to assign the project to the delivery team. The manager should be formally nominating and advising the project manager of the project. Other interested parties such as Quality Assurance will also need to be notified. The project manager should be tasked with preparing at least an initial plan as the highest-priority item.

Process control

Process control addresses the need to control production to ensure that quality requirements are achieved. The processes are the activities we perform in order to produce a unit of product or provide an instance of a service. Contract review, design, and so forth are also processes that must be controlled in order to achieve the organization's objectives. Process control includes the requirement to plan the production and installation processes in order to maximize production and minimize defects. This includes the need to specify any controlled conditions in the form of methods and work instructions.

Process control also calls for monitoring and control of process and product characteristics during the production process. These may include temperature ranges, size tolerances, and defect rates. Once meaningful characteristics can be identified and measured then a whole range of statistical quality measures can be implemented based on Shewhart control charts and the work of W. Edwards Deming and others. In software development the subject of metrics is becoming increasingly important as many quality improvement programs fail to eventuate or flounder in our lack of ability to measure what we do and whether we are doing it better when we change the processes. ISO 9126 defines the terminology we should use, such as *reliability* and *maintainability*. The international SPICE project is extending the work of the Software Engineering Institute of Carnegie Mellon University in the field of process maturity measurement, and this is leading to a clearer definition of the processes (methods) to be applied and measured in quality programs. Over the next few years this attention to process improvement and measurement should start to impact the commercial world of software development. Processes and equipment that affect quality and require verification before being performed or used should be controlled by an approval mechanism prior to the process being commenced and at selected intervals during performance of the process. Examples of these are cleanliness of food preparation areas and ensuring enclosed spaces are free of explosive gases before hot work.

A quality plan must include information on deliverables and review points. To enforce the creation of a quality plan a project should not proceed until the quality plan has been accepted by all project participants. The plan is the basis for subsequent monitoring (process control) activity, including routine monitoring of project status, participation in key reviews within the project, and formal project audits. The planning process must systematically evaluate all anticipated project work, including special or unusual contractual requirements, documentation requirements, inspection, validation, verification and review requirements, and specific quality plan requirements.

The plan documents the practical implementation of the agreement to execute the project. It should be a comprehensive document that tries to solve any problem that may arise in the future and thus allow us to avoid confrontation and disagreements at later stages. It is far easier to examine and decide action to be taken over future events when we are in the first flush of courtship, marriage, or honeymoon than it is to try and resolve property settlements during a divorce. Consider the plan a prenuptial agreement for a project and you won't go far wrong. The plan defines what is to be delivered (in terms of products, services, and documentation, not in terms of requirements), how the project will be performed and managed, the reviews to be performed, the costs and schedules, and who will provide which resources and facilities. The plan should also be used to agree on staff commitments and availability from all sides. A project quality plan may be sufficiently sophisticated to allow a project to achieve certification in its own right

Finally, there is a need for standards of workmanship, which should be specified in writing or by means of samples of work already done or pictures of good and bad work. The hospitality industry, especially resorts in developing countries, make extensive use of photographs to show the standards for room makeup, table settings, and food presentation,

It is a requirement that programming standards exist, in writing, that define both recommended and prohibited practices for program design, development, testing, and integration. These standards form part of the quality management system documentation. Note that usefulness is more important than quantity. How can anybody guarantee they have taken cognizance of a fiftypage standards manual when they have been translating a specification into programming on a keyboard? Remember, the objective of standards is to achieve the functionality, including reliability and maintainability, and not to overcontrol programming.

This section of the standard also calls for the identification of special processes. These are processes that can produce defects that the testing and inspection cannot be confident of finding. These processes must be subject to regular, formal monitoring and control to make sure they are followed correctly in order to minimize the possibility of defects being produced. Records must be kept of processes and equipment that need to meet special conditions or controls (qualified processes and equipment). records must also be maintained of qualified personnel, that is, personnel who have special training, skills, or experience that allows them to perform qualified processes.

In the software development business the environment used to generate programming product is part of the process that if altered may result in a change to or a requirement to change the design. Process control must be exercised over the development environment, including secure maintenance of libraries of development software; authorized backups of software under development; the identification, storage, and handling of media containing software under development; and the control of software development tools, techniques, and processes.

Policies

Typical policies addressing process control requirements of ISO 9001 include the following:

Quality planning

The documentation associated with the project shall be reviewed for quality issues including the work breakdown structures to be adopted, deliverable items to be produced and any specification or contractual issues relating to quality or deliverables. The products to be developed, phases of the development methodology to be followed and other quality related issues shall be documented as a project execution strategy.

This calls for a review of all issues relating to quality and the preparation of a strategy identifying the major project issues and the approach to be adopted in executing the project including the preparation of plans. This twostep approach (strategy, then plan) provides a checkpoint between the decision on how the project will be executed and the preparation of the detailed plan. This prevents a common project management problem where the project manager decides *this* project is *different and* ignores the quality management system methodologies and standards when preparing the plan. The project manager then defends the plan against change (lack of time; the customer already accepts it) and the project has now taken its first leap toward a catastrophe. Experience shows that following such a procedure usually takes only a few minutes and has the longterm benefit of committing the project to the organization's approved method of working. Of course, it may expose a fundamental deficiency in the quality management system requiring new methods and standards; at least this will be recognized and their development included in the plans.

WHEN REQUIRED BY THE PROJECT STRATEGY, A PROJECT QUALITY PLAN SHALL BE PREPARED FOR COMPLETING THE PROJECT. THE PROJECT QUALITY PLAN SHALL REFLECT THE FULL REQUIREMENTS OF THE CONTRACT, WHERE ONE EXISTS, AND SHALL ALSO REFLECT THE REQUIREMENTS OF THE PROJECT EXECUTION STRATEGY. THE PROJECT QUALITY PLAN SHALL INCLUDE DESIGN AND DEVELOPMENT PLANNING AS APPROPRIATE.

A planning procedure is required. Rather than talk about project plans and quality plans, which will evoke preconceived ideas of content, refer to these plans as project *qualityplans.* These plans are the first deliverable document for a project and should be as comprehensive as possible. The need for design and development planning is included to show where these requirements from ISO 9001 are addressed.

THE PROJECT QUALITY PLAN SHALL BE REVIEWED AND APPROVED BY NOMINATED PERSONNEL AFTER EXAMINATION FOR ADEQUACY IN TERMS OF CONTRACT CONDITIONS AND THE QUALITY MANAGEMENT SYSTEM.

As with any deliverable, the project quality plan must be formally reviewed and approved.

THE APPROVED PROJECT QUALITY PLAN SHALL BE AUTHORIZED BY THE MANAGER AND SHOULD BE ACCEPTED BY THE CUSTOMER.

The plan must be authorized as a baseline for the project and, obviously, agreed to (accepted) by the customer. Notice the use of the word *should* when referring to the customer instead of the word *shall* used in reference to staff. The reason for this is that we can demand our staff do something and take action when they don't, but we would be silly to leave ourselves open to quality management system nonconformances by demanding our customer do something they may not want to do.

Dangerous but true: We often complete projects without the customer signing *anything*.

THE PROJECT QUALITY PLAN IS PART OF THE QUALITY MANAGEMENT SYSTEM DOCUMENTATION AND SHALL BE SUBJECT TO DOCUMENTATION CONTROL. A BACKUP SHALL BE RETAINED ON COMPUTER READABLE MEDIA.

The procedure for distribution control of documentation is to be applied to the plan.

AT THE END OF EACH PHASE OR GROUP OF PHASES MANAGED TOGETHER, AND WHEN ANY SIGNIFICANT INFORMATION IN THE PLAN CHANGES, THE PROJECT QUALITY PLAN SHOULD BE REVISED AND UPDATED TO REFLECT ACTUAL RESULTS AND MORE DETAILED PLANS FOR THE NEXT PHASE.

The plan will be updated at least at the end of each phase of development.

Process control

Before commencing production the version of the processes to be used shall be verified.

There is a need to baseline the quality management system elements to be used in a project. This is later extended to other items such as software. We do this because changes to baselines of any sort have the potential to seriously disrupt a project.

WHERE WORK IS BEING UNDERTAKEN AS A PROJECT THEN THE PROJECT MANAGER SHALL PREPARE REGULAR REPORTS ON THE STATUS OF, AND PROGRESS MADE ON EACH PROJECT. THESE REPORTS SHALL INCLUDE THE ACHIEVEMENT OF TARGETS, COMPLIANCE WITH THE DEVELOPMENT PLAN AND THE STATUS OF INTERNAL MANAGEMENT MILESTONES.

Status reporting provides evidence of process control and is part of the visibility needed to assure good project management and to provide customer and management comfort.

Software development

A project quality plan shall be prepared which describes the methods, procedures, standards and guidelines to be adopted to achieve the quality objectives specific to the project. This plan shall also describe the means by which adherence to the plan is to be achieved. The plan shall also describe how the process of software development, including the preparation of requirements specifications and the design of the software is to be managed. The plan shall ensure that records are maintained for qualified processes, equipment and personnel

This is an alternative policy for planning that more closely aligns to IEEE 1298 for software development. It is a little more prescriptive than the more general planning policy aligned to ISO 9001. Either policy should be acceptable.

Before commencing development the programming standards and the development environment to be used shall be documented showing the current release of each item of development (system) software to be used.

This is a more prescriptive policy defining the need to baseline standards and tools (software) to be used during development.

When a new or changed item of software support, tools, techniques, methodologies, etc., is to be used then it shall be accepted on the basis of historical performance or tested to ensure it operates correctly.

Another IEEE 1298 requirement is to make sure that any tools you use actually work. How often do we see people leap onto the next release of a development tool only to have the project severely slow down or have major rework and recovery. If you did not plan on using a new version, don't waste your time and money changing unless you are confident it will increase productivity. Extra functionality should not be an issue. If you started a project with tools that did not have the functionality you needed and had not planned on the new software release then you are a very adventurous (and foolish) project manager.

REGULAR BACKUPS SHALL BE MADE OF LIBRARIES CONTAINING SOFTWARE UNDER DEVELOPMENT. ALL MEDIA CONTAINING BACKUPS OF SOFTWARE UNDER DEVELOPMENT SHALL BE CLEARLY LABELED TO ENABLE RESTORATION OF THE LIBRARIES. MEDIA SHALL BE HANDLED AND STORED IN ACCORDANCE WITH THE MANUFACTURER'S INSTRUCTIONS.

Again we see some commonsense requirements from IEEE 1298 in the need to back up our work and make sure we can recover from loss

Installation and implementation

THE APPROACH TO BE TAKEN FOR INSTALLING PRODUCTS ON A CUSTOMER'S SITE SHALL BE DEFINED. THIS INCLUDES THE INSTALLATION TEST PLAN.

Here we have a policy requiring us to plan for installation and also to plan for proving the installation was successful.

The results of testing applied during installation shall be reviewed and approved by suitable authority.

After installation make sure somebody signs off that you have completed what was planned. Implementation shall be performed as defined. The services being provided shall be regularly reviewed and any required actions initiated. This policy calls for implementation to be performed in accordance with some defined (documented) processes and for the results of the processes to be regularly reviewed to ensure we are doing what we committed to do.

Training

Training shall be provided as defined in the contract or in the project quality plan. Persons attending training sessions should provide feedback on the quality of the course and the trainer. The trainer shall provide feedback on the persons attending the course, the materials, venue and other relevant issues.

This policy is for the provision of training as a service. This training may be either part of implementation or it may be training as a business (the education business). The need for assessment of the quality of training provides a mechanism on which to base improvement. There should be a procedure to implement this policy.

Special processes

By its very nature software cannot be fully inspected and tested prior to release of the product. As a result the process of developing software is a qualified special process and all software developers shall conform to the documented processes specified for the project. All software developers shall be qualified on the basis of skills, education, training and experience. The process of developing software shall be continuously monitored in accordance with the defined processes.

This statement is required under ISO 9001, which calls for us to qualify special processes and calls fbr us to maintain records of qualified processes (this policy is a suitable record), equipment (covered under the development software baselines), and personnel (covered by our training records).

Other contractual services

Where a contract calls for other services not defined in our quality management system then the project quality plan shall document the services required. Procedures to deliver these services shall be documented or referenced in the plan. The procedures shall be required to generate evidence that they have been followed.

This is a useful catchall that makes sure we trap any novel quality requirements and develop suitable processes to meet them. It also identifies the need for such processes to generate evidence that the process has been followed.

Design control

Design can be considered to be any process that creates a new process, service, or product. To this end, people in the software development industry recognize that programming and user documentation (including help text and operations manual) are also design; we do it only once (or should) and the result is a service in the form of a computer system that others can use in their daytoday business operations. The importance of design can be seen in its place in the ISO 9000 series of standards. Design is the only requirement that makes the difference between ISO 9001 and ISO 9002. If you do not design your products and services then you would be looking to conform to ISO 9002 rather than ISO 9001. Only about 10 percent of companies seek ISO 9001 conformance, and this is therefore seen as some form of superachievement. Software developers do not have a choice. Design, programming, and user documentation are all ISO 9001 activities.

As reports, manuals, training materials, and documents are produced only once, they are also covered by design control. There must be standards for the preparation of documents and means of ensuring compliance with those standards. Consultants and authors will need to be cognizant of this need. Developing computerbased material, including drawings, computerbased training, and so on, is also design. Computer programming is another form of design and is subject to design control. In this book, a threelevel signoff mechanism is used. The first signoff is the review signoff or quality assurance signoff where the deliverable is approved for release to the customer for acceptance. The second signoff is acceptance by the customer or some other party on behalf of the customer. Finally, the project manager signs off the deliverable as a baseline for use in the next phase or for delivery. ISO 9001 does not require any signatures per se on design, so you should find a mechanism that suits your organization.

Requirements

One of the hardest issues we need to come to grips with in most endeavors is determining customers' needs *(requirements).* We seem to think that a good design is the solution to our problems but forget that we often fail to determine what the problem is. It comes as quite a surprise to discover that the designers of a new automobile were considered radical when they went to their potential customers and found out what they wanted to buy. The designers of a new camera were thought to have come up with a great new concept by first developing a model customer and then designing a camera for that customer. Most of us probably harbor the belief that large companies really know what their customers want. This is not so; it is actually quite common for people to produce a solution without first understanding the problem.

How do you know what the customer wants? You work with the customer to prepare a requirements specification! After all, what gives us the right to dictate an answer? We therefore come back to the fundamental determinant of quality specifying customers' needs. It is a painful fact that most companies fail to determine customers' needs but design what they want to design and then spend huge sums of money convincing customers that they need the product.

There is a need for practical, workable processes (methods and possibly tools) to specify requirements, review the specification, and ensure the specification is understood and accepted by the customer. Requirements definition is the most misunderstood part of any endeavor. If you don't know what customers want, how can you give it to them? If you don't know what you are trying to achieve, how will you know when you have achieved it?

An important issue with specifications is that they are feasible, that is, we can actually design a product or service to satisfy the requirement. A further crucial issue is that of testability: How will we know when we have satisfied the specification? What tests will need to be passed so that we know we have finished? There is nothing more futile than embarking on a project when you have no way of knowing when you have finished! Of course, the customer may be paying for research and development with such matters as completion being left open. This is satisfactory if the commitment is open-ended on both sides. One of the major tragedies still seen regularly in the computer software industry is the fixed-price contract with no definition of completion (especially the idea of a fixed-price contract to specify the requirements). What you will get is $X of requirements, an unhappy customer, a bankrupt or disgraced supplier, or other disaster. What you *will not* get is satisfaction and what you want. Still the myth goes on, from the big accounting firms to the backyard operators, and the misery continues. Caveat emptor you get what you pay for and every other cliche is true: Don't stint on requirements specification (either as a customer or a supplier) or you will be dissatisfied; this is a guarantee.

Design and development planning

Design and development planning should form part of the project quality plan and should ensure that all activities, including quality assurance (design reviews, design verification, and design validation) activities, are planned. People assigned to perform design work should be competent to perform such work and records should be available to provide evidence of their competency. People reviewing design should also be competent to perform such reviews and again this should be evidenced. It would be unacceptable, for instance, to have a hydraulic engineer review and approve an electrical design.

Organizational and technical interfaces

The *project organization* should be defined as part of the quality plan. This should show the structure of the project, including the management and reporting structures. The means of communication between the development people and the customers must be described.

Design input

It is imperative that the design process start with adequate input, and therefore a procedure is required to review the *design input.* If an agreed on requirements specification is not available there is serious doubt as to whether the design should proceed. There must be identification, documentation, and review of items input to the design process (e.g., requirements specification, design manuals, product/tools manuals), Design input may include prototypes ' code generated by researchers, and other novel forms. Don't be constrained by convention but aim for the best design inputs to achieve your objectives.

The design team, supported by suitable outside expertise, should review the design as it evolves. When properly managed, *design reviews* provide a valuable training mechanism as experts participate in the review process and feed their expertise to the less skilled team members. In software development the use of design reviews is the principal means by which conformance of the software product to the requirements is evaluated. Design reviews should specifically address reliability and maintainability as well as the safety of the delivered system. Design review activities should form part of the quality plan.

The format and content of the *design output* must be defined. This may include a documentation table of contents or a definition of the computer model to be produced.

Design verification

Design reviews are the mandated mechanism for *design verification.* However, where appropriate, the suitability of the design may be verified using other techniques as well. The techniques to be used should be defined in the quality plan. In software development, techniques for evaluating software are beginning to be developed, and include automated verification tools.

One of the significant requirements for a design is that it must conform to all relevant regulations "whether or not these have been stated in the input information." This means it is the designer's responsibility to know local laws and regulations and not the customer's responsibility to tell the designer!

Design validation

Design validation in software is usually referred to as testing. This is the process of ensuring that what we have developed conforms to the requirements specification.

Design changes

Once a design has been placed under configuration management there must be a formal mechanism for controlling changes.

Policies

Typical policies addressing the design control requirements of ISO 9001 include the following:

Requirements Specification

Control of requirements specification shall be documented as part of the project quality plan. The approach to defining requirements shall ensure that adequate consultation exists between ourselves and our customer to specify the requirements.

The plan should identify the methods, tools, and guidelines that should be followed to specify the requirements. If you have one methodology, then the relevant phase may be identified in this policy statement and reference to the plan removed. The methodology, tools, and guidelines should ensure that the specification phase is a consultative process. Be careful that the use of analysis tools does not destroy the consultation process.

As each major activity or change in requirements definition has been completed to the stage where it can be inspected it shall be issued for review to ensure that the requirements are feasible and can be proven to have been satisfied.

The whole specification, each section of the specification, or changes to the specification should be subject to a formal review process. The review should ensure that the specification really does specify the requirements and that we can build a system to implement the requirements and that we have sufficient information to be able to prove that we have developed a system to implement the requirements. This is one of the major issues affecting software development and comes from IEEE 1298 (it does not exist in ISO 9001). The major issues are completeness (so that we can limit specification creep) and testability (so that we can prove we have finished). Few software developers are good at specification. Most are too keen to get onto the technical design and development phases. The need to properly specify requirements is one of the greatest contributors to producing the right system and should be used by all quality practitioners as the lever to shift emphasis from technical solutions to finding out what the customer wants. We must stop building technically perfect but functionally flawed systems.

When the original or changed requirements specifications have been completed, reviewed in their entirety and approved then they shall be provided to the customer for review to ensure the specifications reflect the requirements. The customer shall review the requirements specifications and, if satisfied, shall accept the requirements specifications.

When we are satisfied that we have addressed all the requirements, that a system can be built, and that we can prove we have built it, then we look for final confirmation of the requirements by the customer. We should not proceed until this is obtained, except where the customer agrees to write off all wasted time if the specifications are subsequently rejected. If the product requirements specifications are not acceptable to the customer then corrective action shall be initiated.

While at first glance it may seem a bit strict to call for corrective action if the customer does not accept the specification the first time, it is actually a very important quality issue. If the customer does not accept the specification we have wasted our time and have probably failed to involve the customer in the consultative process. We should look at our analysis techniques and make sure that the next time we do analysis we get it right the first time. Be careful that your use of tools and techniques during analysis really does include consultation with customers and does not just leave them with their heads reeling and a desire to get rid of you until the completed system is ready for them to change to what they really want. Note that ISO 9001 does not call for this level of control and you may prefer to leave corrective action as something to initiate after the release of the specification. It is your quality management system and it's up to you what improvement opportunities to take. You can always change the rules as you get better.

THE PRODUCT REQUIREMENTS SPECIFICATIONS SHALL BE SUBJECT TO DOCUMENTATION CONTROL. A BACKUP SHALL BE RETAINED ON COMPUTER READABLE MEDIA.

The requirements specification is subject to configuration management as documentation. This means keeping track of the distribution of versions of the specification. A backup is always a good idea, so state your policy here. Changes to the product requirements specifications after release shall be performed under formal change management processes. The changes shall be subject to a complete review of the impact of the change before being scheduled for inclusion in the next version of the requirements specifications.

Obviously, there is no point in properly controlling the original specification and then letting changes happen without control. Changes should be performed under configuration control. Reviews and siginoff should be performed to the same standards applied to the original specification. Controlled release of progressive baselines enables continuous control of development rather than the anarchy of uncontrolled change.

Design and development

Design and development planning shall be part of the project quality plan. The plan shall also specify the use of defined design and development processes. ISO 9001 addresses the specific need for design and development planning and this statement shows us where to find it. Some organizations have separate plans but it is usually easier to have one document that consolidates all the project planning.

Design activity assignment as well as the organizational and technical interfaces for review and approval of design shall be specified in the project quality plan. Tasks shall be assigned to suitably skilled, trained or experienced personnel. Groups for task assignment shall be the project team, the customer quality assurance representatives and subcontractor design leaders unless otherwise specified in the project quality plan.

This statement defines the need to document the project structure (IT staff, users, and management) so that everyone involved knows where they fit in the team and what the roles and responsibilities are. The identification of the groups addresses a specific ISO 9001 requirement. The need to allocate suitably skilled staff repeats the requirement we have already seen under training and process control. You should be able to show a plan (e.g., Gantt chart) with personnel assignments. The personnel/training records should record the education, training, or experience of the personnel to perform the activities to which they are assigned. This seems at first glance to be rather trivial but it is very common to allocate warm bodies rather than skilled personnel to keep team numbers up.

Input to design will usually be the requirements specification or the contract. Other input may be provided or used, for example specific product design manuals. All input to design shall be recorded and reviewed for suitability. A review of previous designs shall, where appropriate, form part of the review of design input.

Design input is a complex issue. Most of us think of design input as being the specification and our intellect. Behind that intellect there is a lot of other material, including books and manuals. If you want to produce a good design (this includes programming) you may want to read some books on the subject or refer to manufacturer's guidelines. These are all design inputs and listing them is part of the demonstration of your professionalism and competence. After all, if your customer sues you for a poor database design you should at least have some evidence that you tried to do the right thing by using suitable reference material. You may have a standard list of design input material. If you do, please make sure your people read it (this is called training). Design input may be in novel forms. If you have a creative genius whose output is working code then you may use their nonstandard undocumented code as input to the formal process of designing and developing a product.

The approach to design is described in the project quality plan and shall follow documented processes previously approved as being suitable for designing the product or service.

The methodology, tools, and guidelines to be used to design, develop, and document the system should have been approved as acceptable and suitable. Your process control system should enforce them. Any changes to the methodology, tools, and guidelines should be controlled as documentation changes. Changes may be initiated by request or as a result of corrective action finding deficiencies in the methodology, tools, techniques, and guidelines.

AS EACH MAJOR ACTIVITY IN THE DESIGN CYCLE HAS BEEN COMPLETED OR EACH DESIGN CHANGE HAS BEEN PROCESSED TO THE STAGE WHERE IT CAN BE VERIFIED THEN IT SHALL BE ISSUED FOR DESIGN REVIEW. THE REVIEW SHALL ENSURE THE DESIGN IS SAFE, RELIABLE AND MAINTAINABLE AND CONFORMS TO REGULATORY REQUIREMENTS. THE PROJECT MANAGER, TECHNICAL SPECIALIST, QUALITY MANAGEMENT REPRESENTATIVE, MANAGER OR CUSTOMER MAY, AT ANY TIME, CALL FOR A DESIGN REVIEW TO BE CONDUCTED OUTSIDE OF THE SCHEDULE. THE DESIGN REVIEW PROCEDURE SHALL INCLUDE A DESCRIPTION OF THE OBJECTIVES OF THE REVIEW, AN IDENTIFICATION OF THE QUALIFICATIONS OF THE REVIEWER(S) AND MECHANISMS FOR RECORDING REVIEW RESULTS AND ENSURING RECOMMENDATIONS RESULTING FROM THE REVIEW ARE IMPLEMENTED. SHOULD ANOTHER FORM OF DESIGN VERIFICATION BE DEEMED APPROPRIATE THEN THIS SHALL BE DESCRIBED IN THE QUALITY PLAN. SUCH VERIFICATION METHODS MAY INCLUDE CARRYING OUT ALTERNATIVE CALCULATIONS OR COMPARING THIS DESIGN WITH A SIMILAR PROVEN DESIGN.

This specifies the need for design reviews and addresses the mechanism for initiating unscheduled reviews. This policy extends the ISO 9001 design review requirement with the requirements specified in IEEE 1.298. Design reviews/verification should be applied to design, programming, and user documentation (including manuals, reports, and training materials). If you operate a training business or a consultancy, design reviews are the process by which you determine the suitability of your deliverable.

THE FORMAT, CONTENT AND STRUCTURE OF THE DESIGN OUTPUT SHALL BE DEFINED IN THE PROJECT QUALITY PLAN. DESIGN OUTPUT SHALL SATISFY THE DESIGN INPUT, CONTAIN OR REFERENCE ACCEPTANCE CRITERIA INCLUDING MEETING THE PRODUCT REQUIREMENTS SPECIFICATIONS, CONFORM TO ALL REGULATORY REQUIREMENTS AND IDENTIFY THOSE CHARACTERISTICS OF THE PRODUCT OR SERVICE WHICH ARE CRUCIAL TO SAFE AND PROPER FUNCTIONING OF THE PRODUCT OR DELIVERY OF THE SERVICE.

When the original or changed design has been completed, reviewed in its entirety and approved then the design should be provided to the customer's quality assurance representative or nominated authority for verification. The authority shall verify the design and, if satisfied, shall accept the design. If the design is not accepted then corrective action shall be initiated.

The design should be signed off. This is not an excuse to bully customers into signing off something they do not comprehend. If customers do not have expertise to sign off design then you should sign off (and accept responsibility) on their behalf. (This is akin to a consulting engineer signing off on behalf of a customer.)

THE DESIGN SPECIFICATION IS SUBJECT TO DOCUMENTATION CONTROL. A BACKUP SHALL BE RETAINED ON COMPUTER READABLE MEDIA.

The design specification is subject to configuration management as documentation. This means keeping track of the distribution of versions of the specification. A backup is always a good idea, so state your policy here.

Programming and user documentation is subject to configuration control. A backup shall be retained on computer readable media.

Programming must be subject to configuration control. This is best applied after unit testing and programming standards reviews. The exact point at which you bring programming under configuration control will depend on circumstances. Regularly review your policy as your quality improves. You may start off only having configuration control over production libraries and progressively tighten the rules until you use a *clean room* development, which has configuration control over first-cut code. Documentation should be placed under configuration control after internal quality assurance.

DESIGN VALIDATION (TEST) SPECIFICATIONS SHALL BE PREPARED IN ACCORDANCE WITH. THE PROJECT QUALITY PLAN OR DEFINED PROCESSES TO MEET THE ACCEPTANCE CRITERIA. ACCEPTANCE CRITERIA SHOULD HAVE BEEN SPECIFIED IN THE PRODUCT REQUIREMENTS SPECIFICATION AND/OR THE DESIGN OUTPUT.

Software design validation is usually called testing. There is no specified requirement for unit testing, system testing, integration testing, performance testing, and so on. The only objective is to prove that the system implements the specification (including quality issues and operational issues). Programmers would typically devise and conduct unit testing and itemize a list of the tests applied. The itemized list is reviewed after the event, and if found to be inadequate, the programmer is guided to what additional tests are required. It is then often necessary only to prove functionality to complete the design validation. Look carefully at the use of system and integration testing. Determine whether it is adding value or whether the technical people are performing acceptance testing before the customer is given the system to play with prior to being asked to accept it. Don't duplicate acceptance testing; if you are proving functionality (including performance) then you are performing acceptance testing. Design validation is about proving we have met specification most other testing is really doing the same thing, so if we can get all of them together we can significantly reduce testing costs.

Design validation specifications shall be inspected for adequacy in meeting the validation (test) plans or defined processes and to ensure that all specified test and acceptance criteria are included or referenced.

The validation specifications are another project deliverable and should be reviewed and signed off.

DESIGN VALIDATION SPECIFICATIONS SHALL BE FORMALLY APPROVED AND ACCEPTED. THE RELEASED DESIGN VALIDATION SPECIFICATIONS SHALL BE SUBJECT TO FORMAL DISTRIBUTION CONTROL. A BACKUP SHALL BE KEPT IN COMPUTER READABLE FORM.

The validation specifications should be placed under configuration control and a backup kept

THE DESIGN VALIDATION (TEST) SPECIFICATIONS SHALL BE APPLIED TO THE DESIGN IN ACCORDANCE WITH THE TEST PLAN OR DEFINED PROCESSES AND THE RESULTS COMPARED WITH THE EXPECTED RESULTS. IF THE RESULTS ARE NOT AS EXPECTED THEN CORRECTIVE ACTION SHALL BE INITIATED.

Testing should be performed and not only should defects be rectified but the causes sought out and corrected. This may appear radical to people who accept that errors are a part of software development, but if we never identify causes we are only guessing when we initiate improvement programs.

THE RESULTS OF DESIGN VALIDATION (TESTING) SHALL BE FORMALLY REVIEWED TO ENSURE THE DESIGN HAS BEEN VALIDATED.

The formal review of testing should include a statement of the form "release aaa of the system was tested using release *bbb* of the validation specification to prove that the system met release ccc of the requirements specification." If the testing was successful the development is complete. If you can separate the acceptance of the test results from the decision for the system to go live then you will have made a major breakthrough. When the system meets specification it is finished and we can compare budget with actual. The next decision is whether customers want to use the system as is or whether they want to change it before implementation. These changes are not part of the original system and should be shown to be extra-cost items.

Changes to the design, programming, user documentation or design validation specifications after release shall be performed under formal change management processes. The changes shall be subject to a review of the impact of the change on other work before being scheduled for inclusion in the next version of the design. Changes shall be reviewed and approved by the authority which approved the original design, programming, user documentation or design validation specification unless agreed otherwise.

Again we need to make sure that configuration control is applied to deliverables so that we can build on a series of released baselines rather than a flood of change requests. Note that an excessive number of change requests is a symptom of poor specification and baseline signoff earlier in the project.

Inspection and testing

Inspection and testing defines the requirements for inspecting and testing products and services to ensure they meet specification and comply with technical standards. ISO 9001 again shows its origins with its emphasis on the inspection of goods received from vendors and subcontractors. If you don't use vendors or subcontractors then say so and concentrate on those areas that impact your work. Inspection and testing covers all areas including services and product. Computer software and documentation are best addressed under design validation but the policies required are also documented here. There is a requirement to specify testing, define testing processes and verify that testing was performed in accordance with the processes, and that testing was completed satisfactorily.

An important part of the inspection and testing process is final inspection. No, this does not mean that you have to devise and run a final set of tests. Final inspection requires you to verify that all the inspections, tests, reviews, approvals, acceptances, signoffs, and so on that you had planned or contractually agreed to perform have been performed and the products and services passed them as planned. The final inspection must be performed before a product is shipped or before it is released for customer use. Final inspection, therefore, suggests that appropriate reviews, inspections, and tests are planned and that they should generate records.

Policies

Typical policies addressing the inspection and test requirements of ISO 9001 include the following:

Product testing

Test specifications shall be prepared in accordance with the quality plan or defined processes to meet the defined product acceptance criteria. Product acceptance criteria should have been specified in the product requirements specification and/or the design. This calls for the preparation of test specifications, which should be designed to prove that the acceptance criteria have been satisfied. Where an external supplier is producing the product the specification should be provided to the supplier. An initial reaction to this statement in software development is "but then they will build the product to pass the test." Isn't that what we want? If the supplier has a quality management system we can use their system and their effort to prove to us that the product meets specification and save ourselves doing any inspection and testing.

TEST SPECIFICATIONS SHALL BE INSPECTED FOR ADEQUACY IN MEETING THE TEST PLANS OR DEFINED PROCESSES AND TO ENSURE THAT ALL SPECIFIED TEST AND ACCEPTANCE CRITERIA ARE INCLUDED OR REFERENCED.

The test specifications are another project deliverable and should be reviewed and signed off.

TEST SPECIFICATIONS SHALL BE FORMALLY APPROVED AND ACCEPTED. THE RELEASED TEST SPECIFICATIONS SHALL BE TREATED AS PRODUCT AND SUBJECT TO FORMAL DISTRIBUTION CONTROL.

The test specifications should be placed under configuration control.

THE TEST SPECIFICATIONS SHALL BE APPLIED TO THE PRODUCT IN ACCORDANCE WITH THE TEST PLAN OR DEFINED PROCESSES AND THE RESULTS COMPARED WITH THE EXPECTED RESULTS. IF THE RESULTS ARE NOT AS EXPECTED THEN CORRECTIVE ACTION SHALL BE INITIATED.

Testing should be performed and not only should defects be rectified but the causes sought out and corrected.

Changes to test specifications shall be performed under formal change management processes.

Again we need to make sure that configuration control is applied to deliverables.

Customer inspection and confidentiality

The customer shall have the right to inspect products and processes at our premises or our supplier's premises. The customer should make all such arrangements through us. The customer shall be required to protect the confidentiality of all information made available for examination, inspection an review.

This addresses a requirement of ISO 9001. The standard introduces the topic with "as required by the contract." It is a largely useless statement to have in a standard because we must do whatever we agree to in the contract and ISO 9001 adds no value with this statement. The major point is to make sure your policy protects you by calling on all arrangements between your customer and your supplier to include you so that you are not squeezed out of the agreement.

Purchased goods and services inspection and testing

The need for actual inspection and testing or acceptance based on supplier records shall be defined in the quality plan. Purchasing specifications for goods and services should specify the inspection and test required. When purchased goods or services are received, they shall be examined for external damage to packaging before being accepted. Any external damage shall be noted on the delivery docket. The items shall be carefully unpacked (follow any instructions provided) and inspected for physical damage. The item shall then be checked against the purchase specification. Any damage, defects, problems or discrepancies shall immediately be notified to the supplier in writing (facsimile or letter). Where the product is unacceptable then corrective action shall be initiated and the inspection report attached to the nonconforming product.

This is a straightforward statement covering inspection on receipt of goods. You may require much more sophisticated policies and procedures if you do a lot of purchasing.

Software tools and techniques

WHEN SOFTWARE TOOLS, TECHNIQUES, METHODOLOGIES, ETC. ARE TO BE INSTALLED AND THERE IS NO HISTORICAL PERFORMANCE ON WHICH TO BASE ACCEPTANCE THEN THE SOFTWARE SHALL BE SUBJECT TO TESTING TO ENSURE IT PERFORMS SATISFACTORILY.

Do not use unproven software. Either accept it on the basis of "three months in the market with no significant adverse reports" or prove it before you use it.

Final inspection

When all inspection and testing is complete a final inspection shall be made to verify that all tests, inspections, reviews, approvals and acceptances documented in the quality plan, defined processes and otherwise agreed have been completed, authorized and accepted.

This is an audit of the reviews, inspections, and tests to make sure that all the planned activities have been completed. This includes all signoffs, customer acceptances, and quality assurance activities. If any have been missed then go and do them before delivering the system to the customer.

Inspection and test status

Inspection and test status is concerned with recording the status of review, inspection, and test of each product or batch of product at each part of the process. Each process may develop its own product or products, which undergo one or more reviews, inspections, and tests before being released to the next process. Records should be generated by all reviews, inspections, and tests and it is necessary to know the current review, inspection, and test status of the product or batch.

Review, inspection, and test status may be marked on the product or the container in which the product or product batch is transported from one process to the next. Inspection and test status may also be recorded in a log or register, which may be kept on computer.

Policies

Typical policies addressing the inspection and test status requirements of ISO 9001 include the following:

ALL PRODUCT IS SUBJECT TO ONE OR MORE REVIEWS, INSPECTIONS AND/OR TESTS BEFORE BEING SUBMITTED FOR ACCEPTANCE AND RELEASE AS A PRODUCT. EACH REVIEW, INSPECTION, AND TEST GENERATES A RECORD WHICH INCLUDES THE IDENTIFICATION OF THE PERSON WHO RELEASED THE PRODUCT AS HAVING PASSED THE REVIEW, INSPECTION OR TEST.

Another statement of the obvious but a most useful one as it informs your people that everything must be reviewed, inspected, or tested at least once before the work is finished.

THE INSPECTION OR TEST STATUS OF PRODUCT IS RECORDED ON THE PRODUCT, IN THE INSPECTION/TEST RECORDS OR IN A SUITABLE REGISTER,

This points to the relevant procedure for recording the results of reviews, inspections, and tests. This is sometimes called development status. This is another use for our product register along with configuration management and control of nonconforming product.

Control of inspection, measuring, and test equipment

Inspection, measuring, and test equipment means any equipment used for inspection, or testing. It can vary from a simple ruler to a sophisticated simulator. The objective of this section is to ensure that the equipment used is capable of performing the measurements and testing it is supposed to perform and that measurements are to the level of accuracy required.

Be very careful when documenting the requirements of this section that you do not accidentally include measuring equipment you did not intend. Statements such as "all inspection measuring and test equipment shall be calibrated" includes such things as the ruler in your desk drawer and the toy thermometer next to the air conditioning duct. Qualify your statement in a form such as "all inspection measuring and test equipment used in the production processes shall be calibrated."

Inspection measuring and test equipment may include hardware and software simulators such as power station and aircraft simulators. It is rather difficult to borrow an airplane to test a fly-by-wire computer program. Would the programmer want to do it before the software has been tested on a simulator? Similarly, anything you develop to test products also needs to be verified as being capable of performing the tests. Computer software developers will find a problem here because it means that quick-and-dirty programs written to support the testing of other programs must first be tested and proven before they can be used. The quality plan or defined processes must ensure that the suitability of inspection, measuring, and test equipment is verified at suitable intervals and the verification results recorded.

If your business does not require you to make use of inspection measuring, and test equipment you need only address this requirement of ISO 9001 by a statement of this form:

THE NATURE OF OUR BUSINESS IS SUCH THAT THERE IS NO REQUIREMENT TO

MAKE USE OF INSPECTION, MEASURING AND TEST EQUIPMENT. SHOULD THIS CHANGE THEN EITHER POLICIES AND PROCEDURES WILL BE DEVELOPED OR THE PROJECT QUALITY PLAN FOR THE PROJECT SHALL SPECIFY THE CONTROLS TO BE APPLIED.

Omitting such a statement may be construed by an assessor as an oversight or a failure to address this section of ISO 9001.

Policies

Typical policies addressing the inspection, measuring, and test equipment requirements of ISO 9001 include the following:

VERIFICATION OF INSPECTION, MEASURING AND TEST EQUIPMENT SHALL BE PERFORMED IN ACCORDANCE WITH DOCUMENTED PROCESSES DESIGNED TO CONDUCT SUCH VERIFICATION. THESE PROCESSES SHALL PRODUCE SUITABLE EVIDENCE THAT THE EQUIPMENT IS CAPABLE OF DEMONSTRATING THE CONFORMANCE OF THE PRODUCT TO THE SPECIFIED REQUIREMENTS.

If you use equipment that needs calibrating, you need to point to a procedure that addresses calibration or proof that the equipment (including software) works. Calibration of inspection, measuring and test equipment shall be done by a source which provides traceability to national standards.

Physical measurement must be traceable back to national (and therefore international) standards of physical measure.

INSPECTION, MEASURING AND TEST EQUIPMENT SHALL, WHERE PRACTICABLE, BE VISIBLY MARKED WITH ITS CALIBRATION STATUS AND A DATE ON WHICH IT IS TO BE RE-CALIBRATED.

Use tags or stamps to show calibration status and expiration date.

EQUIPMENT WHOSE CALIBRATION CERTIFICATE HAS EXPIRED SHALL NOT BE USED FOR INSPECTION, MEASURING OR TESTING.

If the expiration date has passed you must not use the equipment until it has been re-calibrated.

EQUIPMENT WHICH HAS BEEN STRAINED, DAMAGED OR SUBJECTED TO ROUGH TREATMENT SHALL NOT BE USED FOR INSPECTION, MEASURING OR TESTING.

If the equipment has been subject to conditions that may invalidate the calibration, it must not be used until it has been re-calibrated.

Statistical techniques

The statistical techniques referred to in ISO 9001 are the ones used to prove products are satisfactory. If you use sampling techniques rather than 100-percent inspection, the techniques you use should be statistically correct for the confidence level you need to achieve. If you test 10 percent of a product there are two things you need to know: First, is 10 percent the right sample size for the confidence you need, or would 20 percent be better, or would 5 percent be sufficient? Consult your statistician for verification. Second, the mechanism used to take the sample must be correct, otherwise you may not be getting valid results. If you take every tenth item as a 10 percent sample, your people may be tempted to make sure that every tenth item is a good one. Again, consult your statistician. As you develop your performance statistics, describe them here and identify how the data is going to be collected, analyzed, and used.

This is a contentious area because there is an increasing movement toward metrics in software development. These metrics are defined in ISO 9126 and various programs are under way to develop objective means of measuring quality. If you do full testing of your systems, you are not using statistical techniques in the ISO 9001 sense. If your customer accepts the system on the grounds that 10 percent has been proven to work, therefore we assume the other 90 percent works, then you are using statistical techniques.

We must assume that few if any software developers use statistical techniques to validate software. In this case, you need only address this requirement of ISO 9001 by a statement of the form:

THE NATURE OF OUR PROCESS IS SUCH THAT SOFTWARE IS VALIDATED BY A 100% INSPECTION AND TEST. AS SUCH STATISTICAL TECHNIQUES ARE NOT USED.

Policies

Sampling for inspection and testing shall be performed using statistically valid techniques and sample sizes to meet the confidence level required. Statistical techniques shall be subject to independent validation and verification by a suitably qualified statistician.

Make sure techniques for selecting the samples will achieve the level of confidence required to release all the product as satisfactory. Make sure you are using statistically correct techniques by having expert assessment of your techniques.

Where deviations occur from statistical norms then corrective action shall be initiated.

Servicing and software maintenance

Servicing and maintenance deals with the support of products after they have been delivered and, if required, installed. For software it is almost a disappointment that such a large part of our effort can be addressed with so few words. Servicing may be limited by contractual conditions or may be a business in its own right. Servicing covers the rectification of defects, work required due to normal wear and tear, and changes in functionality and performance by applying design changes.

Handling of customer complaints and the use of them to improve processes and therefore products and services should not be ignored or taken lightly. The customer is the reason for our existence as an organization and this part of the process should be one of its driving forces.

Policies

Typical policies addressing the servicing and software maintenance requirements of ISO 9001 include the following:

THE PERSON RESPONSIBLE FOR SUPPORTING A PRODUCT SHALL MODIFY THE PRODUCT WHEN REQUESTED BY A CUSTOMER. THESE MODIFICATIONS SHALL BE PERFORMED UNDER FORMAL CHANGE MANAGEMENT PROCESSES.

Do maintenance the same way you did the original development.

The response to defect notification shall be in accordance with defined processes or as specified in the project quality plan. Nonconforming product controls shall be used to manage the rectification of defects.

Control the rectification of errors in the same way you did during development. Be careful of blindly following corrective action when a defect arises. In very old systems there may be no benefit in finding out that the programmers twenty years ago were ineffective-especially if one of the programmers is now the IT manager!

Requests for assistance (help desk or response center calls) and customer complaints shall be dealt with promptly and the details recorded for future analysis in accordance with corrective action.

One of the biggest sources of information for improvement programs comes from customer feedback. Help desks, response centers, network support centers, and other customer contact points are invaluable sources of information. Make sure you have procedures to capture that information, preferably ones that don't tie your customers up in bureaucracy and paperwork.

3

Concept of Hardware Management

This chapter is about hard disk organization. It covers different ways to arrange and order the files on your drive, primarily by using subdirectories.

Files and subdirectories

Fortunately, DOS is flexible when it comes to the subdirectory organization of your disk. There are no required subdirectories, no specific design you must follow. You're totally free to build the kind of hard disk structure best suited to your needs. However, there are several things you should consider before taking the leap into hard disk management with subdirectories. They are

- the DOS subdirectory commands
- the reasons behind file organization
- how to take advantage of the path

DOS subdirectory commands

There are only a few commands to deal with subdirectories. They are

- MKDIR
- CHDIR
- RMDIR

Remember that each command has an abbreviated form:

- MD
- CD
- RD

The two forms of each command perform the same task in the same way.

MKDIR and MD are used to Make subdirectories. Subdirectories are named just as DOS files are, and the same naming rules apply. You can make a subdirectory in any directory on your drive. However, if you don't specify a full pathname, the subdirectory is created in the current directory.

CHDIR and CD are used to Change from one directory to another. Either command is followed by the pathname you wish to make the currently logged directory. CD entered by itself displays the pathname of the currently logged directory. CHDIR and CD are really the workhorses of the *DOS* subdirectory commands.

RMDIR and RD are used to ReMove subdirectories. They work just like the DEL command, which removes files. You follow RMDIR with the pathname of the subdirectory you want to remove. The only limitations to RMDIR and RD are that you cannot delete the current subdirectory and you cannot delete any subdirectory unless it is totally empty of files.

There are two subdirectory commands that would be nice to have but that *DOS* doesn't give you: a command to rename a subdirectory and a command to move a subdirectory. Sadly, once you make a subdirectory, there's no way to rename it. Not by using *DOS,* at least. However, there are utilities and special programs that do allow you to rename a subdirectory. But if you don't have one, you're stuck with using the method DOS prescribes: Make a new subdirectory with the name you want, then COPY all the files and directories from the first subdirectory into the appropriately named one.

Fortunately, there is one quasi-solution. In DOS version 3.2 a special command for COPYing, XCOPY, was introduced. XCOPY is a better, more "intelligent," and faster version of the COPY command. It has the same basic format but many more options. First, it copies all the files you specify into memory, then it writes them all back out onto disk. This works much faster than COPYing files one at a time, as COPY does.

One of XCOPY's options is /S. When you specify/S, XCOPY copies all files in the current directory as well as any files in any subdirectories in the current directory. For example, the command

```
XCOPY C:\DOS\*.* C:\SYSTEM\DOS /S
```

effectively copies an entire branch of your hard disk tree structure to a different location. However, this still leaves you with the problem of deleting the original files and their subdirectories.

Why organize files?

If you've worked on a disorganized hard disk, then the question "Why organize files?" seems rather innocent. But there are several reasons: some result from limitations of DOS, others from plain common sense.

- DOS puts a limit on the number of files you can put into the root directory. For most hard disks, this limit is 512 files. Even if your hard disk still has quite a bit of free space on it, when you hit 512 files, you'll get a "Disk full" message.
- Keeping too many files in the root directory, or in any subdirectory, slows down

the performance of DOS. Although the root directory limits the number of files you can put there, normal subdirectories don't. When the subdirectory becomes full, DOS extends it. Accessing that extension really slows down the system. You will notice this if you ever use the DIR command on a large subdirectory; it will grind to a near halt as the file list nears the end.

- When you have a lot of files in one directory, you encounter naming conflicts. There are millions of combinations for filenames. However, only a few are really useful. The more files you have in a subdirectory, the more likely there are to be naming conflicts.
- By putting related files into their own subdirectories, you can easily locate the files you need. You won't need to hunt them down in a large directory. Remember, with only eight characters in a filename plus a three-character extension, it can be hard to make a name descriptive. But put related files in a subdirectory, and everything is neat and organized.

Above all, the most important edict of file organization is

```
KEEP THE ROOT CLEAN
```

That means "Keep as few files as possible in the root directory."

Yeah, subdirectories are fine, but restrict them. Three dozen subdirectories are too many for the root directory. At most, try to keep fewer than a dozen, with six being a workable number. Keep a maximum of three files in the root directory: AUTOEXEC.BAT, COMMAND.COM, and CONFIG.SYS. Of those three,

COMMAND.COM can be placed into a subdirectory if you use the SHELL command in CONFIG.SYS. That leaves you with two files in the root directory, but only if you use them in your system—they're both optional.

There is no limit to the amount of organization you can apply to a hard disk. For example, you can divide your word processing files into PERSONAL and WORK subdirectories. Further subdirectories can divide those categories up. PERSONAL can have LETTERS, POEMS, BOOKS, THOUGHTS, and other categories underneath it; LETTERS can have QUERIES, FAMILY, FRIENDS, PENPALS, and so forth under it. You can go as "deep" as you want to. In fact, any subdirectory with more than two dozen files in it can stand some sort of organization. If you're fussy about organization or think you don't really need to start out that organized, then create a MISC subdirectory. Put into it anything that falls into the miscellaneous category or lacks any category of its own. Then, as the MISC subdirectory collects more files, splinter related files off into their own appropriately named subdirectories. As long as you have set up an effective and flexible scheme, organization becomes a snap.

How to use PATH to best advantage

On a hard disk, you can have dozens of programs. And if you're organizing things, you can have dozens of programs in dozens of subdirectories. How can you deal best with the situation?

The answer is that there is no effective way to deal with dozens of programs in dozens of subdirectories. You can use the CD command to change to the proper subdirectory and then run the program. But there are certain programs that you always want to have access to. For example, it would be useful to always have FORMAT, CHKDSK, XCOPY, BACKUP—the DOS commands—available from any location on your hard disk. Also, it would be nice to be able to access your word processor, spreadsheet, database, or whichever program you use most often from whichever subdirectory you happen to be logged to.

Note that it's not necessary to be able to access all your programs at all times. Sure, it would be neat. But if you could access all files at all times you'd defeat the purpose of having subdirectories. It's much better to keep just a few programs—utilities and DOS—so that you can access them at any time. You do this with the PATH command.

The PATH command sets a search path for DOS. When you type a command at the command prompt, DOS checks from one to three places:

- First, it checks to see if the command is an internal DOS command. If so, it's executed; if not, the search continues.
- Second, DOS checks to see if the command is a filename with either a COM, EXE, or BAT extension in the current directory. If so, the file is loaded and executed; if not, the search continues.
- Third, DOS checks each subdirectory listed after PATH for the COM, EXE, or BAT file matching the name you typed. If found, DOS loads and executes that file.

You can see how taking advantage of PATH can really simplify operation of your hard disk. By putting after PATH the names of subdirectories that contain your most popular and necessary programs, PATH, you can access those programs from any location on your hard disk.

But, before going nuts with PATH, temper yourself. Putting every subdirectory on the search path is not effective hard disk management. It will work—DOS will look everywhere and eventually find the program you want to run but—it could take some time. DOS will also use the path when you mistype names. For example, suppose the cat walks across the keyboard, types ASXCYUJ and presses ENTER. DOS will look in those same three places, including all the subdirectories on your PATH, before it comes back to give you a "Bad command or filename" message. Again, that could take some time. It's best to be tidy with PATH.

At the most keep only three subdirectories on the path. Nearly everyone puts the DOS subdirectory on the path. For example, your three subdirectories might be

1. DOS subdirectory
2. Utility subdirectory
3. Program subdirectory

or

1. DOS subdirectory
2. Program1 subdirectory
3. Program2 subdirectory

Or, if you use only three programs on your hard disk, you might expand the path slightly:

1. DOS subdirectory
2. Program1 subdirectory
3. Program2 subdirectory
4. Program3 subdirectory

The point is to keep the path brief and efficient. Also, remember that PATH is an environment variable. It's always possible to reset PATH to something else—for example, to use batch files.

Examples of subdirectory organization

You can read about hard disk organization until your PC becomes obsolete. But what will really help you understand it are some good solid examples. The examples in the rest of this chapter will illustrate different approaches to hard disk organization. Remember, some approaches are more efficient than others. But the effectiveness of your approach depends on your situation and what you want to get out of hard disk management.

Assume that you're starting with a blank slate. However, you can modify any subdirectory structure on your hard disk to fit into one of the following categories. Simply take those ideas that you find interesting and apply them to your own situation. Then, feel free to wander and explore. Adapt what you need; discard what doesn't work. After a while, you'll develop your own personal feel for organization. The following examples will help you on your way.

The DOS subdirectory

True enough, every hard disk will have a root directory. The next subdirectory created should be one for DOS. The DOS subdirectory is the most important one on your hard disk.

Traditionally, the DOS subdirectory is poised off the root directory. All the DOS files and associated supplemental programs should be tossed into that subdirectory. Everything. Don't ever make the error of putting DOS programs into the root directory. That's the worst error of judgment you can make.

To create the DOS subdirectory off the root directory, type

```
C> MKDIR \DOS ENTER
```

To move to the DOS subdirectory, type

```
C> CD \DOS ENTER
```

To COPY files from DOS diskettes in drive A, use the following command:

```
C> COPY A:*.*
```

Note that some recent versions of DOS come with installation programs. These programs ask into which subdirectory you wish to place DOS. Specify DOS or whichever subdirectory you desire as the DOS destination. Each program type is given its own subdirectory under SYSTEM. So, in my personal computer, DOS is in the DOS subdirectory of SYSTEM. You may choose a similar scheme based on which of the following design examples you prefer. The examples illustrate various approaches to using subdirectories for hard disk organization. When you use these approaches in your own system, remember that you'll be substituting your own program and subdirectory names. Feel free to elaborate on, subtract from, or take only those ideas that will work best in your situation.

Program and data subdirectories

The program and data subdirectories design is the one most installation programs set up for you. In those subdirectories go any data files you find necessary to put there. When you add new programs to this scheme, you simply create a new subdirectory off the root and put the files there. Any additional data subdirectories go underneath those new directories.

The path for this type of subdirectory structure might look like this:

```
PATH=C:\DOS;C:\1-2-3;C:\MLTIMATE;C:\DB3
```

All the programs in the four main directories are always on the path. You can be in any subdirectory on any drive, type the name of a program, and have DOS run it for you,

A better path is

```
PATH=C:\DOS;.
```

It's much shorter and does the same thing. See if you can guess what it means before reading the next paragraph.

The dot-dot,.., is an abbreviation used by DOS to indicate the parent directory. When you create a subdirectory it automatically contains <DIR> files,

```
<DIR>  11-30-91  11:26A
<DIR>  11-30-91  11:26A
```

The single dot,., is an abbreviation for the current subdirectory. Dot-dot means the parent directory. For example, to move to the parent subdirectory, type

```
C> CD.. ENTER
```

The same type of logic can be applied to the path. There dot-dot means the parent directory as well. When it appears on the path, DOS looks in the parent directory for files.

Can you see the drawback to this type of subdirectory structure? After you gather about 12 different applications, you have 12 subdirectories hanging off the root directory. That's inefficient organization, and it makes expansion difficult. However, for office systems or computers that do only one or two tasks, this type of structure is perfect.

Categorical subdirectories

This is a really tight system. 'Me only four subdirectories that will ever be in the root are SYSTEM, MISC, BD4, and PROJECTS. Period. Expansion takes, place in each of them, as opposed to in the root directory.

The SYSTEM subdirectory contains any nonapplication-type programs, each of which is held in its own subdirectory. SYSTEM contains DOS, a subdirectory for DOS; UTIL, for general utilities; and MEMRES, for memory-resident software. Other subdirectories that go here may contain backup software, mainstream utilities, and applications that control expansion boards, memory options, and other hardware.

The MISC subdirectory is always a good one to have, and it's good to keep it in a convenient location, such as off the root. MISC contains miscellaneous stuff, temporary information, and files you don't want to delete just yet. Other names for MISC could be TEMP, JUNK, or STUFF. A MISC subdirectory shouldn't contain any other subdirectories or any permanent files.

The BIN subdirectory serves the same purpose as the root directory of the previous example. It contains subdirectories that contains a your major applications. In those subdirectories are data subdirectories. If you need to add another application to your system, you just stick it in the BIN subdirectory. The total number of files in the root will not change.

The PROJECTS subdirectory was added as a place to put commonly related files. For example, if you're working on a project that involves data from both your spreadsheet and database, you can create a subdirectory specifically for that project in the PROJECTS subdirectory. This is an optional subdirectory, but it does solve a few problems that may arise.

Choosing the path for this type of system is a coin toss. It's not practical to put every subdirectory on the path. So, you have to decide which subdirectories you always want to have access to. For example, the path

```
PATH=C:\SYSTEM\DOS;C:\SYSTEM\UTIL;C:\BIN\WORD
```

gives you access to the programs in your DOS and UTIL subdirectories as well as to the word processor in the WORD subdirectory. If you're a writer or work a lot with your word processor, then this setup is just fine. If you work more with the spreadsheet, then replace C.\BIN\WORD with C:\BIN\CALC.

The only drawback to this type of design is, in fact, the path. It offers organization and allows expansion, but the PATH statement can get messy. You just have to decide which files you need to access from any spot on the hard drive, then put those file's subdirectories on the path. But the next structure provides an even better solution.

Batch file subdirectories

Batch file subdirectory design provides the best way to run a hard disk. It uses the same approach as the categorical subdirectories but allows for maximum flexibility.

There are specific areas for my two major activities: programming and word processing. A subdirectory exists for communications. The MISC subdirectory handles miscellaneous applications and stuff. There's a TEMP subdirectory for temporary files and so forth. And then there's a SYSTEM subdirectory with 13 subdirectories.

Note the BATCH subdirectory of the SYSTEM subdirectory. It's what makes the whole arrangement possible. Into that subdirectory are placed about three dozen batch files. Those batch files run every other program in the system. How? Take a look at the path:

```
PATH=C:\SYSTEM\DOS;C:\SYSTEM\UTIL;
C:\SYSTEM\BATCH
```

The DOS and UTIL subdirectories are on the path. Additionally, the BATCH subdirectory is there. That subdirectory contains batch files that run every other program in the system. For example, the WP batch file runs WordPerfect. The contents of the file are

```
ECHO OFF
C:\WORDP\WP
```

DOS first looks for W, a" internal command, then in the current directory, then in the directories on the path. It will then find WP.BAT and run WordPerfect. If the 123 spreadsheet were on the drive somewhere, then the 123.BAT program could be written to run it. Likewise with any major application. Just write a batch file to run the application and stick it in the BATCH subdirectory of the SYSTEM subdirectory.

This arrangement can handle special cases. The subdirectories in the PROGRAM directory each have many other subdirectories associated with them. Those subdirectories contain the data files associated with each programming language. To make this work effectively, a special batch file adjusts the path. For example the batch file to run TURBOC contains

```
ECHO OFF
SET PATH=C:\PROGRAM\TURSOC;C:\SYSTEM\DOS;
     C:\SYSTEM\UTIL;C:\SYSTEM\BATCH
CD \PROGRAM\TURBOC
T C
```

This batch file adjusts the path so that the TURBOC subdirectory is on it. You can be in any data directory under TURBOC and still access the Programs there. Other applications that need the same attention can have the path modified by a batch file as well.

```
ECHO OFF
SET PATH=C:\SYSTEM\DOS;C:\SYSTEM\UTIL;
C:\SYSTEM\BATCH
```

Again, since this batch file is in the batch file subdirectory, it can be accessed from anywhere in the system.

Multiple-user subdirectories

No matter the subdirectory strategy employed, certain computers are used by more than one person. To keep each person's data separate, it's a wise idea to give each user a private subdirectory.

Each of the four people using the computer has a private subdirectory under the 123 directory. Batch files can be used so that each user need type his or her name only. For example, the ANN batch file looks like this:

```
ECHO OFF
C :
CD \1-2-3\ANN
PATH=C:\DOS;C:\1-2-3
123
```

This batch file logs Ann to her subdirectory under 123, sets a path, then runs 123. Similar batch files allow each of her co-workers to do the same thing.

Hard disk maintenance

Once you choose a hard disk organization that works for you, the rest is easy. Only simple maintenance is needed. This consists of

- routine file maintenance
- backing up software
- installing new applications

Routine file maintenance

Routine file maintenance takes place during the daily operation of your computer. It involves some bits of organization for example, creating new subdirectories when they become necessary. But for the most part, file maintenance consists of deleting old and unused files; writing new batch files as needed; and COPYing, or archiving, unused but still needed files to floppy diskettes for safekeeping.

Software backup

Backing up software, next to effective hard disk organization, is the best thing you can do for your computer. Backing up software isn't just running the backup program. It's developing a good backup strategy and then carrying it out on a regular basis.

Installation of new applications

Installing new applications is the only major field of hard disk management that remains somewhat unpredictable. You must know what you're installing and its hardware requirements and know how to fit it into your subdirectory structure.

The requirments of new software

Just like boxes of breakfast cereal, most software boxes list the system requirements. Read that information, then mentally compare it with your knowledge of your computer to make sure that everything fits correctly. There's nothing more disappointing than bringing your computer a piece of new software and then finding out that it just doesn't work.

Before you buy a new application for your system, know the requirements of the software and the capabilities of your computer. Know

- the type of system required (an IBM PC AT 386, for example)
- the minimum version of DOS required
- the diskette format needed
- how much disk space the software cats (if provided)
- how much memory the software demands
- what type of graphics is required
- any special peripherals needed (expanded memory, a mouse, modem, and so on)

Mentally make a note of how the requirements apply to your computer.

Make a similar table about your computer system. Know what you have. Then, before you buy the software, make sure your system has what the software needs to work properly.

One of the most important items to consider is often not stressed on the software box: the amount of space that must be available on your hard drive. When you first bought the hard drive, the size seemed just about right. But, like most users, you may have filled it up rather quickly. If storage space on the hard disk is at a premium, then count those megabytes before you install a new application. Most of today's software takes at least 1MB of space on the hard disk and that doesn't count the data files you will create. Keep the amount of available space in mind when you go shopping for software.

Where the software goes

Deciding where to put the new application is a snap: It goes into its own subdirectory. But deciding where to put that subdirectory depends on how you've organized your hard drive. If you're using a simple organization, then put the application off the root directory. If the organization goes deeper, decide on an appropriate place. This may depend on the application type as well as the other programs you'll be using with the application.

Remember that there's nothing wrong with making some severe modifications if you notice three applications that really belong together in the same branch of your hard disk tree. Feel free to move those subdirectories by recreating them and using XCOPY to place the files in their new locations. If your hard disk was well organized initially, this won't be a problem. And doing so isn't a sign of bad hard disk management

How the software is installed

There are two ways you can go with installing a new application on your system. You can do it yourself or you can run the installation program that comes with the application.

When you do it yourself, you're basically doing what an installation program would do for you. In fact, most installation programs are mere batch files, which you can examine using the DOS command TYPE. They simply create a directory and COPY the files there. You can do the same thing on your own. Simply follow these steps:

1. Make a subdirectory for the application.
2. COPY the application its files to that directory.
3. Update CONFIG.SYS or AUTOEXEC.BAT as needed.
4. If needed, write a batch file to run the program.

Remember that some applications require you to update CONFIG.SYS or AUTOEXEC.BAT. The instructions and options for doing so are probably in the application's manual. Pay special attention to them! Also, remember that most manuals provide additional information on installation and options in appendixes and in other chapters besides the chapter about installation.

If your hard disk's subdirectory structure is using batch files to get the work done, you may want to write a batch file to run the new application. If so, make sure you make the proper settings in the batch file, then have it log to the correct subdirectory and run the program. Remember to put the batch file into your BATCH subdirectory and keep that subdirectory on the path.

If you're so inclined, you can let a new application's installation program do things for you. This will only happen on two occasions: when you don't know any better and when it won't let you do it any other way.

Most new DOS users and the DOS-timid opt to run the automatic installation programs. These programs usually create a subdirectory for the application on your hard disk, COPY the files there, and even modify CONFIG.SYS and AUTOEXEC.BAT. Some even write their own batch files and stick them in the root directory for you. You know better; avoid this type of installation program.

Of course, there are times when you can't avoid using an installation program. For example, some programs come on a dozen or so diskettes. Other programs may need to be "assembled" in RAM by the installation program. In these cases you have no choice but to run the installation program. Just answer the questions and pray that it will let you install the application in the subdirectory you want it in.

There may be a bit of patching required after some of those automatic installation programs do their damage. For example, you may have to remove the lines it adds to your AUTOEXEC.BAT file. Or you may want to remove any files it puts in the root directory. In all cases just keep a keen eye on things and you should be able to return your system to normal—even after the most calamitous of installation programs has mucked with your hard disk.

DOS and the hard drive

Hard disks present problems that don't exist with floppy disks. The most obvious hard drive problem doesn't seem like a problem: where to put all the files and data. Yet, when you consider the massive storage available, you can see that the potential for conflicting filenames an general sluggishness-both due to the sheer number of files-is great. The solution to dealing with so many files on a hard drive is to divide the hard drive up into minidrives, or separate work areas. Files in one area exist independently of others. This avoids filename conflicts and keeps everything neat and tidy in the process. DOS refers to these separate areas as subdirectories.

This chapter is about subdirectories-how DOS allows you to deal with massive amounts of files on a hard drive. The subdirectory system DOS uses is largely what hard disk management is all about. To deal with subdirectories, you need to know what a subdirectory is and how it works and the commands that manipulate subdirectories. The concept of subdirectories is not the simplest to grasp. They can be compared to floors in a building or boxes within boxes, but only by dealing with them firsthand will you discover their value.

The DOS commands you'll use to manipulate subdirectories are

- MKDIR or MD
- CHDIR or CD
- RMDIR or RD

Know these commands and how to use them with subdirectories, and the rest is relatively easy.

Subdirectories

To properly deal with subdirectories, you must first understand what a subdirectory is and how it can be useful. In the previous chapter, you saw how all DOS commands and files can be placed into their own subdirectory. Why not just copy them over to drive C? What's the advantage of subdirectories? In answer, consider an axiom: Subdirectories provide a way of dealing with many files on your hard disk.

DOS normally categorizes files by the directory. Remember the DIR command? That command displays a directory of files on disk. In the old days, before hard drives were affordable, the concept was one disk-one directory. When you typed the DIR command, it listed file on the floppy drive. But with hard drives, subdirectories give you one disk-many directories. The drive can be divided up into smaller directories-directories within directories. The DIR command lists only the contents of the current directory; the files in that directory exist independently of other files.

Ever since DOS version 2.0, you could divide up a disk, hard or floppy, into as many directories as you desire. Each directory can have directories of its own. The mental image most people make of this concept is an organization chart. Using subdirectories, you can organize your hard drive, putting related files into their own subdirectories, safe and secluded from everything else. The DOS manual provides an excellent interpretation of this concept. The next section describes practical applications of it.

The root and the tree

No, this isn't a dissertation about gardening. "Root" and "Tree" refer to subdirectory structure. The subdirectories on your hard disk are like branches of a tree. The main directory the only directory if subdirectories didn't exist—is called the root directory. But, unlike a tree, the root is really at the top of the, subdirectory structure. All other directories branch off downward from the root.

The symbol DOS uses for, the root directory is the backslash character: V That's the name of the root directory. When you refer to the root directory in programs, applications, spray-paint graffiti, and in DOS, you use.

DOS neither creates nor requires directories other than the root. However, the root directory itself has space for only 512 files or subdirectories. Fill up those 512 spaces, and even though you may have 66MB of available space on the disk, DOS gives you a "Disk Full" message.

An important point to consider here is that subdirectories are essentially files on disk. For example, making a subdirectory takes up one of the 512 file slots in the root directory. But once you get past the first level, you can have as many files as you want in the subdirectory.

A well-organized hard drive has maybe half a dozen subdirectories. To those subdirectories, the root directory is the "parent." In fact, the term parent is commonly used to refer to the directory just "above" the current directory. The subdirectories can be considered the root directory's "children," though the common convention is to refer to them only as subdirectories. Additional subdirectories can fall below the first level, and more subdirectories can branch off even lower. Voila! Can you see the upside-down tree? When programmers talk about a tree structure, this is the kind of structure they mean. Note that each branch of the subdirectory is independent. You cannot cross-connect subdirectories; two parents cannot share one child directory.

The pathname

DOS refers to subdirectories by their names, just as it refers to files. The location of the subdirectory is given as its pathname. The pathname is the full name of the subdirectory, the drive that the subdirectory is on, and all subdirectories above it. For example:

```
C:\PASCAL
```

The name of the subdirectory is PASCAL. It is a subdirectory of the root directory, \, on drive C. If PASCAL has a subdirectory called TURBO, then its pathname is

```
C:\PASCAL\TURBO
```

TURBO is a subdirectory of PASCAL, which is a subdirectory of the root directory. Note that the backslash character,\, is used to separate directory names in the pathname.

A filename can also be part of a pathname. For example, assume LESSON1.PAS is a file in the TURBO subdirectory. In that case, its pathname is

```
C:\PASCAL\TURBO\LESSON1.PAS
```

Note again that the backslash is used to separate names in the path. This time the backslash separates the name of a file from its subdirectory. The same holds true for all files, For example:

```
C:\AUTOEXEC.BAT
```

The preceding is the full pathname for the file AUTOEXEC.BAT in your root directory. AUTOEXEC.BAT is not the name of a subdirectory. However, if that file appears in a subdirectory, say the MISC subdirectory, then its pathname is

```
C:\MISC\AUTOEXEC.BAT
```

This tells you that the file AUTOEXEC.BAT is in the subdirectory MISC off the root directory in drive C.

But how can you tell if you're dealing with a subdirectory or file? You can't.

Remember, files and subdirectories are essentially the same thing to DOS. A subdirectory is simply a special type of file, representing another directory on disk. In fact, the only way you can tell which is which is to examine the output of a directory listing. For example:

```
VOLUME IN DRIVE C IS TOO LOUD
DIRECTORY OF C:\STUFF
.<DIR> 11-30-91 11:26A
..<DIR> 11-30-91 11:26A
MISC <DIR> 9-28-91 11:37P
TEMP <DIR> 9-24-91 4:26P
GO BAT 864 7-21-91 2:59P
4 FILE(S) 18872320 BYTES FREE
```

In the preceding sample output of a DIR command, you'll see that some files have the <DIR> symbol by them. This indicates that they are subdirectories, not files.

You'll also notice that. and are <DIR> files as wen. These are special directory files used by DOS—and you can use them as well. They're subdirectories on your disk. The single dot is an abbreviation for the current directory. The double dot is an abbreviation for the parent directory.

Finally, before moving on, note that the drive letter and colon are sometimes not used in a pathnarne, especially if the file or subdirectory to which you're referring is the current drive. For example:

```
\AUTOEXEC.BAT
```

refers to the file AUTOEXEC.BAT in the root directory of the current drive. If you're using drive A, then A:\ is assumed.

Directory manipulation commands

There are only three commands DOS uses to manipulate directories.

After making subdirectories with MKDIR you'll use CHDIR to move between them. CHDIR is the most common command. RMDIR is not used that often, but it is necessary when you wish to remove a directory. The two-letter abbreviations are used more frequently than the full names. Both serve the same function.

Note that the normal file manipulation commands in DOS do not function on subdirectories. You cannot use REN, DEL, ERASE, or COPY with a subdirectory-only on files within the directory. And, yes, this means there's no way to use DOS to rename a directory once it's been created.

DOS Commands for manipulating subdirectories

Command	Abbreviation	Function
MKDIR	MD	make a subdirectory
CHDIR	CD	change subdirectories or show current directory
RMDIR	RD	remove (erase) a subdirectory

Creating directories

Directories are created by using the MKDIR command or MD. The format of the command is

```
MKDIR  pathname
OR
MD  pathname
```

In the preceding example, "pathname" is the name of the subdirectory you're creating. In creating a subdirectory you must follow the same rules you would for naming a file. The name can contain eight characters, plus and optional period and a three character extension. You can use any character when naming the subdirectory, except for the followig:

```
\ / \ [ ] : * < > + = ; , ?
```

In addition, the name cannot contain any spaces or any control characters. These are the same rules that apply to naming any file on disk.

The pathname can also specify a location on any disk in any existing subdirectory. Normally, you create subdirectories for the current directory only. For example, if you're in the root directory and you want to create a subdirectory named WP, you type

```
MKDIR WP
```

and press ENTER. This creates the subdirectory whose full pathname is C\WP. To create the same subdirectory from another drive, you type

```
MKDIR C:\WP
```

After pressing ENTER, a subdirectory named WP is created in the root directory of drive C.

If \WP already existed, you can create a subdirectory named MISC by typing the following command:

```
MD  \WP\MISC ENTER
```

The MISC subdirectory is be placed "under" the subdirectory WP in the root directory of drive C. Normally, however, subdirectories are only one level deep. How is that possible? And what is a "current directory"? Hold tight. The answers lie in the next section, which focuses on the CHDIR command.

There is one limitation to naming subdirectories that doesn't apply to naming files: The total pathname of the subdirectory can be no more than 63 characters long. (In fact, that's the only limit on the depth to which you can make subdirectories.) For example:

```
\BIN\WORDS\MANUSCPT\PROJECTS\BOOKS
\EDUCATE\BMR\HDM\CHAPTER1\FIG
```

The above pathname is exactly 63 characters long. If you try to add any more subdirectories, DOS gives you an error message. But chances are you'll never get that deep within your subdirectory structure.

Making Subdirectories

The purpose of this lab is to let you become familiar with the concept of making subdirectories by using the MKDIR command. Normally, you'll probably be making only one or two subdirectories at a time. However, this lab has you make an entire disk at once a very rare occurrence in the typical life of a computer. Your task will be to duplicate that structure on the data diskette. You won't be putting any files into the subdirectories, so they all will fit on the data diskette. Insert the data diskette in drive A and boot the computer, using the data diskette as the source of DOS. Enter the date and time.

1. At the command prompt type LAB4X and press ENTER
2. Use MD to make the directories. Remember that you can make different levels of subdirectories at a time; however, create the first level before you make the second.
3. After using MD to make the subdirectories, use the DOS command TREE to verify your work. Type

   ```
   A:\> TREE A:\ ENTER
   ```

   This will display a copy of the tree structure in drive A from the root directory down.
4. Produce a hard copy of your work by printing the output from the TREE command. To do this, turn your printer on and type the following:

   ```
   TREE A:\ > PRN ENTER
   ```

If possible, keep the data diskette in the drive for the next lab. If it's not possible, don't erase from the hard drive the structure you've just created.

Moving between directories

CD, the abbreviation for CHDIR, performs two different functions. When used without a pathname, CD displays the current directory. When followed by a pathname, CD changes to the named directory.

When CD displays the name of the current subdirectory, it is acting as part of the DOS "logging" function. For example, recall that typing A:ENTER sends you off to drive A. Typing C: ENTER sends you to drive C. Logging is the process of specifying the active drive. You can say that you're"logged to" a specific drive. The same term applies to subdirectories.

When you first use a disk, you're logged to the root directory. You use the CD command to change to a subdirectory, providing you type the name of that new subdirectory after CD. However, when you type CD without the name of a subdirectory, you get the name of the directory you're logged to. For example, if you type

```
C> CD ENTER
```

the computer reports the current subdirectory by displaying

```
C:\WP\MISC\HDM
```

To change to a different directory, type the pathname of the new directory after typing CD. For example:

```
CD \DATABASE ENTER
```

moves access from wherever you are to the DATABASE subdirectory. Even if you are way, way down in the subdirectory structure, buried in some lowly subdirectory, the preceding command instantly moves you to the DATABASE subdirectory. Beginners make the innocent mistake of assuming they must use the Hansel and Gretel approach-in other words, to get out of the forest of subdirectories, they think they must retrace the steps they took to get in. This approach is inefficient; instead, just type CD, the pathname of the desired directory, and press ENTER.

If you are in the root directory, you need only type

```
CD DATABASE
```

to get to the DATABASE subdirectory. When you don't include the leading backslash, DOS assumes you mean a subdirectory within the current subdirectory. For example, suppose HDM is a subdirectory in MISC, which is a subdirectory of WP. If you're in MISC, then you can type

```
CD HDM ENTER
```

to log to HDM.

Before moving on to the lab, note that with some versions of DOS the CD command works only on the current drive. You cannot change directories across drives. Consider an example:

```
CD A:\TEMP
```

With some versions of DOS, the preceding command displays the current directory for that drive only. Other versions of DOS interpret the command as "Change to subdirectory TEMP on drive A." Test your version of DOS to see if you can change directories across drives.

Changing directories

The purpose of this lab is to familiarize you with the CD command. If you've been away from the computer since the previous lab, insert the data diskette in drive A and boot the computer, using the data diskette as the source of DOS. Type LAB4X at the prompt and press ENTER. Otherwise, move on to step 1.

1. Turn your printer on. To print all the information on your screen, type CTRL-P. This command activates "printer echo" in DOS. To prove it, hit ENTER a few times.
2. In the sequence of tasks that follows, you will practice using CD to move around the directory structure in drive A. It may help to have the hard copy of the tree structure, which you produced for the previous lab. Perform tasks a through i, making sure all your work is noted on the printer.
   a. To make sure you're logged to the root directory, issue the CD command that logs you to it. Next, issue a CD command to display and print the current directory.
   b. Log to the PROGRAM subdirectory. Use the CD command to display and print the name of the current directory.
   c. Log to the BASIC subdirectory. Use CD to display and print the current directory.
   d. Log back to the root directory.
   e. Log directly to the FICTION subdirectory.
   f. Log to the POEMS subdirectory. Use CD to display and print the current directory.
   g. Log back to the FICTION subdirectory.
   h. Log to the DOS subdirectory. Use CD to display and print the current directory.
   i. Log to the root directory. Use the DIR command to get a directory listing for the diskette in drive A.
3. Type CTRL-P again to turn off the printer echo. Press ENTER a few times to make sure the echo is off.
4. If possible, keep the data diskette in the drive for the next lab. If it's not possible, don't erase from the hard drive the structure you've just created.

Removing directories

Directories are removed by using the RMDIR command, or RD. The format of the RD command is

```
RMDIR  pathname
```

or

```
RD  pathname
```

where pathname is the name of the subdirectory you're removing. It can be a full pathname or the name of the subdirectory beneath the current directory.

There are two rules regarding the removal of a subdirectory with RMDIR:

- The subdirectory must be empty.
- You cannot delete the current directory or the root directory.

If the subdirectory you're deleting with RD contains files or other subdirectories, DOS will not erase it; you'll see an error message. You must delete all files from the subdirectory before using RD.

For example, assuming DATA is a subdirectory in the current directory, you can remove it with the following:

```
C> DEL  DATA

ARE  YOU  SURE  (Y/N)?Y

C> RD  DATA
```

The first command deletes all files in the subdirectory DATA (under the current directory). Note that there's no need to specify *.*, as in DATA*.*. Why? Because DATA, the name of the directory, is the same as *.*; both are equal in the eyes of DOS. The RD command deletes the now empty subdirectory.

You cannot delete the current directory, nor can you delete the current directory's parent directory (you can't "orphan" a subdirectory). The root directory on a drive cannot be removed either.

Zapping directories

The purpose of this tab is to familiarize you with the RD command. If necessary, insert the data diskette in drive A, type LAB4X at the prompt and press ENTER

1. As in the previous lab, activate printer echo by typing CTRL-P.
2. Remove the following subdirectories from your disk.
   a. TURBOC, which is a subdirectory of PROGRAM
   b. FICTION, which is a subdirectory of WP
3. Deactivate printer echo.

4. You're now through with the data diskette for this chapter. Type CLEAN and press ENTER to prepare the data diskette for the next chapter's tabs. Then put the data diskette away in a safe place.

File manipulation between directories

Subdirectories and pathnames add a level of complexity to certain DOS commands. Most of the file manipulation commands can accept full pathnames as the filename parameter. For example, recall that you can copy all files from drive A to drive B with the following command:

```
COPY A:*.* B:
```

This means "Copy all files from drive A to drive B." If you're currently logged to drive B, then you can type

```
COPY A:*.*ENTER
```

Since you're already logged to drive B, it's assumed to be the destination. The B part of the COPY command is implied in this instance. Subdirectories, and the file manipulation commands for moving between them, am handled in the same manner.

Suppose you want to copy all files from drive A to the BASIC subdirectory of the subdirectory in drive C. You can use the deliberate method or the "implied" method.

The deliberate method specifies both the origin and destination for the files:

```
COPY A:\*.* C:\PROGRAM\BASIC
```

This COPY command can be issued from any drive or subdirectory. All files from drive A are copied to the subdirectory of the PROGRAM subdirectory in drive C.

The implied method is a two-step process that involves making sure you're already in the subdirectory in drive C. The first command is

```
CD \PROGRAM\BASIC
```

The second command copies the files:

```
COPY A:*.*
```

These file manipulation methods work between subdirectories as well. Suppose you want to copy all the *.TXT files from one subdirectory to another. The command

```
COPY \DOS\*.TXT \WP\WORK
```

copies all the *.TXT files from your DOS subdirectory to the work subdirectory of the WP subdirectory.

Suppose you're logged to the WP subdirectory and you want to delete all the *.TXT files in the WORK subdirectory. You can type

```
DEL WORK\*.TXT (ENTER)
```

Note that the full pathname, \WP\WORK*.TXT need not be specified. This is because you're already logged to WP. WORK, in this instance is a pathname, and DOS assumes you mean the WORK directory in the current subdirectory. All the file manipulation commands can be used within and between the various subdirectories.

Hard drive installation

The hardware installation involves physically installing the hard drive and controller card into the computer. This includes connecting the cables, power supply, and so forth. The software installation involves formatting the disk and preparing it so that DOS recognizes and deals with the hard drive.

There are many steps to take to install a hard drive into a computer. Because of space considerations and because few computer labs are set up so you can install your own drive, you will read about installing a hard disk rather than doing it. The steps involved in the process follow.

1. Turn off and unplug the computer.
2. Remove the computer's housing.
3. Connect the data and control cables to the hard drive unit.
4. Slide the hard drive unit into an open drive bay.
5. Connect the hard drive to the power supply.
6. Anchor the hard drive into place. Note that with some systems you screw the hard drive directly into the drive bay mounts. With other systems, mostly ATs, you first attach mounting rails to the drive. Then you anchor the drive by using restraining braces at the front of the drive bay.
7. Locate an open slot for the controller card. Position is unimportant, though the closer to the hard drive the better.
8. Connect the data and control cables to the controller card.
9. Remove the slot cover from the back of the PC and slide the hard drive controller card into position. Make sure it connects into the slot, making full contact. Press down firmly to ensure that the card is in the slot. Anchor the controller by tightening the screw on the slot cover. Put the housing back on the computer and plug it in.

When you turn the power on, the light by the hard drive comes on, flashing for a moment. If your hearing is good, you will notice the sound of the hard drive as it revs up to the full 3,600 revolutions per minute (rpm). But don't expect anything else to happen. The hard drive hasn't been initialized. That's the second part of installation: the software setup.

Right after you connect a hard drive, you may see an error message on the screen telling you about a 1701 error; that means something is wrong with the hard drive. In most cases, what happened is that you put the cables on wrong-or forgot to connect the cables altogether. When that happens, redo the installation, making sure all the cables are properly connected. Otherwise, take the easy way out and have a professional install the drive.

Software Installation

Software installation is necessary to let DOS know about the hard drive and prepare it for use. All hard drives come "naked," as all floppy drives do. So, the major operation in the software installation is formatting. As with floppies, you use the FORMAT command.

Software installation of a hard drive involves these four steps:

1. low-level formatting
2. using FDISK
3. DOS formatting
4. installing DOS

To perform these, you must put a DOS diskette or a copy of it into drive A. To boot that diskette, either turn your computer on or reset it. After your computer does its memory check and beeps at you, DOS asks you to enter the date and time. Then, at the A> prompt, you begin setting up the software for your hard drive.

Low-level formatting

Hard drives, like floppies, don't come formatted. The two parts of formatting a hard drive are Low-level and DOS formatting. Both prepare the disk for storing data. The low-level formatting is done by the controller card. The controller card and the hard drive make up the hard drive system. Both of them may have been purchased separately, and odds are pretty good they're made by different manufacturers. You must introduce the hard drive to the controller card by performing low-level formatting.

In logical terms, low-level formatting simply defines the cylinders of the drive, It does not set down sectors or identify sectors or tracks. The DOS formatting does that. The program used for low-level formatting is kept on a ROM chip on the hard drive controller. Some hard drive controllers come with a program on a floppy disk that subsequently runs the program on the controller's ROM chip. Other hard drive controllers rely upon the DEBUG program in DOS to go into the controller's memory and run the program manually. This is tricky.

The DEBUG program in DOS is a programmer's tool used to debug programs. It's not for the timid. DEBUG is one of the truly cryptic, arcane programs of yesteryear. But you need it for low-level formatting.

Bug spray

The following steps will not reformat the hard drive.

1. For the sake of realism, playact; pretenend you just installed a hard drive into the belly of computer. Turn the computer off.
2. Put the data diskette into drive A and turn the computer on. Close the drive door.
3. Dos boots the computer, displaying various messages. Enter the date and time when it tells. After entering the time, you should see the A> prompt.
4. At the A> prompt type

DEBUG

which is the name of the DEBUG program, Press ENTER. The DEBUG program is very cryptic. Its prompt is a single hyphen:-. At the hyphen you type in one letter commands. Number values used in DEBUG are in base 16 hexadecimal.

5. The first thing you should do is to look at the ROM of your hard drive controller. Traditionally, it sits at a memory location in your computer referred to as C800:0. To display this location, type at the "-" prompt:

DC800:0 ENTER

You may see six lines of information displayed on the screen. Your display may be different. However it looks, the DEBUG screen display is the first part of the low-level formatting program. If you were really going to format your system's hard drive, you would continue by running the program displayed on your screen. All it takes is one more command in DEBUG.

6. To prove to humankind that you've gone into DEBUG and successfully displayed it, turn on the printer and do a screen dump of the DEBUG display. Remove the printed sheet from the printer and mark it "Lab 3. 1, step 6."
7. At the hyphen prompt, type Q and press ENTER to exit (quit) DEBUG. Unless you plan on programming, the only time you'll ever use DEBUG is when doing low-level formatting for a hard drive.
8. If possible, leave your computer as it is; the DEBUG display is the starting point for the next lab.

So why do you need to use DEBUG? Why didn't they just write a low-level formatting software program you could run from a floppy? Because all controllers are different. The general approach is the same for each of them, but the command you enter in DEBUG to initiate the low-level formatting is different. You get that specific command from the user manual for the hard drive controller.

Some computers do come with a program on disk that runs the low-level formatting software. This program essentially does the same thing that you can do with DEBUG. The low-level formatting routine is always on the hard disk controller card.

```
WX2 Format Revision 6.0 (C) Copyright Western Digital Corp. 1985
(AH)  = Relative drive number (0 - 7)
(AL)  = InterLeave factor (3 is standard)
Press "y" to begin formatting drive C with interLeave 03
```

The display resulting from the lowlevel formatting program of an IBM PC XT. Press Y after this message and you would erase any data on your hard disk. Be careful! For controllers compatible with the IBM PC XT, the command has traditionally been

```
G=C800: 5
```

After the user presses ENTER, the command runs the low-level formatting program that's on the ROM of the hard drive controller. The command means "Go to memory location C800:5 and run the program there." Controller ROMs from different manufacturers may be in different locations; the ROM provides the appropriate DEBUG command. If an IBM PC XT user had typed G=C800:5 and pressed ENTER. From this point some programs have you set values by using DEBUG; others may even display a menu for you, allowing you to choose other options such as drive type and interleave factor. Generally speaking, the correct options have already, been selected. All you need to do is follow the instructions and proceed with low-level formatting, After it's done, the computer may reset or it may just return you to DOS. If you're returned to DEBUG, type Q to quit.

Running FDISK

The next step in setting up the hard drive is to prepare it for use by DOS. Do this with the FDISK command. FDISK deals with partitions. A partition divides up your hard drive into separate logical units-or just one logical unit, if you wish. There are three reasons you may want to establish partitions:

- to put DOS in a partition
- to use another operating system on another part of the drive
- to make the single hard drive work as more than one logical drive

One partition always contains DOS for your first hard drive. FDISK writes identifying code on the hard drive to let the computer know that it's a DOS partition and that the computer should address that partition to boot up. A non-DOS partition may contain either data or other operating systems.

If you're using your computer with both DOS and a secondary operating system, such as XENIX or UNIX, then you can use FDISK to divide your hard drive UP into two partitions: one designated as the DOS partition and another for the other operating system. FDISK lets you allocate space on the hard drive for each.

FDISK is also used to divide up one large hard drive into smaller logical units. This is necessary with DOS versions 3.3 and earlier, because those versions can deal only with a hard drive capacity of 33MB or less. So, if you have a 40MB drive, you must use FDISK to split it into two 20MB logical drives, or to make a 30-10 split, or to make whatever allocation you desire. You'll then designate one of the logical drives, say C, as your DOS partition and the second, D, as a non-DOS logical partition.

Suppose you've just finished the low-level formatting of your new hard drive. Your next duty is to run FDISK to assign the DOS partition and any additional partitions you may want on your drive. You've just installed the hard drive, so you'll be running FDISK from your DOS diskette in drive A. At the A> prompt type

```
F D I S K
```

and press ENTER.

Normally, if you were installing a hard drive for the first time, you would press 1 to create a DOS partition. FDISK would report the number of cylinders in your hard drive and ask you how many to assign to the DOS partition. You would then enter the number of cylinders for the DOS partition and then allocate any additional data partitions. Once this was done, FDISK would record the information on the hard disk and your computer would reset.

```
IBM Personal Computer
Fixed Disk Setup Program Version 3.30
(C)Copyright IBM Corp. 1983,1987
F D I S K Options
Current Fixed Disk Drive:1
Choose one of the following:
  1. Create DOS Partition
  2. Change Active Partition
  3. Delete DOS Partition
  4. Display Partition Information
Enter choice:  [1]
Press ESC to return to DOS
```

Peeking at the Partitions

The purpose of this lab is to show you how FDISK works. Rather than using FDISK to establish partition information, as you would if you were initially installing a hard drive, this lab will show you your system's hard-drive partition data. The data diskette that accompanies this text should be in drive A and the A> prompt should be the last message on the screen.

1. Type FDISK at the A> prompt and press ENTER.
2. To view the partition information about the hard drive in your computer, press 4 and ENTER or whichever option says "Display Partition Information." The resulting display should look something, which indicates that drive C is partition 1, that the status is A, that the type is PRI DOS. There are 611 cylinders in the drive. The cylinder numbers start at 0 and go up through 610.

```
    Display            Partition   Information
    Current            Fixed       Disk  Drive:1

Partition     Status     Type         Start   End       Size

C: 1          A       P R I D O S       0     610       611

    Total disk space is 611 cylinders.
```

Press ESC to return to FDISK Options

The FDISK display of partition information for a 20MB hard drive with a single DOS partition.

If your computer has two or more partitions, FDISK may ask if you want to see the information about the EXT DOS (Extended DOS) partition. If so, it will show you how that partition is divided up into logical drives, that is, logical drives C, E, F, and so on.

3. With your printer turned on, get a screen dump of your system's FDISK display. Remove the sheet from the printer and label it, "Lab 3.2, step 3'
4. On the sheet with your screen dump, describe how your hard drive is divided into partitions and what each partition does.
5. Keep pressing Esc until you see the A>. Before removing the data diskette to put it away, type DONE ENTER at the A> prompt. This sets the data diskette up, preparing it for the next lab.

```
Partition   Status    Type      Start    End     Size
C: 1        A         PRI DOS   0        384     385
   2                  EXT DOS   385      1021    637
```

Partition Information for a hard drive with multiple partitions.

DOS formatting

Finally, after low-level formatting and "FDISKing" the drive, you're ready to do the DOS formatting. Remember, after doing FDISK your system resets. However, you need to boot from a diskette in drive A until the hard drive has been formatted by DOS and DOS has been transferred there. Until DOS formatting is complete, you cannot use the hard drive. The other two steps, low-level formatting and using FDISK, are only preludes to setting up the hard drive. Only after DOS formatting can you start using the hard drive. It's DOS formatting that lays down the tracks, cylinders, and sectors on the drive. From there, you can start using the drive as a storage device.

Since most computers boot from the hard disk, you have the option of installing DOS on the hard disk when you first format it. DOS consists of two hidden DOS files as well as COMMAND.COM. If you specify that the hard disk is to hold DOS, then the FORMAT command automatically copies those files to the hard disk for you, making it possible for the computer to boot from drive C.

From drive A, you would format the hard disk by entering the following command:

```
FORMAT C:
```

If you wanted to install the system, you would use the /S parameter.

```
FORMAT C:/S ENTER
```

The preceding command would copy the basic system files to your hard drive, making it a boot disk.

After typing the FORMAT command with or without the S parameter, you may see a message such as

```
WARNING, ALL DATA ON NON-REMOVABLE DISK
DRIVE C: WILL BE LOST!
Proceed with Format (Y/N)?
```

This terrifying message is to let you know you're about to format the hard drive. If the hard drive already has data on it, the effect will be disastrous-hence, the cautionary note. Some versions of DOS even have you enter the drive's volume label before proceeding with the format, just to be on the safe side.

If you truly wanted to format the hard drive, you would type Y and press ENTER. DOS will take a few minutes to go through the drive and prepare all the tracks, sectors, and bytes for your use. Note that some versions of DOS do recognize that the hard drive is unformatted. In those cases, the error message won't be displayed.

Once formatting is complete, you would perform the traditional reboot from the hard drive. You would remove any disk from drive A and reset the machine. If the hard drive was properly set up and DOS installed, your computer would then boot from it. If you added other logical drives, you would also need to format them at this time.

Installing DOS

DOS consists of only three programs. In PC-DOS, the two hidden programs are IBMBIO.COM and IBMDOS.COM. In MS-DOS, the hidden program are IO.SYS and MSDOS.SYS. Though the names of the programs in the two versions of DOS differ, the program in one DOS version is nearly identical to its counterpart in the other version. The visible program is COMMAND.COM. Together, the hidden programs and COMMAND.COM give you DOS.

In addition to the three basic DOS programs, DOS comes with other programs and files. These are external commands, device drivers, and a host of other files that allow you to customize DOS for the computer you're using. If you're setting up a hard drive, install the DOS files before you start installing software. This involves copying all the DOS programs and files from the distribution diskettes to your hard drive. This is the point where most users make their first fatal error in hard disk management. To avoid this error

Never install files and programs in the root directory.

Recommendations about the root directory are given in later chapters. For now, know that your DOS files and programs should be put into a special subdirectory, their own private location on your hard drive.

The Constituent Programs Of DOS

File (PCDOS)	*File (MS-DOS)*	*Function*
IBMBIO.COM	IO.SyS	interfaces DOS with low-level information in your computer's hardware
IBMDOS.COM	MSDOS.SYS	actually operates the core computer system, or kernel
COMMAND.COM	COMMAND.COM	interfaces DOS with you, the human

To finish hard drive installation, you must take two more steps. You must create a DOS subdirectory and copy your DOS files into the subdirectory.

Creating the DOS subdirectory is done with the DOS command MKDIR:

```
MKDIR DOS
```

The command MKDIR stands for *make directory;* another form of the same command is MD. After you press ENTER, DOS creates a subdirectory named DOS on the hard drive.

To copy the DOS files from the distribution diskettes to the DOS subdirectory, you need to use the COPY command. Insert the first DOS diskette into drive A, close the drive door and type

```
COPY A:*.* C:\DOS ENTER
```

'This command means "Copy all files (*.*) from the diskette in drive A (A:) to subdirectory DOS (DOS) on drive C (C:)." After you press ENTER, DOS Copies all the files from drive A to their new home in the DOS subdirectory on your hard disk. If you have a second or third DOS diskette, remove the first diskette from drive A and replace it with the next one. Retype the copy command and press ENTER to copy the DOS files from the second diskette to the DOS subdirectory.

If you know your DOS editing keys, you know you can press (F3) to "retype" the previous command line.

That finishes basic hard drive installation. The hard drive now exists as a large empty field on which you can start setting up your software. The manner in which you do that, as well as how you organize and maintain your software, constitute the basics of hard disk management. The next concept that requires your attention is the subject of subdirectories, which has been only lightly touched upon to this point.

Hard disk manager

Requirements

The system requirements for the use of these programs are minimal. There are no system memory requirements because none of these routines is memory resident. The only requirements are as follows:

1. The user's hard disk must contain all of the DOS programs (the DOS disk and the Supplemental Programs disk). The user must know the directory location of DOS on the hard disk. The DOS version may be 2.0 or later.

2. It is assumed that all individuals using *Hard Disk Manager* are using a hard disk system with a C drive.

If the user can answer "yes" to the above requirements, the installation of all of *Hard Disk Manager* is a straightforward process. If the hard disk does not contain the DOS programs, the DOS manual should be consulted for instructions on how to install all of the DOS programs on the hard disk.

It should also be noted that the program disk does not contain any operating system files; the computer cannot be started using this program disk as a "boot" disk.

Installing the entire program

The amount of disk space occupied by the *Hard Disk Manager* varies with the size of the hard disk. For example, on a 20-MB hard disk, the program uses approximately 700 KB of disk space. A directory structure is created and the files are copied into these directories. There should be no overlap with any existing directories since there is only one directory created at the second level under the root directory: \HDU. All of the other directories created are subdirectories of \HDU.

Steps

The only information required of the user is the directory containing the DOS files. During the installation process, the user is prompted for this information. Otherwise, the process is as follows:

1. Turn on the computer. After the DOS system prompt (the C > symbols) is displayed, insert the *Hard Disk Manager* disk in drive A.

2. Enter the following command:

   a: install

3. An information screen that describes the installation process will be displayed. A "Strike any key when ready" message appears at the bottom of the screen; press a key for the installation process to proceed.

4. After a few moments, a prompt for the name of the directory containing the DOS program files appears. You must:

Enter the directory name (including the drive and path). The path should include all path parameters currently on your disk.

Press the < F6 > function key.

Press < Enter >.

Pressing the < F6 > key causes the symbols ^ Z to be displayed; this is normal. The installation process then continues.

5. A check is made to determine if the DOS directory input is valid (i.e., if the specified directory does indeed contain the DOS program files). If the input is not valid, an error message is displayed and the installation is aborted.

6. If the DOS directory specification is valid, the installation proceeds to create the necessary directories and to copy program files into them. This section takes about 5 to 10 minutes, depending on the speed of ones system.

7. A message is displayed when the installation is complete. Figure 3.1 shows the final installation message.

8. You must then reboot the computer (press < Ctrl > < Alt > < Del >).

9. To start the program, change the current directory to the root directory (by entering the command CD\).

Then, enter the command

hdu

to display the *Hard Disk Manager* main menu.

That is all there is to the installation of *Hard Disk Manager*. Be sure you make a backup copy of the program disk. The program is always started by executing the command hdu from the root directory. The following section describes the action that is taken during the installation process.

The installation of all of *Hard Disk Manager* begins with INSTALL.BAT and is completed with CONTINUE.BAT.

Installation is now complete. To start the program...

1. Remove disk from drive A
2. Reboot the system (by pressing [Ctrl] [Alt] [Del])
3. Enter the command CD\
4. Then, enter the command HDU

Figure 1. Hard Disk Manager Final Installation Message

Basically, the installation can be divided into the operations listed:

1. The directory containing the DOS program files is specified by the user.
2. The user's DOS directory input is added to a file that becomes CONTINUE.BAT.
3. The validity of the DOS directory information is checked.
4. The ANSI.SYS file is copied to the root directory.
5. The necessary directories are created.
6. The *Hard Disk Manager* programs are copied into the new directories.
7. A check is made to determine if a CONFIG.SYS file exists. (CONFIG.SYS is a configuration file required to run some of the *Hard Disk Manager* utilities.) If CONFIG.SYS does not exist, this file is copied to the root directory; if it does exist, then the command DEVICE= ANSI.SYS is appended to the existing file.
8. The DOS directory information is appended to a PATH command that is stored in a separate file for future use. This PATH command also is added to the beginning of the HDU.BAT file. This is the batch file that calls up the *Hard Disk Manager* main menu.

Installing part of Hard Disk Manager

For users interested in installing only certain components of *Hard Disk Manager,* the installation process is somewhat different. A directory structure is created, but only the directories necessary for the desired utility are created. Like the complete installation, there should be no overlap with any existing directories since there is only one directory created at the first level under the root directory: \HDU The other directories created are subdirectories of the \HDU directory.

The partial installation process can be divided into two parts. The first part is automated, whereas the second part is menu driven. The automated process performs the initial configuration routines that are necessary for all the programs on *Hard Disk Manager.* It is executed only once.

Steps

The first part of the installation performs the following operations: The user is asked to specify the location of the DOS program files; the validity of the user's entry is checked; a CONFIG.SYS file is created or the command DEVICE= ANSI.SYS is appended to an existing one; the \HDU directory is created; and some key files are copied to the new directory. Here are the specific steps.

1. Turn on the computer. After the DOS system prompt (the C > symbols) is displayed, insert the *Hard Disk Manager* disk in drive A.

2. Enter the following command:

   a: partial

3. You are prompted for the name of the directory containing the DOS program files. You must:

   Enter the directory name (including the drive and path).

   Press the < F6 > function key.

   Press <Enter >.

   Pressing the < F6 > key causes the symbols ^ Z to be displayed; this is normal. The preparation routine then continues.

4. A check is made to determine if the user's DOS directory input is valid (i.e., if the specified directory does indeed contain the DOS program files). If it is not valid, an error message is displayed and the preparation process is aborted. (The user should refer to the "Troubleshooting" section of this chapter.)

5. If the DOS directory specification is valid, the necessary directories are created and certain files are copied into them. This section takes a few minutes. A message informs the user when the preparation routine is complete. Pressing any key will display a menu of installation options.

6. The Installation Menu contains the following options:

   Install Disk/Directory Utilities

   Install Customized Display Utilities

   Install Screen Design Utility

   Install Backup/Restore Utilities

   Install File Management Utilities

   Install HELP Utilities

Install All Utilities

Exit To DOS

You may select one or more of these components of *Hard Disk Manager* for installation. All utilities may be installed even if individual components have previously been installed.

7. When the desired portions of *Hard Disk Manager* have been installed, select the Exit To DOS option.

8. Each selected utility is now installed. The following commands call tip the menu associated with the specific utility from the \HDU directory:

Disk/Directory:	DISK
Display:	DISPLAY
Screen Design:	DESIGN
Backup/Restore:	BACK
File Management:	FILE
Help Utilities:	HELP

9. *You must then reboot the computer* (press <Ctrl> <Alt> <Del>).

10. Then, change the current directory to C:\HDU and execute the appropriate command.

Installation Menu

1.	InstallDisk/Directory Utilities
2.	InstallCustomized Display Utilities
3.	InstallScreen Design Utility
4.	InstallBackup/Restore Utility
5.	InstallFile Management Utilities
6.	InstallHELP Screen Utilities
7.	InstallALL Hard Disk Utilites
8.	Exit to DOS

Troubleshooting

This section briefly covers some problems that may be encountered during installation and use of *Hard Disk Manager*.

Invalid directory specification

This is the problem when the user encounters the error message "Your DOS directory specification was not specified correctly." Here are some possible errors:

1. The specified directory does not contain DOS. Check to make sure that the directory really contains DOS. Run the DIR command and look for files such as FORMAT, TREE, DISKCOPY, and EDLIN. If DOS is not found, you must copy the DOS program files into a directory on the hard disk and rerun the installation.

2. The pathname entered with the directory name was invalid. The complete path must be specified. For example, if the directory containing DOS is \DOS, the directory should be entered as

   C:\DOS

   If the root directory contains DOS, the directory would be specified as

   C:\

   Also, be careful of typing errors.

Strange characters after the prompt

Odd characters may appear at the bottom of the menu as a prompt, below the ENTER SELECTION line, such as

[1, 59; "return", 13p; [22; 18H

This is a result of an absent CONFIG.SYS file. If this file does not exist on your system when *Hard Disk Manager is* installed (either partially or totally), the installation routines should create it. If you have just installed *Hard Disk Manager* utilities, you must restart (reboot) your system before using any of the utilities. The CONFIG.SYS file is only read by DOS at start-up time. If you have already done this, here are some possible solutions:

1. Enter the following command:

   type c:\config.sys

   The contents should contain the following line:

   device = ansi.sys

2. If DOS responds with a "File not found" message, then place the *Hard Disk Manager* disk in drive A and enter this command:

copy a:\hdu\disk\auto\config.tmp c:\config.sys

3. If the CONFIG.SYS file exists, but does not contain the line shown above, the~ place the *Hard Disk Manager* disk in drive A and enter this command:

copy c:\config.sys + a:\hdu\disk\auto\config.tmp

4. If the CONFIG.SYS file exists and contains the required line shown above, then try entering this command:

dir c:\ansi.sys

If a "File not found" message is the response, then you must copy the ANSI.SYS file from your DOS directory to the root directory, as in:

copy c:\dos\ansi sys c:\

One of the above steps should solve the problem. Be sure to reboot the system after performing any of the above steps.

Conflicts with additional PATH Commands

In order for Hard *Disk Manager* to work, it is necessary for the user to specify the directory containing the DOS programs. This information is placed in a PATH command at the beginning of a file called HDU.BAT. (This is the command file that calls the *Hard Disk Manager* program.)

If the user's system contains an AUTOEXEC.BAT file, and that file also contains a PATH command, there may be problems if the specified paths are not the same in both files. The problems will only be evident when the other programs are executed after *Hard Disk Manager* has been run. Here are the steps for investigating this possibility.

1. Enter the following command:

type c:\hdu\ hdu.bat

The first line of this file should contain the PATH command.

2. Now enter this command:

type c :\autoexec.bat

If your system responds with the message "File not found," or no PATH command is found in the displayed file, then the PATH command is not causing a problem.

3. However, if there is a PATH command in the AUTOEXEC.BAT file, compare its contents to the same command in the HDU.BAT file. Disregard differences in upper- and lowercase letters or the presence or absence of the "equals" (=) sign.
4. If any directories are shown in the AUTOEXEC.BAT file's PATH command, these should be added to the HDU.BAT file. For example, suppose the HDU.BAT file contains the command

path c:\; c:\dos

and the AUTOEXEC.BAT file contains this PATH command:

path c:\; c:\dos; c:\utility

5. The additional directory (c:\utility) must be added to HDU.BAT. Here is the procedure for editing HDU.BAT

   a. Change your current directory to the directory containing your DOS program files.

   b. Enter the following command:

      edlin c:\hdu.bat

   EDLIN will respond with the message "End of file."

   c. To edit the first line, enter the number 1. EDLIN will display the contents of the existing line 1.

   d. Type the existing line exactly as it appears, and add the additional directory at the end of the line; then press <Enter>.

   e. End the EDLIN session by entering the command

   E

Pressing <Ctrl> <Break>: No Menu, No Prompt

The user may encounter problems when the < Ctrl > < Break > is activated during the running of some of the utilities. Under normal execution, all the utilities will return to a menu screen. However, if <Ctrl> < Break > is pressed during the execution of a utility and a menu does not reappear, the user can press the < Fl > key to redisplay the menu.

Removing all utilities from the hard disk

If the user, alas, wishes to remove all of the *Hard Disk Manager* from his or her hard disk, a batch file has been included on the program disk that will do the entire process. This routine will erase all files in the directory system of the *Hard Disk Manager*. If any nonprogram files are stored in those directories, they too will be erased. After the directories are emptied, they will be removed. There will be no trace of Hard *Disk Manager* on the user's system.

Hard Disk Manager is removed by placing the *Hard Disk Manager* program disk in drive A, and entering the following command:

a:remove

Of course, if the user later decides that this was folly, the *Hard Disk Manager* can simply be reinstalled.

INSTALL.BAT

```
echo off
cls
```

```
type a:title.scr
pause
cls
a:
echo      This routine installs all of Hard Disk Manager on your
echo      hard disk. The program is installed on drive C.
echo      DOS must already be installed on the hard disk. You will
echo      be prompted to enter its path and directory name.
echo      Those unfamiliar with DOS should read Chapter 3 prior to
echo      proceeding. The installation process is explained in this chapter.
echo      To abort the installation, press [Ctrl] [Break], and
echo      then a "Y" in response to "Terminate batch job (Y/N)?"
pause
cls
type dospath.scr
copy con:dospath.tmp
if not exist dospath.tmp goto ABORT
copy dospath1.txt + dospath.tmp + continue.txt continue.bat
continue
:ABORT
echo DOS directory information was not specified correctly;
echo installation aborted.
echo Please refer to Chapter 3 for installation procedures.
c:
```

Install.Bat Batch File

File management utilities

Since a large number of files may be created and stored on a hard disk, these files must be organized and maintained. Unlike a manual filing system in which one can glance at documents for information, electronic storage of data means that files must be retrieved from disk and read into memory to review their contents. Thus, electronically stored files can be difficult to identify and access without some sort of file management system. Periodically, old or infrequently used files must be archived to make room for new ones. Such tasks are the "housekeeping" functions with which every user must contend.

The File Management utilities are basic functions used in the maintenance and "housekeeping" functions of a hard disk system.

What are the file management utilities?

There are six File Management utilities. They include routines for:

- copying files
- moving files from one directory to another
- combining files and performing text searches for character strings
- locating a file on the hard disk
- assigning files as Read-Write or Read-Only access

Why are they used?

Although routine "housekeeping" functions are not difficult to perform, they require a working knowledge of many DOS commands. As a result, some functions are not performed as often as they should be. The File Management utilities are designed to provide the user with a standard set of easy-to-use routines for maintaining a hard disk system.

How to use the utilities

The File Management utilities are accessed when selection 5 is chosen from the *Hard Disk Manager* main menu. This selection changes the directory to \HDU\FILE and displays the File Management menu. Any of the six selections on the screen can be chosen simply by typing the number of the desired utility. After the selection is made, the utilities prompt the user for any required input; informational screens, when necessary, guide the user through the utility. If at any time the user chooses not to proceed with a utility, the < F1 > key can be pressed to return to the previous menu.

For the user who would like additional information on file management and hard disk maintenance, overviews of these topics can be found at the end of this chapter.

Organization of the file management utilities

The batch files and information screens for all of the File Management utilities are found in a single directory: \HDU\FILE. There are no subdirectories for any of the File Management utilities. Because there is no multiple usage of the "Continue (Y/N)?" prompt by these utilities, there is no need for separate directories for the corresponding Y.BAT and N.BAT files.

The contents of the \HDU\FILE directory are shown in Figure 1. As can be seen in Figure 1, there are only three types of files in the \HDU\FILE directory. The numbered batch files start the individual utilities. Each of these displays an appropriate instruction screen (the SCR files). Finally, as indicated by the instruction screen, the user activates the specific utility by entering a command followed by any required parameters. This command is the name of a batch file that performs the given operation (e.g., ARCHIVE.BAT).

```
C:\HDU\FILE<DIR>
1. BAT     ARCHIVE. BAT    ARCHIVE. SCR
2. BAT     COMBINE. BAT    COMBINE. SCR
```

```
3. BAT        MOVE. BAT        MOVE. SCR
4. BAT        SEARCH. BAT      SEARCH. SCR
5. BAT        LOCATE. BAT      FILEMENU. SCR
6. BAT        DOLOCATE. BAT    LOCATE.SCR
7. BAT        DODCOPY. BAT     NOINPUT. TXT

C:\HDU\PROTECT    <DIR>

 PROTECT.BAT       PROTECT.SCR
 UNPROTEC.BAT      INSTRUCT.SCR
 Y.BAT        N.BAT
```

Figure 1: Directory and file structure for the file management utilities

Activation of the uilities

Selection 5 on the main menu accesses the File Management utilities by activating the 5.BAT file in the \HDU\FILE directory. It contains the following commands:

```
5. BAT
echo off
cls
cd file
type filemenu. scr
echo ENTER SELECTION:
prompt $e[22;18H
setscrn
```

As can be seen from the above commands, the principal function of this batch file is to change the current directory to the \HDU\FILE directory and to display the File Management screen (FILEMENU. SCR). The last line resets the screen display attributes with SETSCRN. BAT. The File Management menu screen is shown in Figure 2.

File Management Menu

1. File Archive
2. Move File
3. File Combine
4. Text Search
5. Locate File
6. Diskcopy (A: to A:)
7. File Protect/Unprotect (Dos 3.0 or higher)

<<Press F1 to Return>>

Figure 2: File management utilities menu

The file management utilities

The file archive utility

The File Archive utility allows the user to copy hard disk files onto a floppy disk in drive A. It provides a structured approach to the DOS COPY command. When a 1 is entered by the user from the File Management screen, an information screen is displayed. Figure 3 shows the text of this screen.

As can be seen from Figure 3, the user is given instructions on how to enter the ARCHIVE command and directions and suggestions in the use of pathnames and global filename characters. The user must enter the command ARCHIVE followed by the pathname/filename of the file(s) to be archived. Before the copy is attempted, a message is displayed showing the user what filename was entered.

Normal DOS messages are displayed if the copy is successful or unsuccessful. The File Management menu is redisplayed regardless of the outcome.

```
                         File Archive
With this utility, you may copy one or more files from the hard
disk to a floppy disk in drive A. If the file is too large for one
floppy disk, or you wish to copy more files than will fit on the
floppy, use the Partial Backup option under the Backup/Restore
Utilities.
To archive a file, enter the command ARCHIVE followed by the path
and filename. To archive more than one file, use global filename
characters.
For example, to archive a file in the \WP directory called MEMO.
DOC, the command is entered as
          archive \wp\memo.doc
     <<<<< Press F1 to Return >>>>>
```

Figure 3: File archive information screen

Undoubtedly, experienced users will find it easier to simply go straight into DOS to run the COPY command. However, for the less experienced, the information screen in the File Archive utility can be a useful reminder of the necessity of using directory paths, and of the convenience of using global filename characters.

The file archive program files

Two batch files and one information screen make up the components of the File Archive utility. Its execution begins when the user enters 1 from the File Management menu. This causes the 1.BAT file in the \HDU\FILE directory to be executed. The commands in this file are as follows:

```
     1. BAT
1:   echo off
2:   cls
3:   type archive.scr
4:   echo ENTER COMMAND:
5:   prompt $e[22;16H
```

The above batch file simply displays an information screen (ARCHIVE.SCR) and positions the cursor after the ENTER COMMAND prompt. The information contained on ARCHIVE.SCR is shown in Figure 3.

When the user enters the command ARCHIVE along with the pathname/filename of the file to be archived, this executes the ARCHIVE.BAT file. This file contains the following commands:

```
      ARCHIVE.BAT
 1:   echo off
 2:   cls
 3:   if "%1 "=="" goto ERROR
 4:   echo Copying %1 to disk in drive A.
 5:   copy %1 a:
 6:   goto DONE
 7:   :ERROR
 8:   echo You must specify the name of the file with
      the ARCHIVE command. Try again.
 9:   pause
10:   cls
11:   type archive.scr
12:   echo ENTER COMMAND:
13:   goto END
14:   :DONE
15:   pause
16:   cd \hdu\file
17:   cls
18:   type filemenu.scr
19:   echo ENTER SELECTION:
20:   prompt $e[22;184
21:   setscrn
22:   :END
```

The IF command in line 3 checks to see if the user has included the argument with the command. The ECHO command in line 4 is a confirmation of the filename the user is attempting to copy. The pathname/ filename that is entered with the ARCHIVE command is substituted for the %1 replaceable parameter in this line as well as the COPY command in line 5.

There is no suppression of output so all DOS messages are displayed if the COPY is successful or unsuccessful. The last five lines redisplay the File Management menu.

The move file utility

Using the Move File utility, a user can copy a file from one location on the hard disk to another location, and then erase the file from the original location. This routine combines the DOS commands COPY and ERASE into one operation.

The process begins when 2 is entered at the File Management menu. This activates the display of an information screen. Figure 8.4 shows the text of this screen. The user must enter the command MOVE together with two arguments: the source directory/filename and the target directory. The filename is not allowed as a part of the target directory specification; a file automatically will be assigned the same filename in the new location.

Multiple files may be moved using global filename characters in the source information. For example, the following command would move all .WKS files from \123DATA to \NEW123:

```
move \123data\*.wks \new123
```

```
                              File Move
With this utility, you may move one or more files from one directory
to another. The file is first copied into the target location and
then erased from the source location. Multiple files may be moved by
using global filename characters in the source filename designation.
To move files, enter the command MOVE followed by the path and
filename of the source file, and then the target directory.
For example, to move a file in the \WP directory called REPORT.DOC
to the \WP\DATA directory, the command is entered as
             move \wp\report.doc \wp\data
       <<<<< Press F1 to Return >>>>>
```

Figure 4: File move screen

After the MOVE command is entered, a confirmation message appears that displays the source and target arguments entered by the user. For example, the above command produces the following message:

```
Moving \123data\* wks file(s) to \new123..
```

The user must enter the MOVE command with both arguments. If the first argument is absent or invalid, DOS error messages are displayed. If the second argument is absent or invalid, in addition to DOS error messages, the following additional message appears:

```
Target directory invalid or not specified. Try again.
```

The user is then returned to the Move Utility Instruction screen. When the file has been successfully moved, the File Management menu is redisplayed.

The move utility program files

The Move File utility is composed of two batch files and one instruction screen. The operation begins with the entry of 2 on the File Management menu. This executes the 2.BAT file in the \HDU\FILE directory. This file has the following commands:

```
      2. BAT
1:    echo off
2:    cls
3:    type move.scr
4:    echo ENTER COMMAND:
5:    prompt $e[22;16H
```

The TYPE command (line 3) displays the instruction screen, MOVE.SCR, and positions the cursor after the ENTER COMMAND prompt.

When the user enters the MOVE command, the MOVE.BAT file is executed. The commands in this file are as follows:

```
      MOVE.BAT
1:    echo off
2:    cls
3:    if "%2" "= ="" goto ERROR
4:    echo Moving %1 file(s) to %2 . . .
5:    cd %2
6:    if exist move .bat goto ERROR
7:    copy %1 %2
8:    del %1
9:    pause
10:   cls
11:   cd \hdu\file
12:   type filemenu.scr
13:   echo ENTER SELECTION:
14:   prompt $e[22;18H
15:   setscrn
16:   goto END
17:   :ERROR
18:   echo Target directory invalid or not specified. Try again.
19    pause
20:   cls
21:   type move.scr
22:   echo ENTER COMMAND:
23:   prompt $e[22;16H
24:   :END
```

Line 3 uses the IF command to ensure that the user entered the second argument. This prevents the DEL command (line 8) from erasing the source file without it first being copied. Line 4 generates the confirmation prompt. The %1 and %2 replaceable parameters are obtained from the arguments that the user supplies when the MOVE command is entered.

The function of the CD and IF commands in lines 5-6 is to check that the user has entered a valid directory for the second argument. This prevents the disastrous course of events in which the DEL command (line 8) erases the source file without it first being copied. If the specified directory is not valid, the current directory remains \HDU\FILE. Then, if the MOVE.BAT file is found to exist in the current directory, this means that the current directory has not been changed and an error has occurred; control is then passed to the ERROR portion of the batch file. Otherwise, it can be assumed that the %2 parameter has been entered correctly; DOS thus executes the COPY and DEL commands in lines 7-8.

There are two different "endings": If the ERROR condition occurs, the error message is displayed and the user is returned to the Move File instruction screen. Note that this does not occur if there is a problem with the first argument: DOS error messages are displayed and the File Management menu is redisplayed. This menu is also displayed when the operation is completed successfully.

In all cases, a pause occurs with the message "Strike a key when ready" before the screen is cleared.

The file combine utility

This utility allows the user to utilize the file concatenation abilities of the DOS COPY command. A lesser known function of the COPY command is its file combination or concatenation facility. Using conventional file specifications, several of the COPY command switches, and " + " signs, any number of files may be linked together. With this utility, the user may combine two ASCII (text) files.

The utility is activated when 3 is entered on the File Management menu. This displays the information screen shown in Figure 5. As indicated in the instructions, the second file is appended to the first. The user must enter, the command COMBINE followed by the two arguments: the source file and the file that is to be appended to it. Drive specifications and/or pathnames must be included with each filename.

When the file combine is complete, the following message is displayed:

```
File combine is now complete. Combined files are stored in
```

```
                          File Combine
This routine will combine two ASCII (text) files. The files will be
combined in the first (source) file and stored under that filename.
If you wish to combine more than two files, repeat the process with
the results of the first combination.
To combine the files, enter the command COMBINE followed by source
file, and then the other file that is to be appended to the to the
source file. Include any necessary drives and/or paths.
For example, to combine two files in the \123DATA directory called
```

```
REPORT.PRN  and  SUMMARY.PRN,  where  the  first  file  is
added  to  the  second,  the  command  is  entered  as  combine
\123data\summary.prn  \123data\report.prn
      <<<<< Press F1 to Return >>>>>
```

Figure 5: File combine screen

The blank space in the message at the bottom of page 156 contains the name of the source file. After a pause, the File Management menu is redisplayed.

The file combine program files

The File Combine utility is comprised of two batch files and one information screen. It is activated by the 3.BAT file in the \HDU\FILE directory. This file contains the following commands:

```
     3.BAT
1:   echo off
2:   cls
3:   type combine.scr
4:   echo ENTER COMMAND:
5:   prompt $e [22; 16H
```

The above commands display the COMBINE.SCR information screen (fine 3) and position the cursor after the ENTER COMMAND prompt (fines 45). The program continues when the user enters the COMBINE command with the two required arguments.

```
COMBINE.BAT
echo off
cls
if  "%1"= =""  goto ERROR
if  "%2"= =""  goto ERROR
copy  %1  +  %2  %1
echo File combine is now complete. Combined files are
stored in %1
goto DONE
:ERROR
echo You must specify both arguments after the
command. Try again.
pause
cls
type combine.scr
echo ENTER COMMAND:
goto END
:DONE
pause
```

```
17:  cd\hdu\file
18:  cls
19:  type filemenu.scr
20:  echo ENTER SELECTION:
21:  prompt $e[22;184
22:  setscrn
23:  :END
```

The two IF commands in lines 3 and 4 check for inclusion of the two required arguments. The COPY operation in line 5 uses the two arguments entered by the user with the COMBINE command for the replaceable parameters %1 and %2. The last five lines redisplay the File Management menu. Line 22 resets the screen display attributes with the SETSCRN.BAT file.

The text search utility

With the Text Search utility, the user may search ASCII files (text files) for specific character strings. It utilizes the DOS FIND filter. A filter is a command or program that transforms input data and outputs the results to a file or a device such as a printer. Through the use of global filename characters and the FOR command, more than one file can be included in the search. It is important to note, however, that this routine is upper and lowercase sensitive (e.g., the letters "a" and "A" are considered different characters).

```
                         Text Search
This routine will search through one or more ASCII (text) files for
the occurrence of a specified string. To search more than one file,
use global filename characters in the filename specification (e.g.,
*.prn).
The command is entered in the following format: SEARCH <directory
location> <filename> <string>
For example, to search all batch files (*.BAT) in the \UTILITY
directory for the occurrence of the string "a:", the command would
be entered as
          search \utility *.bat a:
String may not have spaces. To print results, press [Ctrl) (Prt3c]
before entering command; repeat when done to turn off printing.
     <<<<< Press F1 to Return >>>>>
```

Figure 6: Text search screen

The utility begins when 4 is entered from the File Management menu. The user must enter the command SEARCH followed by three arguments: the directory location of the file(s), the filename(s), and the character string that is the subject of the search.

The command is entered in the following format:

```
SEARCH <directory Location> <Filename> <string>
```

Each argument is separated by spaces, and the specified string may not contain any space characters. For example, if the user wished to search all .PRN files in the \123DATA directory for the occurrence of the word "Budget," the command would be entered as:

```
search \123data *.prn Budget
```

A confirmation of the arguments entered by the user is displayed at the top of the screen.

```
Searching...   Directory: \hdu\protect  FILE:  *.scr  STRING:
"example"
-------- INSTRUCT.SCR
[5]  (if any) and the name of the file. For example, to protect a
-------- PROTECT.SCR
Search is now complete.
The numbers in brackets are line numbers in the file(s).
```

Figure 7: Screen output from search utility

```
Searching ... DIRECTORY: \123data FILE: *.prn STRING:
"Budget"
```

If the specified directory or filename is not valid or does not exist, an error message is displayed and, after a pause the Text Search information screen is redisplayed.

If the directory and filename entries are valid, the search process begins. The file is listed on the screen as it is searched. Under the filename is listed each line in the file that contains the specified string. The line number appears in brackets at the beginning of each line. Figure 7 shows the screen output generated by search through all SCR files in the \HDU\PROTECT directory for the string "example." Note that the second file had no occurrences of the "example" string, but the filename is listed anyway.

When the search is finished, the message "Search is now complete" appears. After a pause, the File Manage-ment menu is redisplayed.

The text search program files

The Text Search utility is made up of two batch files and one information screen, all located in the \HDU\FILE directory. The utility is activated by the 4.BAT file, which contains the following commands:

```
4. BAT
echo off
cls
```

```
type search.scr
echo ENTER COMMAND
prompt $e[22;16H
```

There are no special tricks in the above batch file; its main function is to display the SEARCH.SCR file. The program continues when the user enters the SEARCH command and the required arguments. This activates the SEARCH.BAT file.

How SEARCH.BAT works

Refer to Figure 8 to see a listing of the SEARCH.BAT file. Lines 35 check for user input of the required arguments; control is passed to the ERROR1 section if all three have not been entered with the command. Line 6 provides a confirmation prompt that displays the arguments, using replaceable parameters.

```
     SEARCH.BAT
1:   echo off
2:   cls
3:   if  "%1"= =""  goto ERROR1
4:   if  "%2"= =""  goto ERROR1
5:   if  "%3"= =""  goto ERROR1
6:   echo Searching DIRECTORY: %1 FILE: %2 STRING: "%3"
7:   cd %1
8:   if exist search.bat goto ERROR2
9:   if not exist %2 goto NOFILE
10:  for %%x in (%2) do find /n "%3" %%x
11:  echo?
12:  echo End of search.
13:  echo The numbers in brackets are line numbers in the file(s).
14:  pause
15:  cd \hdu\file
16:  cls
17:  type filemenu.scr
18:  echo ENTER SELECTION:
19:  prompt $e[22;IBH
20:  setscrn
21:  goto DONE
22:  :ERROR1
23:  echo You must specify all three arguments after command. Try
     again.
24:  goto END
25:  :ERROR2
26:  echo ... your directory does not exist. Try again.
27:  goto END
```

```
28:  :NOFILE
29:  echo Specified file(s) not found. Try again.
30:  :END
31:  pause
32:  cd \hdu\file
33:  cls
34:  type search.scr
35:  echo ENTER COMMAND:
36:  prompt $e[22;16H
37:  :DONE
```

Figure 8: SEARCH.BAT File Listing

The CD and IF commands in lines 79 of SEARCH.BAT are attempts at making the routine somewhat "idiot-proof." If the directory argument is not valid, then the current directory remains \HDU\FILE and the subsequent IF command finds SEARCH.BAT to exist. Control then is passed to the ERROR2 section of the batch file and an error message is displayed. Likewise, the second IF command checks to see if the specified file exists; if not, control is passed to the NOFILE section for the display of an appropriate error message. In both cases, the SEARCH.SCR file and prompt are redisplayed.

If the specified arguments pass these little tests, the search is performed with the FIND command that is embedded in the FOR command (line 10 of SEARCH.BAT). The FOR command is used so that multiple files may be searched when global filename characters appear in the filename parameter. Each filename is displayed on the screen as it is searched. Lines containing the specified string appear under the filename. Nothing is displayed if the string is not found in a file.

When the search is finished, the ECHO commands display some messages, a pause occurs, and the File Management menu is redisplayed (lines 12-19 of SEARCH.BAT). Line 20 resets the screen display attributes with SETSCRN.BAT. Control is shifted to the last line in the file with the GOTO command in line 21 of SEARCH.BAT so that the error conditions are not executed. The ECHO command in line 11 forces a blank line; the "text" of the command is actually an unprintable character, <Alt> 255.

The file locate utility

Every hard disk user suffers the frustration of misplacing a file in the hard disk occasionally. (" . . . I know it's here somewhere.") This utility eliminates the necessity of wading through one directory listing after another in search of the elusive file. It works by using two DOS commands: the CHKDSK (Check Disk) command, and the FIND filter. Using the /V switch with the CHKDSK command generates a list of files (and their paths) on the hard disk; this output is redirected to a file that is then searched by the FIND filter.

The program begins when 5 is entered on the File Management menu. This produces the information screen shown in Figure 9. The user must enter the command LOCATE followed by the filename. The filename must be specified in uppercase letters. This is because the CHKDSK commands generates its output in uppercase; the FIND command is case sensitive (i.e., it differentiates between an "A" and an "a").

```
                         Locate file
This routine searches directories on your hard disk for a specified
file or files. The filename MUST be entered in upper case.
The command is entered in the following format: LOCATE <filename>
The filename may be with or without extension. If only the extension
is entered, all files with that extension will be located. For
example, to locate a file called TCRESUME.WK1, the command would be
entered as locate TCRESUME.WK1
Again, note that uppercase letters must be used for the filename.
        <<<<< Press F1 to Return >>>>>
```

Figure 9: File locate screen

The command is entered in the following format:

```
LOCATE <FILENAME>
```

Global filename characters are not permitted. However, by entering only an extension, or other portions of the filename, a list of all files containing those characters is displayed. For example, to locate all files whose first four characters are MEMO, the command is entered as

```
locate MEMO
```

Or, to find all files with extensions of ..DAT, the command is

Locate DAT

After the command is entered, a confirmation prompt appears at the top of the screen. If the specified directory or filename is not valid or does not exist, an error message is displayed and, after a pause, the Text Search information screen is redisplayed.

```
Starting search. A full disk may take a few minutes; be patient...
Looking for file 3CH8C.
--------- Result
 C:\123DATA\3CH8C.WKS
 C:\123DATA\3CH8C.WK1
End of search.
Strike a key when ready . . .
```

Figure 10: Screen output from locate utility

If the directory and filename entries are valid, the program begins the attempt to locate the file(s). The drive, path, and filename will be listed for every file on the disk that matches the input specified by the user. If no match is found, no file will be listed, only the message "End of search. Press Enter to continue." Figure 8. 10 shows the output when a file called 3CH8C is located on the hard disk. Note that two entries are displayed because there are two different extensions on this filename.

When the search is finished, the File Management menu is redisplayed.

Printing the results

If the output of the Locate File utility exceeds a single screen, the user may send the output to the printer by pressing < Ctrl > < PrtSc > before the command is entered. Be sure to press these keys again when finished to turn off this "slaving" of the printer (as it's called); otherwise, it will continue to print everything that appears on the screen.

The locate file program files

The Locate File utility is made up of three batch files and one information screen, all located in the /HDU/FILE directory. The utility is activated by the 5.BAT file, which contains the following commands

```
5.BAT
echo off
cls
type locate.scr
echo ENTER COMMAND:
prompt $e[22;16H
```

The purpose of this file is simply to display the LOCATE.SCR information screen, shown in Figure 8.9. The program continues when the user enters the command LOCATE.

How LOCATE.BAT works

When the user enters the command LOCATE, followed by the specified filename, the batch file LOCATE.BAT is activated. This contains the following commands:

```
LOCATE.BAT
echo off
cls
if "%1 "==" goto BADINPUT
command /c dolocate %1
echo off
goto DONE
:BADINPUT
echo You must specify a filename after the command. Try again.
pause
cls
```

```
11:   type locate.scr
12:   echo ENTER COMMAND:
13:   prompt $e[22;16H
14:   goto END
15:   :DONE
16:   cls
17:   type filemenu.scr
18:   echo ENTER SELECTION
19:   prompt $e[22;18H
20:   setscrn
21:   :END
```

Line 3 in the above batch file checks if the user entered an argument with the command. If no argument has been entered, control passes to the BADINPUT section, lines 7-14. Note that in line 4, a batch file subroutine is called. It is DOLOCATE.BAT that contains the heart of the location routine. The program has been structured in this way so that a menu will be redisplayed in the event < Crtl > < Break > is pressed before execution is completed. The DOLOCATE.BAT file contains the following commands:

```
      DOLOCATE.BAT
1:    echo off
2:    cls
3:    echo Starting search. A full disk may take a few minutes; be
      patient.
4:    chkdsk /v <no input.txt>result
5:    echo Looking for file %1.
6:    find "%1" Result
7:    echo
8:    echo End of search
9:    pause
10:   exit
```

The CHKDSK command in line 4 has its output redirected to the file RESULT. The ECHO in line 5 uses a %1 replaceable parameter to display the user's input in the message. In line 6, the FIND command performs the search on the RESULT file for the user filename, which is %1. Line 7 forces a blank line to be displayed (the "text" is the unprintable character, <Alt > 255). At the end of DOLOCATE.BAT, the EXIT command returns control to LOCATE.BAT, line 5.

The diskcopy utility

The Diskcopy utility allows the user to duplicate an entire disk. It uses the DOS command DISKCOPY, and it requires the use of only one disk drive (drive A). It is also one of the simplest routines on the program disk.

It is started by entering 6 at the File Management menu. The screen clears, and the following messages are displayed.

```
This  routine duplicates diskettes using a single drive (A) . You
will be prompted to insert the source and target disks . . .
```

After a pause, the operation begins. This user is prompted by DOS to insert the source disk and target disk at various intervals. The target disk is formatted if it is not already. When the diskcopy is finished, DOS displays the message:

```
Copy another (Y/N) ?
```

A response of Y repeats the operation; N redisplays the File Management menu.

The diskcopy program files

There are only two files in this utility: The 6.BAT and DODCOPY.BAT files in the \HDU\FILE directory. The 6.BAT file contains the following commands:

```
         6. BAT
    1:   echo off
    2:   cls
    3:   command /c dodcopy
    4:   echo off
    5:   cls
    6:   type filemenu.scr
    7:   echo ENTER SELECTION
    8:   prompt $e[22;18H
    9:   setscrn
```

In line 3 of the above file, a subroutine batch file, DODCOPY.BAT, is called, using the COMMAND command. This ensures that a menu is redisplayed if the user does a < Ctrl > < Break > before the program is completed. DODCOPY.BAT contains the following commands:

```
         DODCOPY.BAT
    1:   echo off
    2:   cls
    3:   echo This routine duplicates diskettes using a single drive
         (drive A) .
    4:   echo You will be prompted to insert the source and target
         disks . . .
    5:   pause
    6:   diskcopy a: a:
    7:   exit
```

The DISKCOPY command is performed in line 6 of DODCOPY.BAT. In line 7, control is returned to 6.BAT, line 4. The last five lines redisplay the File Management menu when the diskcopy is complete.

The file protect/unprotect utilities

The File Protect/Unprotect utilities can be used to change the status of a file from Read/Write to Read Only, and vice versa. Note that they can be used only if the system is using DOS 3.0 or higher. This is because these utilities use the DOS command ATTRIB (Attribute), which is not available in earlier versions of DOS.

```
                  File Protect/Unprotect Utility
                       (DOS 3.0 or higher)
This routine allows you to protect files from inadvertent erasure or
   alteration. Files that have been "protected" are marked as Read-
   Only, and cannot be erased or changed without first "unprotecting"
   them marking them as Read/Write.
You MUST be using DOS 3.0 or higher. Do not continue if this is not
   the case
```

Figure 11: File protect/unprotect screen

The utilities are accessed by entering 7 from the File Management menu. This displays an information screen that describes the utility and the requirement for DOS 3.0 or higher. The text of this screen is shown in Figure 11. If the user responds to the "Continue (Y/N)? " prompt with N the File Management menu is redisplayed. If Y is entered, an instruction screen is then displayed.

To protect a file, the user is required to enter the PROTECT command followed by the pathname/filename of the file. This makes the file Read Only. Similarly, when the UNPROTECT command is entered followed by the pathname/filename specification, the status of the file is changed to Read/Write. In either case, global filename characters may be used to run the utility on multiple files.

```
                          Instructions
To protect a file, enter the command PROTECT followed by the drive
and/or path, and the name of the file. For example, to protect a
file in the \123\DATA directory called RESUME.WKS, the command is
entered as
                 protect \123\data\resume.wks
To unprotect a file, enter the command UNPROTECT followed by the
drive and/or path, and the name of the file, as in
 unprotect \123\data\resume.wks
      <<<<< Press F1 to Return >>>>>
```

Figure 12: File Protect/Unprotect Instructions

For both utilities, if the directory or filename is not valid, the following error message is displayed:

```
Invalid directory or file does not exist. Try again.
```

The instruction screen then is redisplayed. If there is no problem with the pathname/filename parameter, then a message is displayed indicating that the file has been marked either Read Only or Read/Write. In this case, the user then is returned to the File Management menu.

The protect/unprotect program files

There are a few more files involved in the Protect/Unprotect utilities than others in the File Management section. This utility includes five batch files and two information screens. The utility is activated by choosing selection 7 on the File Management menu. The contents of this file are as follows:

```
   7. SAT
1: echo off
2: cls
3: cd ..\protect
4: type protect.scr
5: echo Continue (Y/N)?
6: prompt $e [.14; 18H
```

With the exception of this batch file, a other files associated with these utilities are located in the \HDU\PROTECT directory. The above batch file makes \HDU\PROTECT the current directory (line 3), displays an information screen (PROTECT.SCR in line 4), and positions the cursor at the end of the "Continue (Y/N)?" prompt (line 6). The Y.BAT and N.BAT files that are activated by the user in response to this prompt are shown below.

```
Y. BAT
echo off
cls
type instruct.scr
echo ENTER COMMAND
prompt $e[17;16H
```

```
N. BAT
echo off
cls
cd \hdu\file
type filemenu.scr
echo ENTER SELECTION
prompt $e[22;18H
setscrn
```

The N.BAT file redisplays the File Management menu, whereas the Y.BAT file displays the instructions for entering the PROTECT and UNPROTECT commands. When the PROTECT command is entered, the PROTECT.BAT file is executed. This file contains the following commands:

```
PROTECT.BAT
1:  echo off
2:  cls
3:  if not exist %1 goto ERROR
4:  attrib + r %1
5:  echo File(s) now marked Read-Only.
6:  pause
7:  cls
8:  cd \hdu\file
9:  type filemenu.scr
10: echo ENTER SELECTION:
12: setscrn
13: goto DONE
14: :ERROR
15: echo Invalid directory or filename does not exist. Try again.
16: pause
17: cls
18: type instruct.scr
19: echo ENTER COMMAND:
20: prompt $e[17;16H
21: :DONE
```

The IF command in line 3 checks for the existence of the specified file. (A directory path can be used because DOS versions 3.0 and later accept pathnames as part of the EXIST conditions.) If the file is not found, control is shifted to the ERROR section (line 14) of the batch file There an error message is displayed and, after a pause, the instruction screen is redisplayed. If the filename parameter is valid, then the ATTRIB command in line 4 is executed on that file, using the file specified for the %1 replaceable parameter. The confirmation message is displayed and, after the pause, the File Management menu is redisplayed. Line 12 executes SETSCRN.BAT, which resets the screen display attributes.

The UNPROTECT command activates the UNPROTEC.BAT file. (The ending "T" in the command is ignored since filenames cannot exceed 8 characters.) The contents of that file are exactly the same as the PROTECT.BAT file except for lines 4 and 5. In line 4, the ATTRIB command is written as

```
attrib - r %1
```

The use of the minus sign in front of the "r" gives the file a Read/Write status. In line 5, the confirmation message indicates that the file is now marked as Read/Write.

Modifying the file management utitlites

File management has different requirements for different users. The authors have no expectations that the utilities included in the File Management Utilities will cover the needs of all users. The utilities that were chosen for inclusion generally met one or both of the following criteria:

the DOS command in its native state is somewhat complicated, easily forgotten, or overlooked

several, DOS operations are required to accomplish the specific task

For this reason, standard DOS file management operations such as COPY, ERASE, and RENAME are not included. These are relatively straightforward operations (for DOS) that are easily executed without the aid of a structured utility. Experienced users will probably find it easier to execute these commands outside of a menu or batch-file environment. (When setting up a main menu, it can be useful to have an "Exit to DOS" menu choice for such situations.)

However, it may be necessary or desirable to totally structure all aspects of file management, particularly if the system is to be used by PC novices. The following section is a "how to" for adding, deleting, or modifying the File Management utilities.

Some *points to* keep *in* mind

Here are a few general suggestions and reminders for commands and operations that may be involved in modifying or creating File Management utilities:

1. When using the COPY command, if the drive or path parameters are not specified in either the source or target files, the default drive is assumed. If the target filename is not specified, the file is given the same filename as the source file.
2. The use of global filename characters can be helpful when applying an operation to multiple files in a directory. This is particularly true for commands such as COPY, ATTRIB, etc. Instruction screens should remind users of the availability of these utilities. Standardized filenaming conventions greatly enhance the applicability of global filename characters.
3. The EXIST and NOT EXIST conditions of the IF command are useful for checking the validity of filename parameters entered by the user. It must be remembered that pathnames cannot be used in this command in DOS versions earlier than 3.0. In such cases, it is necessary to change the directory to the current directory containing the file before the IF command is executed.
4. If it is necessary to make sure that the user has supplied the necessary arguments with a command, the IF command can ne used for this purpose, as in:

   if "%1" =="" got ERROR

   In other words, IF is checking for a blank (or nonexistent) %1 replaceable parameter; if this is true, the GOTO command is executed.
5. The ATTRIB command in DOS 3.0 and later is useful for protecting files from inadvertent erasure.
6. The COPY command can be used to combine files. Files may be appended to a source file, or they may be combined together into an new summary file. Both binary and ASCII (text) files can be combined, using different switch settings in the

7. Execution of the main body of a batch file program through a subroutine batch file is advisable if it is possible that the user may press < Ctrl > < Break > during program execution. This ensures that the utility will return to menu and not leave the user stuck in DOS somewhere.

Adding and deleting menu selections

Adding and deleting menu choices on the File Management menu does not require a great deal of effort. There are only a few preliminary points that need to be made before the reader proceeds to that chapter.

The File Management menu is named FILEMENU.SCR and is located in the HDU\FILE directory. All batch and screen files are located in that directory. When adding new menu choices, all batch and screen files should be placed in the \HDU\FILE directory.

There are no Y.BAT and N.BAT files in HDUFILE. This means that the "Continue (Y/N)?" prompt can be used in one new utility that occupies that directory. If more than one utility requires this feature, then it is necessary to create subdirectories for those utilities. This is because only one set of Y.BAT and N.BAT files can occupy the same directory. Likewise, there are no INSTRUCT.SCR files in this directory.

When creating utilities that use the ERASE command, be particularly alert to the possibility of error or misuse by the novice user. Try to anticipate every possible blunder someone might make in using the utility. Then try to build some controls into the batch file to account for these mistakes.

Some oossible modification and enhancements

A number of changes can be suggested for the File Management utilities. In addition, depending on the user's needs, more utilities can be developed that build upon the existing ones. The user may modify, delete, or add menu selections to the existing routines. This section describes some suggestions for additional menu choices.

Creating an audit trail of file manipulations

The File Management utilities allow the user to archive files, move files, and combine one or more files. In order to keep track of these modifications, the utilities can be altered to automatically print the changes. This can be done by using DOS's redirection of output facilities.

DOS's redirection facilities allow output to be sent to a number of devices, including the printer. PRN is the reserved device name used by DOS to specify the printer. To direct the output to a printer the symbols >PRN must follow the command. For example, entering the command at the system prompt:

```
C>DIR>PRN
```

produces a directory listing of the current directory and outputs the contents of the disk to a printer instead of the display. Consider the first 5 lines of the batch file for the File Archive utility described previously:

```
        ARCHIVE.BAT
1:      ECHO OFF
2:      CLS
3:      IF    "%1"==""  GOTO ERROR
4:      ECHO COPYING %1 TO DISK IN DRIVE A . . .
5:      COPY %1 A:
```

Functionally speaking, the filename(s) that are entered after the command ARCHIVE are inserted as the %1 replaceable parameter. Thus, by using DOS's redirection features, the names of the files that are archived can be sent to the printer by changing line 5 to read:

```
copy %1 a:>prn
```

This same technique can be used on other utilities included in the File Management programs. For example, the user can obtain a printout of the names of files that have been moved, the names of files that have been combined, etc.

Creating an archived file inventory

DOS's redirection facilities also permit the user to output data to a text file. In a process similar to that described above, one can maintain an inventory file of all filenames that have been archived. Using the COPY command, one can continually append newly archived files to an Archived Files Inventory. Consider again the ARCHIVE.BAT file shown above. The output of the archive command can be redirected into a text file (ARCHIVE.TMP):

```
copy %1 a:>archive.txt
```

This temporary file will always hold the most recently archived filename(s).

The " > > " symbols could be used instead of of " > " to append output to an existing file:

```
copy %1 a :>>archive.txt
```

If the output is sent to the file ARCHIVE.TXT, the user then may go to this file and view a list of all files that have been archived. This file can be sorted into ascending or descending alphabetic order.

The user can also "time stamp" the last time/date that files were archived by using another feature of the COPY command. This feature allows the user to change the time and date on the file entry (normally, the time and date are NOT changed when the COPY command is used). Another line is added to the batch file after the append operation:

```
copy archive.txt +, ,
```

The two commas in the example are used to define the end of the source file

(ARCHIVE.TXT). Otherwise, DOS would expect another filename to follow the " + " sign.

Finally, if one wants to be super-organized, the floppy disks that contain the archived files can be numbered. Then, the user can manually edit (with EDLIN or another text editor) the ARCHIVE.TXT file and insert the number of the disk on which the archived file is located.

A few other short utilities

This section describes some possible additions to the File Management menu. These are utilities that use DOS features not covered in the existing utilities or commands found in the later versions of DOS. The descriptions basically only cover the actual program files.

Copy, erase, and rename utilities

These utilities might be helpful for users who wish to structure all aspects of file management in a menu and batch file environment. This may be a necessity if the hard disk system is being used by DOS novices. In the case of ERASE, the user may wish to build into it an audit trail such as the one described for the File Archive utility.

The batch file that runs these routines would not have to be very complicated. For example, the following commands would suffice for a rename routine:

```
1:    echo off
2:    cls
3:    if   "%2"=="" goto ERROR
4:    echo Renaming %1 to %2 . . .
5:    rename %1 %2
6:    goto DONE
7:    : ERROR
8:    echo You must enter two arguments with the command. Try
      again.
9:    :DONE
10:   pause
11:   cd \hdu\file
12:   CLS
13:   TYPE FILEMENU.SCR
14:   ECHO ENTER SELECTION:
15:   PROMPT $E[22;18H
16 : SETSCRN
```

The use of the replaceable parameters would require the use of a preliminary instruction screen to prompt the user for input. The name of this batch file would be the command that preceded the arguments. The IF command in line 3 checks for the required arguments.

A Copy utility could use the same batch file, substituting a COPY command for the RENAME command. The routine for an Erase utility also could follow the same format. Instead of the RENAME command in the above batch file, the ERASE command would be used, with only one replaceable parameter. For users concerned about inadvertent erasure, the ERASE command could be preceded by a "Y/N" prompt asking users if they wish to copy the file to an archive directory. (Or, for the truly paranoid, the files could be copied automatically.) However, if disk space usage is an issue, this may not be a desirable feature.

A multiple directory copy utility

For users with DOS 3.2 or later, a utility can be added that uses the DOS command XCOPY. This command was introduced in DOS 3.2. It allows the user to copy all files in a directory plus the files of any subdirectories of that directory. This command can be particularly useful if the user is copying an entire floppy diskette with multiple directories to a hard disk. Or, if a system has two hard disks, one can use this command to copy large chunks of one disk to another. A final use of the XCOPY command might be to create a backup disk on a removable cartridge (when the BACKUP format is not desired).

The XCOPY command has many switches that involve the use of dates, prompting, the archive bit, and the creation of subdirectories. No attempt is made here to use all of these in the suggested utilities.

A utility that copies a floppy diskette with subdirectories might have the following format:

```
1:   echo off
2:   cls
3:   echo Insert the floppy diskette in Drive A . . .
4:   xcopy a: \ c:\ /s /w
5:   cd \hdu\file
6:   cls
7:   type filemenu.scr
8:   echo ENTER SELECTION
9:   prompt $e(22;18H
10:  setscrn
```

This utility might be called something like "Copy Entire Floppy To Drive C." The XCOPY command in line 4 copies all files on the floppy diskette to drive C. The /S switch includes files in any subdirectories, creating the necessary directories on the hard disk if they do not already exist. The /W switch makes the XCOPY command wait for the user to insert the floppy diskette in the drive before beginning the search for the source files. Together with the ECHO command preceding it, the following message is displayed:

```
Insert the floppy diskette in Drive A ...
Press any key to begin copying file(s)
```

A /P switch could be added that would produce a DOS "Y/N" prompt before each file copied. This would permit copying on a file-by-file basis.

Some background information on file management and hard disk maintenance

When it comes to performing hard disk housekeeping tasks, it is particularly important to be able to quickly locate and identify files. This is because a substantial portion of a user's time must be spent on housekeeping (i.e., moving files from one area of the disk to another, renaming files, combining files, and so on). Since the user is dealing with a fixed-capacity disk, he or she also will periodically want to weed out seldom-used or duplicate files. This can be a tedious, time-consuming task if the user must retrieve every file to determine its contents.

A hard disk system can be organized so that files can be easily identified, located, and manipulated. Using filenaming conventions and a hierarchical directory structure, files can be organized in two fundamental ways:

1. Files may have common identifiers in their filenames so that it is apparent to the user that they have some commonality in content.
2. Files can be logically grouped together in one or more subdirectories, each subdirectory containing files with similar contents.

Using filenaming conventions

Filenaming conventions refer to a general agreement on the usage of filenames to identify and describe the contents of files. A carefully designed filenaming scheme is essential to a well-organized hard disk system for three reasons:

1. Well-designed filenaming conventions describe and/or abstract the contents of a file so that it is meaningful to multiple users. Filenaming conventions also provide a framework for naming subsequently created files.
2. Filenaming conventions greatly increase the efficiency of file management and maintenance if they are used in conjunction with DOS commands and global filename characters.
3. Filenaming conventions allow the user to sort his or her directories and obtain an inventory of relevant files. For example, if date information is included in the filenaming scheme, sorting the directory will provide a list by file type in the date order. Although DOS includes its own date information in the directory listing, the date changes with each update to a file. In contrast, the date information in the filename always reflects the creation or start date of a file.

Filenaming conventions are best established at the time the machine is first installed. This allows one to define a scheme that can be readily understood by multiple users. Users can name new files in accordance with the filenaming conventions, and more importantly, they can quickly locate and identify preexisting files. As the volume of files increases over time, filenaming standards reduce the amount of time required to perform many managerial tasks associated with disk organization and file maintenance.

Using column positions in filenames

Filenaming conventions can be designed in a number of different ways, depending on the needs of the end user and the various types of applications. Perhaps the best way of establishing filenaming conventions is to assign meaning to each of the eight column positions in a filename.

To design a filenaming scheme using column positions, a number of decisions have to be made. Most importantly, the user must decide how to categorize application types (and subtypes, if necessary). Once types and subtypes have been identified, each one must be assigned a unique code (either alpha or numeric).

The user must also decide the detail level that he or she wants to build into the filename. For example, a filename could simply indicate that the file is a memo written on a particular date. Or the filename could contain a reference number to indicate the subject of the memo, the recipient of the memo, and so on.

In designing a filenaming scheme, it is important to construct it with enough flexibility so that more detail may be added at a later time. This could be accomplished by including several "open" positions within the eight-column limitation. When not necessary to the identification of a file, the position(s) could always contain the number "0." If this type of strategy is used, the detail level of the filenaming scheme can be easily modified. Another code number or letter can be added rather than adding or deleting the position itself.

Finally, the user must decide on a logical order of the codes for the various column positions. This order must be consistent for all files on the hard disk. The user then is able to gain maximum benefit from DOS file management features such as directory sorts and global filename characters. This order also should be meaningful to the user. For example, if the most critical identifier of the data files is application type, then this code should precede all others.

Using meaningful syllables in filenames

An alternative to using column positions to establish a filename convention scheme is to use short, meaningful syllables within the filename. Thus, documentation files may be labelled "DOC," model-related files "MOD," and so on. For example, a file containing expenses accrued for the month of February 1987 might be called "EXP0287." Meaningful syllables can be used very effectively under certain circumstances:

1. When all files to be stored on the hard disk are known at the onset; therefore, a great deal of flexibility for handling new filenames is not required.
2. When they are used in conjunction with a highly organized, many-layered, tree-structured directory. In this case, files can be organized into directories and subdirectories by file type, subtype, date, and so on. If the tree-structured directory contains too many levels, however, DOS search and retrieval time will be quite sluggish.
3. The meaningful syllable always appears in the same column positions for each filename. This permits the use of DOS utilities with global filename characters.

The greatest advantage of using this type of filenaming convention is that the first-time user can readily recognize filenames and identify file contents. Extensive documentation on the meaning of each filename column position is not required.

Using global filename characters with filenaming conventions

DOS provides the user with two characters that can be used to perform operations on groups of files rather than individual files. These characters (the symbols? and *) are called Global Filename Characters or wild cards. Use of the? character in a filename or extension means that any character can occupy the position. Use of the * character in a filename or extension means that one or more characters can occupy the position.

Used with a hard disk in which filenaming conventions have been established, global filename characters can be extraordinarily useful when performing operations on groups of like files.

Consider a filenaming convention in which monthly expense files are labelled with the prefix EXP followed by a two-digit month and a two-digit year. For example, the file for February 1987 expense data would be called EXP0287. If one wants to archive all expense files for 1986 from a subdirectory called EXPENSE into a subdirectory containing only expense data for 1986 (called EXPENSE6), the following command would be issued:

```
COPY C: \EXPENSE\EXP?? 86. * C: \EXPENSE6\EXP?? 86.*
```

Once the 1986 expense files are copied into the archive directory (EXPENSE6), they can be erased in the current EXPENSE directory:

```
ERASE EXP?? 86.*
```

Using the? global filename character, the user must include only the prefix code for file type ("EXP") and the year ("86") in the command specification. If, for example, 50 or more files are included in this population, performing this function without using global filename characters could be a highly time-consuming process.

Setting up a hierarchical file and directory structure

Information stored on the fixed disk of the XT and AT can be organized by function and type. This is one of the most important features of DOS, since thousands of files may be placed on the fixed disk. The storage capacity of a 20-megabyte fixed disk is approximately 56 times greater than that of a single 360-KB floppy disk and 17 times that of a high-capacity disk. With a large amount of information stored on the fixed disk, locating a specific file could be a slow process. However, with DOS, quick access of information on the fixed disk can be achieved through the use of hierarchical directories.

The first task in designing a hierarchical directory system is deciding how the directory system is to be structured. DOS gives the user a great deal of flexibility in setting up a hierarchical directory. When a disk is formatted, DOS starts the basic organization of the directory system by creating one main directory. The structure of the directory system after this point is determined by the user.

Structuring a hierarchical directory

The starting point for all hierarchical directories is the root directory. All formatted disks contain a root directory; in DOS versions 2 and 3 the root directory may contain programs, data files, or the names of other directories (subdirectories). However, most individuals prefer to limit the root directory to system or program files. Each directory within the root directory may contain its own set of programs, data files, or directories (subdirectories). This type of organization is referred to as a tree-structured directory. The branching of directories into subdirectories may be extended out as far as necessary.

Hierarchical directories may be structured in any manner that is convenient for the user. To demonstrate how a directory might be organized, consider the following example. The fixed disk on a PC-AT is used to store DOS files, a word processing program, and a spreadsheet program.

The word processing directory (WP) might contain all the files necessary to run *DisplayWrite3* as well as three further subdirectories of its own.

```
\WP\DOC  (Documentation Subdirectory)
\WP\MEMO  (Memo Subdirectory)
\WP\ADMIN  (Administrative Reports Subdirectory)
```

Each of the word processing subdirectories might in turn contain fur. ther subdirectory divisions. For example, the \WP\MEMO subdirectory might contain separate subdirectories by month. Thus, the subdirectory structure might contain:

```
\WP\MEMO\JAN
\WP\MEMO\FEB
\WP\MEMO\MAR
 etc.
```

Hierarchical directory paths

Hierarchical directories allow DOS to quickly locate a specified file. This is because

DOS sees only the files contained in the specified directory when it is searching for a file. The system is able to do this by using a pathname that precedes the filename. A pathname specifies each directory through which DOS must move in order to access the specific file. Each directory in the pathname is separated by the backslash symbol (\). For example, using the hierarchy described above, the path from the Root Directory to a January 19, 1987 memo would be:

```
C:\WP\MEMOS\JAN\NCFX0119.TXT
```

Note that a backslash also separates the directory name from the filename. The filename is NCFX0119. The first two letters indicate the author (Nancy Cain); the second two letters indicate the topic (Foreign Exchange); the last four characters indicate the date (01/19).

A hierarchical directory can contain as many subdirectory levels as necessary. There is no limitation on the number of subdirectories that may be created, except that sufficient disk space must be available. However, DOS cannot accept pathnames that exceed 63 characters, including the backslash characters.

In the three directory levels, many more could be added. Each directory may contain numerous files and subdirectories. The number of files that may be placed in a directory is limited only by the amount of space available on the disk or in the DOS partition.

Managing and organizing a directory hierarchy

A directory system is only as effective as its organization is efficient. A good hierarchical directory should be no more complex than is necessary. Subdirectories should be organized according to the type of files that they will contain. It is best to keep directory names short and simple.

Many applications programs allow the user to store and access data files in multiple subdirectories from within the specific program. If users of such programs are likely to generate hundreds of data files, it is a good idea to create several subdirectories for the program's files. In a program such as Lotus 123, it takes much less time to retrieve a file when the user is not forced to search through a list of all 123 data files stored on the fixed disk.

Disk organisation utilities

How much data can be stored on a disk and how those data are stored are issues of primary concern to users. When a vast amount of data are stored electronically, the user wants some assurance that the data can be retrieved reliably and with a minimal amount of effort. Although the operating system manages how the data are physically stored, it is up to the user to determine the media (hard disk, floppy disk, tape, etc.) and the logical groupings of the data into directories, subdirectories, and files. The

Disk/Directory utilities guide users through the development of a logical directory structure and assist in the management and organization of their storage media.

There are five Disk/Directory utilities. They include routines for:

- setting up a logical directory structure and linking it to a master menu for easy access to any subdirectory
- viewing and/or printing the contents of directories and subdirectories
- formatting floppy disks under a number of different conditions

The key to a well-managed hard disk system is having an easily accessible and well-organized directory and file structure. Particularly when a number of different users will be retrieving and storing data, the administrative tasks associated with maintaining many data files can be overwhelming.

The Disk/Directory utilities address this problem. They provide menu-driven access to all of the necessary directories, subdirectories, and software programs. Such menu-based programs can navigate even the most inexperienced user through a hierarchical directory structure In addition, these utilities eliminate the need to memorize complicated DOS commands and minimize potential errors associated with using certain disk-related commands.

The Disk/Directory utilites are accessed when selection 1 is chosen from the *Hard Disk Manager* main menu. This selection changes the directory to \HDU\DISK and displays the Disk Directory Menu. Any of the five selections on the screen can be chosen simply by entering the number of the desired utility. After the selection ' is made, the user is prompted for any required input; informational screens, when necessary, guide the user through the utility. If at any time the user chooses not to proceed with a utility, the < F1 > key can be pressed to return to the previous menu.

For the those who would like additional information on electronic storage media and DOS's directory capabilities, overviews of these topics can be found at the end of this chapter.

Organization of the disk/directory utilities

The disk organization utilities contained on the *Hard Disk Manager* program disk are made up of numerous files in several different directories. The principal directory is the \HDU\DISK directory. It contains the routines for all the Disk/Directory utilities except the second menu choice on the Disk/Directory menu.

Although there are over 70 files in the \HDU\DISK directory, most of these are used by the Menu/Directory Setup utility. This is a fairly extensive program, and there are two subdirectories also used by this utility: \HDU\DISK\MP and \HDU\DISK\AUTO. The first of these contains the programs for installing the

Miscellaneous Programs option on the main menu. The \HDU\DISK\AUTO directory contains the files used for installation of the main menu onto the system.

C:\HDU\DISK <DIR>			
1. BAT	1DBINPUT. TXT	3DBINPUT. TXT	5DBINPUT. TXT
2. BAT	1EXINPUT. TXT	3EXINPUT. TXT	5EXINPUT. TXT
3. BAT	1HDINPUT. TXT	3HDINPUT. TXT	5HDINPUT. TXT
4. BAT	1MPINPUT. TXT	3MPINPUT. TXT	5MPINPUT. TXT
5. BAT	1SSINPUT. TXT	3SSINPUT. TXT	5SSINPUT. TXT
	1WPINPUT. TXT	3WPINPUT. TXT	5WPINPUT.TXT
A. BAT	2DBINPUT. TXT	4DBINPUT. TXT	6DBINPUT. TXT
B. BAT	2EXINPUT. TXT	4EXINPUT. TXT	6EXINPUT. TXT
C. BAT	2HDINPUT. TXT	4HDINPUT. TXT	6HDINPUT. TXT
D. BAT	2MPINPUT. TXT	4MPINPUT. TXT	6MPINPUT. TXT
E. BAT	2SSINPUT. TXT	4SSINPUT. TXT	6SSINPUT. TXT
F. BAT	2WPINPUT. TXT	4WPINPUT. TXT	6WPINPUT. TXT
G. BAT			
	DBBEGIN. TXT	EXIT 2DOS. BAT	SSBEGIN. TXT
	DISKMENU. SCR	MAINMENU. TMP	WPBEGIN. TXT
	END. TXT	MENU. BAT	SETUP. SCR
	CR. TXT		
	DOCOPYC1. BAT	DOFORM3. BAT	DOFORM5. BAT
	DOCOPYC2. BAT	DOFORM4. BAT	
	SSSTART. TXT	WPSTART. TXT	DBSTART. TXT
	SSSTART. BAT	WPSTART. BAT	DBSTART. BAT
C:\HDU\DISK\VIEW		<DIR>	
1. BAT	INSTRUCT. SCR	VIEW. BAT	DOTREE2. BAT
2. BAT	VIEW. SCR	DOVIEW. BAT	DOTREE3. BAT
3. BAT	PRINT. BAT	DOPRINT. BAT	
C:\HDU\DIST\AUTO		<DIR>	
Y. BAT	MANUAL.BAT	INSTRUCT. SCR	AUTOEXEC. TMP
N. BAT	AUTO.BAT	MAKEAUTO. SCR	RETURN. TMP
	CONFIG.TMP	NURETURN. TMP	
C:\HDU\DISK\MP		<DIR>	
Y. BAT	MP2BEGIN.TXT	MP2. SCR	MISCPROG. SCR

N. BAT	MP3BEGIN.TXT	MP3. SCR	DOCOPYC3. BAT
1. BAT	MP4BEGIN.TXT	MP4. SCR	
MISCPROG. BAT		MP5BEGIN. TXT	MP5. SCR
		MP6BEGIN. TXT	MP6. SCR
		MPBEGIN. TXT	MPLINE. SCR
		MPEND. TXT	MPINSTRU. SCR

Figure 1: Directory and file structure for Disk/Directory Utilities

The \HDU\VIEW directory contains the files that run the second menu choice, Disk and Directory View/Print Utilities.

Above figure shows the structure of the files and directories for the Disk/Directory utilities. As is shown in figure, there are basically three file types used by the Disk/Directory utilities: the batch files (.TXT extensions), information/instruction screens (.SCR extensions), and EDLIN input files (.TXT extensions). The .TXT files serve as input to batch files where the EDLIN program is executed inside the batch file.

Activation of the utilities

Selection of choice 1 on the main utility menu accesses the Disk/Directory utilities by activating the 1.BAT file in the \HDU directory. It contains the following commands:

```
1. BAT
echo off
cls
cd disk
type diskmenu. scr
echo ENTER SELECTION:
prompt $e [22;18H
setscrn
```

```
                    DISK/DIRECTORY MENU
1.   Main Menu and Directory Setup Utility
2.   Disk and Directory View/Print Utilities
3.   Format a Floppy (Data Disk)
4.   Format a Floppy (System Disk)
5.   Format a 360 KB Floppy in High-Capacity Drive
     << Press F1 to Return >>
```

Figure 2: Disk/directory Utility Menu Screen

The functions of this file are to change the current directory to \HDU\DISK, display the Disk/Directory menu (DISKMENU.SCR), position the cursor at the end of the ENTER SELECTION: prompt, and to reset the screen display attributes (setscrn). Figure 2 shows the Disk/Directory screen.

The disk/directory utilities

The menu/directory setup utility

This is one of the key utilities in the *Hard Disk Manager.* This utility allows the user to create a directory structure for common microcomputer applications (such as spreadsheet and word processing programs), and a menu system that accesses these applications. The user decides what the contents of the main menu should be.

The menu choices

The choices that can appear on the main menu include: Word Processing, Spreadsheet, Database, Exit To DOS, Hard Disk Manager, and Miscellaneous Programs. The menu choice Miscellaneous Programs is a submenu to which the user can add any program or application not found on the main menu. The user selects one or more of these six items (in any order) for inclusion in the main menu. The main menu can be installed in the system so that it is displayed automatically every time the system is turned on or restarted, or it may be installed so that it is displayed whenever the user manually enters the command MENU at a DOS prompt. Figure 4.3 shows the appearance of this main menu when all six menu choices have been placed on the menu.

```
                    Main Menu
1.    Word Processing
2.    Spreadsheet
3.    Database
4.    Hard Disk Manager
5.    Miscellaneous Programs
6.    Exit to DOS
```

Figure 3: Main menu screen with six options

It should be noted at the onset that this simple menu system is just that--it is a simple menu structure that is created entirely with DOS commands and utilities. Because it involves no compiled code, it can be modified to meet the needs of individual users. Without the cost of purchasing a menu-creation program, one can create a menu system that gives the average hard disk user the ability to organize and easily access hard disk applications.

Choosing menu selections

The Main Menu Setup Utility screen is displayed when selection 1 is chosen on the Disk/Directory menu. From here, the menu and directory structure is created in a two-step process.

```
                 Main Menu Setup Utility
This utility creates and installs a main menu. Selections A-C will
Prompt you for the following information:
 - The name of the directory where the program resides (the
```

```
    directory will be created if it does not exist)
  - The command that runs the program (e.g., "lotus" for Lotus 1-2-
    3).
Add Selections A-F one at a time, in any order, as needed. You MUST
execute Selection G when the last menu choice has been added.
 A. Add WORD PROCESSING Menu Choice
 B. Add SPREADSHEET Menu Choice
 C. Add DATABASE Menu Choice
 D. Add EXIT TO DOS Menu Choice
 E. Add HARD DISK MANAGER Menu Choice
 F. Add MISCELLANEOUS PROGRAMS Submenu (Directory: \MISC)
 G. Install Completed Main Menu
        << Press F1 to Return >>
```

Figure 4: Main menu/Directory setup utility

1. A menu item can be added to the main menu by entering the letter of the desired item (letters A through F). This step is repeated for each item that is to be placed on the main menu.
2. The last menu choice (letter G, Install Completed Main Menu) is entered after all the desired menu items have been added to the main menu.

These two steps are described in more detail below.

Constructing the menu

In step 1, when selections A, B, C, or F are entered, directories are created for the respective applications. With selections A-C, the user is prompted to supply the name of the directory; in selection F, the directory is automatically called \MISC.

Also, in selections A, B, and C, since these menu selections will activate specific applications programs, the name of the command that calls up that specific program must be entered. For example, if selection A is executed, the user is prompted to enter the command that executes the word processing program. Suppose that program is *MultiMate;* the user must enter the command that calls up the *MultiMate* program, which in this case is wp.

Depending on the speed of ones system, a few minutes may be required each time a menu selection is added to the main menu. During the process, various messages are displayed that provide information about the action being taken. The Menu/Directory Setup screen is redisplayed after a selection has been added. The process is then repeated for another selection. Finally, if there are no further menu additions, the main menu is installed by executing selection G.

Installing the New Menu

The second step in setting up the main menu is the installation. When the Installation routine is started (by entering G from the Setup menu), an information screen is displayed asking the user if the display of the main menu is to be automatic or manual. Figure 4.5 shows the contents of this information screen. An automatic display means that the menu will appear whenever the system is turned on or rebooted. Manual display means that the menu will be displayed only when the user enters the command MENU after a normal DOS prompt (e.g., the C > prompt).

```
                            Instructions
This routine installs your completed menu into your root directory.
The Main Menu can be displayed one of two ways:
 -  AUTOMATICALLY, whenever your system is turned on or a system
    reset is performed; or,
 -  MANUALLY, by entering a command (called MENU) whenever you wish
    to call up the Main Menu.
For automatic menu display, it is necessary to create (or add to) an
AUTOEXEC.BAT file. If this file already exists, the necessary
commands will be appended to the end of that file.
Enter the command AUTO to have the menu displayed automatically.
Enter the command MANUAL to have the menu displayed manually.
                       << Press F1 to Return >>
```

Figure 5: Information screen for installing new menu

The command MANUAL must be entered to set up a manual display of the main menu; AUTO is used for automatic display. When AUTO is entered, the batch file creates an AUTOEXEC.BAT file, if one does not already exist. If this file does exist, then the contents of the file are displayed on the screen.

The user is then asked if additional commands may be added to the end of the file so that the main menu can be displayed. This is done through a confirmation prompt: "Continue (Y/N)?" A Y response adds the necessary commands to the end of the AUTOEXEC.BAT file and completes the installation process. N aborts the AUTO routine and the screen informs the user that the MANUAL option should be used to install the main menu.

When either the MANUAL or AUTO routines are finished, the user is informed that the installation is complete. In both cases, the user is placed in the DOS environment, with the standard DOS prompt (C >). Users who have chosen the AUTO option must reboot their system to see the main menu. If the MANUAL option has been executed, only the command MENU must be entered to see the new menu.

The menu/directory setup program files

The batch files that run the Menu/Directory Setup utility are some of the longer routines contained in *Hard Disk Manager.* The utility begins when selection 1 is entered from the Disk/Directory menu. This activates the 1.BAT file in the \HDU\DISK directory; it contains the following commands:

```
    1. BAT
echo off
cls
type setup. scr
echo ENTER SELECTION:
prompt $e [22;18H
```

The function of this file is to display the Menu/Directory Setup screen.

The files used by this utility can be grouped as follows

1. The letter batch files (A.BAT through F.BAT) in the \HDU\DISK directory; these are used for adding selections to the main menu.
2. The .TXT files, which are used by the letter batch files as input files for EDLIN routines executed in those files; they also are files that are combined with other files.
3. The files in the \HDU\DISK\MP directory, which are used when the Miscellaneous Programs choice is added to the main menu.
4. The G.BAT file and all of the screen and batch files located in the \HDU\DISK\AUTO directory; these files are used during menu installation.

The first three categories relate to the addition of individual menu items to the main menu. The last category involves the installation of the newly completed menu into the system. These are described in detail below.

The program files for adding menu selections

The letter batch files add the individual menu items to the main menu. Although some of these files tend to be quite lengthy (some are over 100 lines), the functions they perform are fairly simple and there is a great deal of repetition.

The A.BAT file and the four files to which it passes control (DOCOPYC1.BAT, WPMORE.BAT, DOCOPYC2.BAT, and WPSTART.BAT) are reproduced. An understanding of the workings of these files will apply to all the other letter files. It should be noted that the program files for selections A, B, and C are more complicated than the other selections because the user is specifying a directory; this is not the case in selections D, E, and F.

Five batch files are executed when A.BAT is selected:

- A.BAT, which calls a subroutine batch file DOCOPYC1.BAT
- A.BAT then calls WPMORE.BAT
- WPMORE.BAT executes WPSTART.BAT
- WPSTART.BAT calls a subroutine batch file, DOCOPYC2.BAT

The subroutine files DOCOPYC1.BAT and DOCOPYC2.BAT are COPY CON routines for: 1) user input of the directory names, and 2) command execution names for the Word Processing program. The same files are also used by the batch files for Selections B and C.

How the program files work

The A.BAT file begins by immediately passing control to the DOCOPYC1.BAT file, where the user is prompted to input the name of the directory containing the word processing program. The first three lines of A.BAT are shown below:

```
A.BAT (beginning)
1: echo of f
2: cls
3: command /c docopycl WORD-PROCESSING wpdir. tmp c:\wp
```

The call is made to the DOCOPYC1. BAT subroutine batch file in line 3 above. There are a number of arguments following the command: the name of the batch file (DOCOPYC1), and three replaceable parameters that are used by DOCOPYC1. The breakdown of components in line 3 is as follows:

Component:	Function
command /c	Invokes secondary command processor
docopycl	This is the batch file subroutine
WORD-PROCESSING	This is the %1 replaceable
parameter in the subroutine,	indicating the directory name
wpdir. tmp	This is the %2 parameter in the
subroutine for a temporary file that	holds the user's input
c:\wp	This is the %3 replaceable
parameter in the subroutine, which	is the text of the example

Note that there is a hyphen in "WORD-PROCESSING." This is because the spaces are interpreted as delimiters between the arguments.

The DOCOPYC1.BAT functions to execute the COPY CON routine for the user input of the directory name. It is structured in a subroutine context so that, should < Ctrl > < Break > be pressed, the user is not left out in DOS somewhere with no menu and no prompt. It contains the following commands:.

```
DOCOPYC1.BAT
1: echo off
2: cls
3: echo  First, you must specify the name of the %1 directory.
4: echo  Use the format shown in the example below. (If you make
   a
5: echo  mistake, press [Ctrl] [Break], and start over.)
```

```
6:  echo (Example: %3)
7:  echo Please ENTER the directory name, PRESS the F6 key and then
    PRESS Enter
8:  copy con: %2
9:  exit
```

In line 3, the %1 variable is replaced by "WORD-PROCESSING." The %3 variable in line 6 is replaced by "c:\wp." In line 8, using the COPY CON command, the batch file becomes user-interactive. The %2 variable is replaced by "wpdir.tmp." The COPY CON command takes the user's input (which is the directory name) and stores it in a file called WPDIR. TMP. In line 9, the EXIT command returns control to the file that made the subroutine call, which in this case is A. BAT. Command execution resumes in A. BAT at line 4. The entire contents of A. BAT are listed as follows:

```
  A. BAT
1:  echo of f
2:  cls
3:  command /c docopyc1 WORD-PROCESSING wpdir. tmp c:\wp
4:  echo of f
5:  cls
6:  if not exist wpdir. tmp goto ABORT
7:  copy wpbegin.txt + wpdir. tmp + cr.txt wpbegin2.txt
8:  copy wpstart. txt + wpdir. tmp wpmore. bat
9:  del wpdir. tmP
10: wpmore
11: ABORT
12: echo Program has been interrupted. Please retry
13:pause
14:cls
15:type setup. scr
16:echo ENTER SELECTION:
17:prompt $E [22;18H
```

Line 4 turns the echo off again, since DOS turns echo on when control moves from one batch file to another. In line 6, a check is made to determine if the subroutine was concluded without a < Ctrl > < Break >. If this is not the case, control shifts to the ABORT section where an error message shown before the menu is redisplayed.

If WPDIR. TMP has been created without problems, in line 7 a text file is created around the user's directory name input. This file, WPBEGIN2.TXT, will be used later on for the batch file that runs the Word Processing menu choice. In line 8, the directory name input is added to a one-line text file, WPSTART.TXT; the result is the batch file WPMORE. BAT.

The contents of WPMORE. BAT are as follows:

```
WPMORE. BAT
1:     wpstart <directory name as %1 variable>
```

Line 1 of WPMORE.BAT executes the WPSTART.BAT file, with the user's directory name input as a %1 variable. Thus, if the user specified his or her word processing directory as c:\wp, then line 1 of WPMORE.BAT would be:

```
WPSTART C:\WP
```

From the WPMORE.BAT file, control is passed to the WPSTART.BAT file. The WPSTART.BAT file begins by displaying a message. Then, six IF commands check for the existence of the numbered batch files (1.BAT through 6.BAT) in the root directory. This is to determine what menu number to give the item that has been selected for addition to the main menu:

```
if not exist 1. bat goto 1 CHOICE
if not exist 2. bat goto 2 CHOICE
if not exist 3. bat goto 3 CHOICE
if not exist 4. bat goto 4 CHOICE
if not exist 5. bat goto 5 CHOICE
if not exist 6. bat goto 6 CHOICE
```

If a 1.BAT does not exist, then the new menu item will be number 1; control is then passed to the 1CHOICE section of the batch file. If it does exist, the test for the existence of 2.BAT is performed, and so on. (Note that the maximum number of menu choices that can be automatically added to the menu is 6: If a 6.BAT file is found to exist, the program will display an error message and return to the Setup menu.)

Next come the individual subsections for the installation of the selected menu item onto the specific location of the main menu (1CHOICE, 2CHOICES, etc.). These sections are similar to one another except for certain variables. The 1CHOICE section contains the following commands:

```
:1CHOICE
cd\hdu\disk
edlin mainmenu. tmp <1 wpinput. txt
cd\
md %1
cd\hdu\disk
cls
command/c docopyc2 WORD-PROCESSING 1. tmp
echo of f
cls
if not exist 1. tmp goto ABORT
copy \hdu\disk\wpbegin2. txt + 1 tmp + \hdu\disk\end.txt \1.bat
```

```
13: goto END
```

In line 3 above, the menu item is added to the main menu, using EDLIN to edit the MAINMENU.TMP file. The input for the EDLIN routine comes from the redirected IWPINPUT.TXT file. In line 5, the directory is created, using as the %1 variable the directory name supplied by the user in A.BAT.

In line 8 above, control is passed to another batch file subroutine, DOCOPYC2.BAT. This subroutine batch file is exactly like DOCOPYC1.BAT except for the text of an ECHO command. In DOCOPYC2.BAT, the user supplies the command that executes the Word Processing program.

Control returns from DOCOPYC2.BAT to line 9 above. As in A.BAT, the IF NOT EXIST command in line 11 checks for successful completion of the DOCOPYC2 subroutine. The COPY command in line 12 sets up a batch file that will run the menu selection. The user's input is combined with WPBEGIN2.TXT and END.TXT, forming the 1.BAT file in the root directory.

In the 2CHOICES section, this combined file would be 2.BAT; for 3CHOICES, it is 3.BAT; and so on. If the user's input from the first COPY CON command was c:\wp and the input from the second COPY CON command was wp,

At the end of each subsection (in this case, 1CHOICE), control is then passed to the END section, where the following message is displayed:

```
Be sure to
-   install the menu (selection G) after adding all your menu choices
-   copy the Word Processing program files into the c:\wp directory
```

This message is different when the Spreadsheet, Database, or other menu option has been added. A %l variable is used for the directory name, so the user's directory name input is displayed in the message. The Setup screen is then redisplayed, and the user is ready to add another menu selection or to install the completed menu.

The program files for installing the menu

The batch files that make up the installation process include G.BAT in the \HDU\DISK directory, and all of the files in the \HDU\DISK\AUTO directory. The function of this routine is to copy the just-completed main menu into the root directory, and to create the process that makes this menu accessible. The process begins when a G is entered from the Setup menu. This activates the G.BAT file, which contains the following commands:

```
G. BAT
    echo off
    cls
    cd auto
    type instruct.scr
```

```
5:    echo ENTER COMMAND:
6:    prompt $e [20;16H
```

After the current directory is changed to the \HDU\DISK\AUTO subdirectory (line 3), an instruction screen is displayed. This instruction screen describes the automatic versus manual option for displaying the main menu.

When the user enters the MANUAL command, the following batch file is activated:

```
MANUAL.BAT
 1: echo of f
 2: cls
 3: echo Copying mainmenu to root directory...
 4: copy \hdu\disk\mainmenu. tmp \mainmenu. scr
 5: copy\hdu\disk\menu.bat
 6: cd \
 7: cls
 8: echo Your menu system has now been installed. To display your
 9: echo menu at any time, simply enter the command MENU.
10: prompt $n$g
```

The above batch file simply copies to the root directory the two files critical to the Manual process: MAINMENU.SCR and MENU.BAT. The AUTO.BAT file, in contrast, is somewhat more complicated.

```
                    AUTO.BAT
 1:   echo off
 2:   cls
 3:   echo Copying main menu to root directory...
 4:   copy \hdu\disk\mainmenu.tmp \mainmenu.scr
 5:   cd \
 6:   if not exist autoexec.bat goto NOAUTO
 7:   goto AUTO
 8:   :NOAUTO
 9:   echo Making AUTOEXEC.BAT file
10:   cd \hdu\disk\auto
11.   copy \hdu\dospath.txt + autoexec.tmp \autoexec.bat
12:   Cls
13:   echo Your menu system has now been installed. Reboot your
      computer
14:   echo (by pressing [Ctrl] [Alt] [Del]) to display the main
      menu.
15:   prompt $n$g
16:   goto END
```

```
:AUTO
cd _\hdu\disk\auto
if exist flag.txt goto HAVEDONE
Cls
echo There already is an AUTOEXEC.BAT file in your root directory.
echo It contains the following commands:
type \autoexec.bat
type makeauto.scr
prompt Continue (Y/N)?
goto END
:HAVEDONE
echo Your new main menu has now been installed. To continue,
pause
cd
cls
type mainmenu.scr
echo ENTER SELECTION?
prompt $e [22;18H
:END
```

Figure 6: Contents of AUTO.BAT for menu installations

The AUTO.BAT file copies the MAINMENU.SCR file to the root directory, and then uses an IF command to determine if the system contains an AUTOEXEC.BAT file. This file is used to automatically display the main menu. If it does not exist, the AUTO.BAT file creates one with the command:

```
copy\hdu\dospath.text + autoexec.tmp \autoexec.bat
```

The path specified by the user when the *Hard Disk Manager* was installed was stored in a file called DOSPATH.TXT This is combined with some other commands to form the AUTOEXEC.BAT file.

If an AUTOEXEC.BAT file already exists, the authors assume that the user may not wish to have the existing one obliterated. A "Continue (Y/N)?" prompt asks permission to append some specific commands to the end of the existing AUTOEXEC.BAT file. The N.BAT file aborts the installation with instructions to install the menu manually. The Y.BAT file is as follows:

```
Y. BAT
echo of f
cls
echo Adding commands to your AUTOEXEC.BAT file...
cd\
copy\autoexec.bat + \hdu\dospath.txt +
```

```
    \hdu\disk\auto\autoexec.tmp
6:  copy \hdu\disk\auto\nureturn.tmp \return.bat
7:  copy \hdu\disk\auto\dospath2.txt \hdu\disk\auto\flag.txt
8:  cls
9:  echo Your menu system has now been installed. Reboot your
    computer by
10: echo pressing [Ctrl] [Alt] [Del], to display the mainmenu.
11: prompt $n$g
```

The long COPY command in line 5 above appends the contents of DOSPATH.TXT and AUTOEXEC.TMP to the existing AUTOEXEC.BAT file. Suppose the DOS path specified by the user was C:\DOS and the existing AUTOEXEC.BAT file simply ran the clock program for an AST board (ASTCLOCK).

The COPY command in line 6 places a new RETURN.BAT file in the root directory. This *will* cause the new main menu to be displayed when the < Fl > key is pressed, instead of the Hard *Disk Manager* menu. The COPY command in line 7 creates a file called FLAG.TXT, its existence simply serves to indicate that the necessary commands have been appended to the AUTOEXEC.BAT file. The AUTO.BAT file checks for the presence of this file to prevent the same commands from being added to the AUTOEXEC.BAT file again if a new main menu is installed.

The miscellaneous programs option

When the Miscellaneous Programs selection is installed on the main menu, a submenu is displayed when this menu choice is selected. The first item on this submenu, "Add A Selection To This Menu," does exactly what its description says. All of the files associated with the Miscellaneous Programs submenu are contained in the directory \HDU\DISK\MP.

Miscellaneous Programs Submenu

---

1. Add A Selection To This Menu Screen

<<Press F1 to Return to Main Menu>>

Figure 7: Miscellaneous programs submenu

Program files for the miscellaneous programs option

When selection 1 on the menu is entered, the following batch file is executed:

```
1. BAT
echo of f
cls
type mpinstru.scr
echo Continue (Y/N)?
prompt $e[17;18H
```

If the user responds with N to the "Continue (Y/N)?" prompt, the Miscellaneous Programs menu is redisplayed. The Y.BAT file adds the new menu item to that menu. This is a long batch file similar to the WPSTART.BAT file described earlier. It performs the following operations:

1. Using a subroutine batch File (DOCOPYC3.BAT), the user is prompted to enter the name of the menu item that is to appear on the Miscellaneous Programs menu screen. This file is similar to DOCOPYC1.BAT described earlier. Using a COPY CON command, the user's input is placed in TEMP.TXT.
2. A check is made of the number of menu items that already exist, using the Exist condition of multiple IF commands:

   ```
   cd\misc
   if not exist 2.bat goto 2CHOICES
   if not exist 3.bat goto 3CHOICES
   if not exist 4.bat goto 4CHOICES
   if not exist 5.bat goto 5CHOICES
   if not exist 6.bat goto 6CHOICES
   goto OTHEREND
   ```

   For example, if a 2.BAT file does not exist, control is passed to 2CHOICES where the new menu item will be labeled "2."
3. In the subsections (2choices, 3choices, etc.), three COPY commands remake the Miscellaneous Programs screen with the new menu pick. The first COPY command adds a menu number to the user's input, and the second COPY command adds this combination to the menu. The last of the three prepares the menu for the next time a selection is added.

   ```
   copy mp2begin.txt + temp.txt temp2.txt
   copy mp1.scr + temp2.txt + mp2.scr miscprog.scr
   copy mp1.scr + temp2.txt + mpline.scr
   goto CONTINUE
   ```

4. Control then passes to CONTINUE. A subroutine batch file (DOCOPYC2.BAT) is executed that prompts the user for the name of the command that runs the program. The COPY CON command again is used to make this a user-interactive batch file. COPY CON places the input in TEMP.TXT.

   ```
   echo ENTER the command, PRESS the F6 key, and then PRESS Enter:
   copy con:temp.txt
   ```

Using the same IF command procedure as before, a batch file is written to run the new menu choice. Depending on what numbered batch files already exist, control is passed to 2BAT, 3BAT, 4BAT, etc.

5. In the 2BAT through 6BAT subsections, the TEMP.TXT input is combined into an appropriate numbered batch file. In the 2BAT subsection, for example:

```
copy mpbegin.txt + temp.txt + mpend.txt 2 bat goto F1 FIRSTEND
```

6. Control passes to FIRSTEND where completion messages are displayed. After a pause, the Miscellaneous Programs menu is redisplayed, containing the new menu pick.

```
                         Instructions
This routine allows you to add menu selections to the MISCELLANEOUS
PROGRAMS SUBMENU Screen. As many as five new menu selections may be
added to the menu. (If you need more than five, refer to chapter 4
of "Hard Disk Manager.")
You will be prompted for the following input:
-The name of the program selection that will appear on the
MISCELLANEOUS PROGRAMS SUBMENU Screen. The menu number will be
supplied automatically.
-The command that executes the menu selection.
<< Press F1 to Return >>
```

Figure 8: Instruction screen for miscellaneous programs option

Resetting the menu

The Menu/Directory Setup utility allows the user to add up to six menu items automatically. On the seventh try, the following error message is displayed:

```
A total of six items has already been installed... program ABORTED.
```

The only time this should happen is if there have been some repetitions, since there are only six choices, A-F. To find out what has gone wrong, the user must do the following:

1. First, examine the temporary main menu. This is done by selecting the Exit To DOS on the *Hard Disk Manager* menu, and then entering the following command:

```
type \hdu\disk\mainmenu.tmp
```

2. Decide which of the menu items is superfluous. Unless a menu item has been placed on the menu manually, there should be some duplications. (Proceed to the next step even if the menu looks all right.)

3. Make note of the numbered items that should be on the menu and then enter the following command:

```
dir\?.bat
```

This should produce a listing of numbered batch files in the root directory (1.BAT, 2.BAT, and so on).

4. Erase the numbered batch file for every menu item that does not belong. For example, to erase the 4.BAT file, the command is

```
erase \4.BAT
```

6. Return to *Hard Disk Manager* (by entering the command HDU) and run the Disk/Directory Setup routine again for the desired menu item. Be sure to install the menu when done (selection G).

To start a main menu again from scratch, select Exit To DOS, and erase all the numbered batch files (see steps 3 and 4 above). Then, copy the file MAINMENU.TMP from the *Hard Disk Manager* program disk back onto the C drive. This is done by entering the command:

```
copy a:\hdu\disk\mainmenu.tmp c:\hdu\disk
```

Now run the Disk/Directory Setup utility from the beginning. When the completed menu is installed, it will replace any existing main menu previously created.

The disk & directory view/print utilities

These routines allow the user to view or print the contents of a disk or directory. When 2 is entered from the Disk/Directory menu, a submenu containing the View/Print options is displayed. The operations performed by the three menu selections are fairly simple.

The view/print contents of a directory utility

To view the contents of a particular directory, the user must enter the command VIEW followed by the directory path. To print a directory, the user must enter the command PRINT, again followed by the directory path.

Disk & Directory View/Print Menu

1. View/Print contents of A Directory
2. View Contents of All Directories
3. Print contents of All Directories

<<Press F1 to Return>>

Figure 9: View/print options menu

```
                         Instructions
This routine allows you to view or print the contents of a specific
   directory.
To view the contents of a directory, enter the command VIEW followed
   by the path and directory name. There will be a pause between
   screens if the contents exceed the size of one screen.
To print the contents of a directory, enter the command PRINT
   followed by the path and directory name.
```

```
To print the contents of the \WP directory, the command is entered
   as
                          print \wp
                  << Press F1 to Return >>
```

Figure 10: Instruction screen for view/print directory contents

The view/print directory program files

The two program files behind View Directory utility are VIEW.BAT and DOVIEW.BAT. Their contents are as follows:

```
      VIEW. BAT
1:    echo off
2:    cls
3:    command /c doview %1
4:    echo of
5:    cls
6:    type view.scr
7:    echo ENTER SELECTION:
8:    prompt $e [22;184
9:    setscrn
      DOVIEW.BAT
1:    echo off
2:    cls
3:    echo Here are the contents of the %1 directory:
4:    dir %\1 /p
5:    echo End of directory listing.
7:    exit
```

In the above batch files, DOVIEW.BAT is a subroutine batch file called by the VIEW.BAT file. In line 3 of VIEW.BAT, the call is made to the DOVIEW.BAT file; the EXIT command at the end of the DOVIEW.BAT file returns control to line 4 in VIEW.BAT. This technique is used to ensure the redisplay of a menu should < Ctrl > <Break > be pressed during program execution. Line 9 of both VIEW.BAT and PRINT.BAT executes the batch file SETSCRN.BAT.

The two program files behind Print Directory utility are PRINT.BAT and DOPRINT.BAT. Their contents are as follows:

```
      PRINT.BAT
1:    echo off
2:    cls
3:    command/c doprint %1
4:    echo off
5:    cls
6:    type view.scr
```

```
7:     echo ENTER SELECTION:
8:     prompt $e [22;184
9:     setscrn
       DOPRINT.BAT
1:     echo off
2:     cls
3:     echo PLEASE MAKE SURE THAT
4:     echo -YOUR PRINTER IS TURNED ON
5:     echo -AND THAT IT IS "ON-LINE"
6:     pause
7:     dir %1 >prn
8:     exit
```

As in the View Directory utility, the DOPRINT.BAT file is a subroutine of the PRINT.BAT file. Line 3 of PRINT.BAT makes the call to DOPRINT.BAT; control is returned to PRINT.BAT with the EXIT command at the end of DOPRINT.BAT.

In the above batch files, the DIR command is the key component. The directory name specified by the user when the PRINT and VIEW commands are entered is substituted for the %1 replaceable parameter. In the DOPRINT.BAT file, a reminder to turn on the printer is displayed with the ECHO commands. The output of the DIR command is redirected to the printer with the " > prn" specification.

The view contents of all directories utility

The second utility on the Disk & Directory View/Print menu allows the user to get a screen listing of the directory files contained on the hard disk. This is a simple, two-file routine. When the user enters 2, the 2.BAT file in the \HDU\VIEW directory is executed.

The view contents program file

The two program files behind the View Contents of All Directories utility are 2.BAT and DOTREE.BAT. Their contents are as follows:

```
       2.BAT
1:     echo of f
2:     cls
3:     command /c dotree2
4:     echo of f
5:     cls
6:     type view. scr
7:     echo ENTER SELECTION
8:     prompt $e [22;18H
9:     setscrn
       DOTREE2.BAT
```

```
1:    echo of f
2:    echo The disk contents will be displayed in a few moments...
3:    echo (Press any key to continue when "More" is displayed in
      Lower corner.)
4:    tree /f | more
5:    echo End of disk listing.
6:    pause
7:    exit
```

The DOTREE.BAT file functions as a subroutine of 2.BAT. Line 3 in 2.BAT makes the call to DOTREE.BAT. In line 7 of DOTREE2.BAT, the EXIT command returns control to 2.BAT.

The central command in the above batch files is the TREE command, with the /F option (line 4 of DOTREE2.BAT). This command displays a listing of all directories on a disk; the /F option includes the files in each directory. The I more specification causes the scrolling to pause after each screen of information.

The View/Print submenu is redisplayed when the listing is completed. Line 9 in 2.BAT executes the SETSCRN batch file.

The print contents of all directories utility

The third utility on the Disk & Directory View/Print menu permits the user to generate a printout of all the directories and files on the ' hard disk. It is executed when the user enters 3 from the Disk & Directory View/Print menu.

The print contents program file

There are only two files associated with this utility: 3.BAT and DOTREE3.BAT. The contents of these files are as follows:

```
3. BAT
echo off
cls
command /c dotree3
echo of f
cls
type view.scr
echo ENTER SELECTION:
prompt $e [22;18H
setscrn
```

```
DOTREE3.BAT
echo off
cls
echo PLEASE MAKE SURE THAT
echo -YOUR PRINTER IS TURNED ON
```

```
5:    echo -AND THAT IT IS "ON-LINE"
6:    pause
7:    echo Printing will begin in a few moments...
8:    tree /f >prn
9:    exit
```

The call is made to the DOTREE3.BAT subroutine in line 3 of 3.BAT. As before, this technique is used to ensure that a menu is redisplayed in the event the user presses <Ctrl > < Break > during program execution.

Like the 2.BAT file, the key command is the TREE command, with the /F option (line 8 of DOTREE3.BAT). The " >prn" specification redirects the output of the command to the printer.

The format utilities

There are two reasons for the presence of these utilities in this package. The first reason is security. It really requires very little effort for an inexperienced user to enter the command FORMAT and inadvertently obliterate everything on a hard disk. Since the hard disk is rarely formatted, these utilities are set up to format floppy disks only. The second reason for the format utilities is convenience. Particularly when high-capacity or system disks are being formatted, it is easy to forget the various switches that must be used with the FORMAT command.

The format a data disk utility

The first of the format utilities, Format a Floppy (Data Disk), will format a 360-KB or high-capacity floppy disk for normal usage as a data disk. When a 3 is entered from the Disk/Directory menu, the 3.BAT file in the \HDU\DISK is activated.

The format a data disk program file

The Format a Floppy (Data Disk) utility consists of two program files: 3.BAT and DOFORM3.BAT. The second batch file is a subroutine that is called by 3.BAT. By placing the FORMAT command in the subroutine, a menu will be displayed should the user press < Ctrl > < Break > before the utility is completed.

The contents of these batch files are as follows:

```
      3. BAT
1:    echo of f
2:    cls
3:    command /c doform3
4:    echo of f
5:    cls
6:    type diskmenu. scr
7:    echo ENTER SELECTION:
8:    prompt $e [22;18H
```

```
9:    setscrn
      DOFORM3.BAT
1:    echo of f
2:    cls
3:    echo This prepares 360 KB or High-Capacity floppies for use as
      data disks.
4:    format a:/v
5:    exit
```

The DOFORM3.BAT file is called as a subroutine in line 3 of the 3.BAT file. Note that the FORMAT command in line 4 in DOFORM3.BAT is written to format a disk in drive A. The /V switch will cause DOS to prompt the user for a volume label. The EXIT command at the end of DOFORM3.BAT returns control to line 4 of the 3.BAT file. The Disk/Directory menu is then redisplayed. Line 9 executes the batch file SETSCRN.BAT.

The format a system disk utility

The second format utility, Format a Floppy (System Disk), performs the same operation as the first, except that the disk can be used as a boot (system) disk. This means the computer can be started using this disk because all of the operating system files required for a system start-up will be copied onto the disk during formatting.

The format a system disk program file

Two program files are executed when the user selects this menu pick: 4.BAT and DOFORM3.BAT The difference in these batch files and the 3.BAT and DOFORM3.BAT files described above is only the message that is displayed and the use of an additional switch in the FORMAT command. The message indicates a system disk is being formatted; the FORMAT command includes the /S option:

```
format a:/s/v
```

The /S switch indicates to DOS that the disk is to be formatted as a system disk. It should be noted that a disk should not be formatted in this way unless it really will be used as a boot disk. This is because an unnecessary amount of disk space will be occupied by the system files.

The format a 360-KB/high-capacity disk utility

The third format utility on the Disk/Directory menu is useful only if the user's system includes a high-capacity disk drive. This utility allows a user to format a 360 KB floppy disk in the high-capacity drive. This disk can then be used by that drive. (In certain situations, the reliability of these disks may be an issue; the reader should refer to "The Compatibility of Storage Media" in section 4.3 later in this chapter for a discussion of these circumstances.) When the user enters 5 from the Disk/Directory menu, the 5.BAT file in \HDU\DISK is executed.

The format a 360-KB/high-capacity disk program file

Like the two other Format utilities, there are two program files associated with this menu choice: 5.BAT and DOFORM5.BAT. The commands in the 5.BAT and DOFORM5.BAT files are the same as the commands in the above utilities, with two exceptions: The message that is displayed refers to the high-capacity drive, and the format command is written as

```
FORMAT A:/V /4
```

The /4 option puts the high-capacity drive into the 360-KB formatting mode.

Modifying the disk/directory utilities

Although the Disk/Directory utilities cover many aspects of disk and directory management, the authors believe that many users will have requirements that will not be met by a generic package such as this. There are some operations that were intentionally not included. For example, there is no provision for use of the MD (Make Directory) or RD (Remove Directory). These commands are fairly easy operations for DOS. Experienced users will probably find it easier to execute these commands outside a menu or batch-file environment. The "Exit to DOS" menu choice can be useful for such situations.

However, if the system is to used by PC novices, it may be necessary or desirable to totally structure all aspects of disk and directory management. This section describes how to add, delete, or modify the Disk/Directory utilities.

Here are a few general suggestions and reminders for commands and operations that may be involved in modifying or creating disk organization utilities. Most of these tricks were used in the Disk/Directory utilities.

1. The COPY CON command can be used in a batch file as a way of obtaining user input without interrupting the execution of the batch file. The command is preceded by instructions, and the user presses < F6 > and < Enter > when finished. The input is stored in the filename that follows the COPY CON command.
2. User input obtained with the COPY CON technique can be combined into batch files or menu screens using the COPY command to append files to one another.
3. Using the EDLIN program with a redirected input file is a technique for automatically remaking a menu screen in a batch file. The input file must contain all the commands and data that would be entered if EDLIN were used manually for the same editing process.
4. The EXIST and NOT EXIST conditions of the IF command are useful for checking the validity of filename parameters entered by the user. Pathnames cannot be used in this command for DOS versions earlier than 3.0; it is necessary to change the directory to the current directory containing the file before the IF command is executed.

5. The MORE command is a useful way of controlling the scrolling of the screen displays exceeding the size of one screen. Piping is used to pass the output of a command through MORE, as in:

```
type info.scr | more
```

6. In circumstances where it is possible that the user may press < Ctrl > < Break > before a utility is completed, it may be useful to call the main body of the batch-file program as a subroutine batch file. This is done through the use of the command

```
COMMAND /C <batch filename>
```

If the commands following COMMAND redisplay a menu, these commands will be executed if the user presses < Ctrl > < Break> while the subroutine is executed.

Adding and deleting menu items

Adding or deleting menu items in the Disk/Directory menu will not present many difficulties. The only area where the task may be a bit more complicated is in the Menu/Directory Setup utility, mainly because of the number of files involved. The reader should consult Chapter 10 for a step-by-step approach to adding and deleting menu items.

Some possible modifications and enhancements

There are any number of changes and modifications in the Disk/Directory utilities that can be made. The user may modify, delete~ or add menu selections to the existing routines. This section describes these procedures and provides some suggestions for possible modifications and new additions. These arc utilities that use DOS features or commands not covered in the existing utilities. The descriptions basically cover only the actual program files.

A directory sort utility

This is an easy utility to add to the Disk & Directory View/Print menu. It allows the user to see or print directory listings sorted by date, size, or filename. It uses the VIEW.BAT and DOVIEW.BAT files from the View/Print Directory Contents utility, almost intact. Here are the two original files:

```
VIEW.BAT
echo of f
cls
command /c doview %1
echo of f
cls
type view.scr
echo ENTER SELECTION:
prompt $e [22;18H
setscrn
```

```
DOVIEW.BAT
1:   echo of f
2:   cls
3:   echo Here are the contents of the %1 directory
4:   dir %1 /p
5:   echo End of di rectory Listing.
6:   pause
7:   exit
```

The files could perhaps be renamed DIRSORT.BAT and DOSORT.BAT. (The filename in line 3 of VIEW.BAT would have to be changed to whatever filename replaces DOVIEW.BAT.)

The DIR command (line 4) in the DOVIEW.BAT file is the key component that must be modified. First, the SORT command is added to the end of the DIR command:

```
dir %1 /p | sort
```

This allows the user to alphabetize the directory listing by passing the directory information through the SORT filter in the above command. To sort directory listings by date or file size, the /+n switch is added to the end of the SORT command. (The "n" represents the screen column number that is to be the primary sort key; the default is column 1.) For example, to sort by file size, the switch would be set as / + 14:

```
dir %1 /p | sort /+14
```

For a sort by date, one has to choose between a sort by month, day, or year, since only one column number can be entered. To sort by month, for example, the switch setting is / + 24.

It should be noted that the use of the SORT command in the above examples does not permanently alter the order of the directory listing. Subsequent issuance of the DIR command alone would produce an unsorted directory listing.

A remove directory utility

This utility is for users who wish to structure the removal of directories in a batch-file and menu environment. The RD command requires that a directory be empty of any files or subdirectories before it is removed.

Before executing the RD command, it would probably be a good idea to precede the operation with some instructions indicating that an empty directory will have files listed. Suppose the specified directory was TEST. The listing for that directory would appear as follows:

```
Directory of C:\test
.      <DIR> 8-30-86   2:14p
..     <DIR> 8-30-86   2:14p
 2 File(s) 1052672 bytes free
```

4

Batch File Programming

Batch file programming plays a big part in hard disk management, bigger than you'd think. Aside from using AUTOEXEC.BAT, the most important batch file in your system, there are dozens of ways you can put batch files to work in a hard disk system. Learning about batch files and how to create them is easy. In fact, it's so simple no more than one chapter is necessary to tell you the basics. All that's left for you to do is then learn how to apply batch files to your system. Once that's done, you'll find they come in handy all the time and really extend your control over the computer.

Types of DOS programs

Extension	*Program Type*
COM	Binary image program. Loaded directly in to memory and executed by the microprocessor. Program can be no more than 64K in size.
EXE	Executable file. Loads in to memory in separate pieces, so it's slower to load than a COM file. EXE files can be any size. Most modern applications are EXE programs.
BAT	Batch file. Contains text instructions that are given to COMMAND.COM and executed. The slowest type of program but one of the most useful.

This chapter is about batch file programming. It shows you how to create batch files and how to put them to work. There are three areas of concentration:

- the nature and purpose of batch files
- batch file commands
- batch file variables

What is a batch file?

Batch files are the simplest type of program run under DOS. There are only three types of programs DOS can run. The names of the types are based on the filename extension. Batch files, which have the extension BAT, consist of text, as opposed to the other types of programs, which contain instruction code for the computer's microprocessor.

Batch file text is in the form of DOS commands and special batch file programming instructions.

DOS reads batch files one line at a time. Each line is then interpreted by COMMAND.COM, almost as if that line were typed at the DOS prompt. The command is then executed, and the next line in the batch file is read. You can store commonly used program names and sequences of DOS Commands in batch files. Since they're just text files, you can create them on disk by using a word processor or by using the COPY command with the CON device as input. Just name the text file with a BAT extension, and DOS executes it as a batch file.

Batch file creation

Nearly anything you normally do at the DOS prompt can be done using a batch file. Batch files come in especially handy when it comes to entering a repeated command line or a series of repeated command lines. Rather than type the same few lines each time, you simply type the name of the batch file.

For example, suppose you always type the same commands to start your database program. First you type

```
CD  \DB3   ENTER
```

which accesses the DB3 subdirectory. Then you type

```
DBASE  ENTER
```

which loads your database. Since you type these commands often, you can write a batch file to do the job. The batch files can save you quite a few keystrokes.

To create a batch file, you have two paths to take. You can

- use a word processor, or text editor
- use the COPY CON function

Using a word processor, or text editor, is the best way to create a batch file. You enter the application, then type the lines you want in your batch file. For example, type the following:

```
CD  \DB3  ENTER
DBASE   ENTER
```

Then you save the file in text format. Remember to give the file a meaningful name, plus the extension BAT. The preceding batch file can be named DBASE.BAT, for example.

The COPY CON function uses simple I/O redirection to make the file on disk. The drawback is that, using COPY CON, you cannot go back and edit previous lines. You must type in the complete, correct batch file the first time. If you make an error, you can use a text editor to correct the mistakes later or just start all over with COPY CON.

To use the COPY CON function, type the COPY command at the DOS prompt, the CON device (the device providing input for the file), and the name of the file you want to create. Then enter the lines in the batch file. Signal the end of the file by pressing CTRL-Z. For example, your screen may look as follows:

```
C> COPY CON DBASE.BAT
CD \DB3
DBASE
CTRL-Z
C>
```

To cancel file creation, press CTRL-C.

The simplest way to run the batch file is to enter the batch file name, DBASE, at the DOS prompt. DOS then reads the lines from the batch file and executes them. You can also run a batch file from any disk drive or subdirectory by entering the batch file's full pathname. And, finally, you can put the batch file in a subdirectory listed on the path.

The net effect of the preceding batch file is to run a program on the hard drive. Other batch files can be written to perform system maintenance, do backups, configure a system, or perform a repetitive DOS task over and over.

Batch file commands

Batch files can contain two types of batch rile commands: commands you enter at the DOS prompt and special batch file programming commands.

Batch File Commands at the DOS Prompt

The commands you enter at the DOS prompt are just that. A batch file can contain any number of command lines to run programs in this manner.

Batch file programming commands

Batch file Command	Function
CALL	Runs a second batch file, then returns control to the batch file currently executing
ECHO	Displays information on the screen or controls the echoing of text. The most commonly used batch file command.
FOR	Executes a DOS command for specified files.
GOTO	Branches execution of the batch file to another line in the batch file.
IF	Tests a certain condition and, if the condition is true, executes a DOS command.
PAUSE	Causes the batch file to pause and display a message prompting the user to press a key.
REM	Allows remarks in the batch file.
SHIFT	Accesses the next command line variable.

Batch file programming commands

The special batch file programming commands enhance the performance of batch files. They give it the power of an unsophisticated programming language; they can do repetitive tasks, make decisions, and use simple forms of variables. Each one of these terms carries out some command or function within the batch file, making your batch files "smarter."

These commands can be divided into two groups: simple commands and not-so-simple commands. A simple command performs a single task. Simple commands are the ones you'll use most often in your batch files. Not-so-simple commands offer advanced features to batch files. You'll probably use these commands for complex tasks, but not for general system operation.

Simple Commands

The following batch file commands are the most commonly used and simplest to understand. These simple batch file commands

- ECHO
- GOTO
- PAUSE
- REM

extend the power of batch files beyond the ability to process only DOS commands.

ECHO: ECHO is both a switch and a command. It's traditionally the command used to start a batch file. For example:

```
ECHO OFF
```

means that the contents of the batch file are not echoed to the display as DOS executes them. In most of your batch files in Lab 6. 1, every command in the batch file was displayed on the screen as the batch file ran. However, for those batch files that started out with ECHO OFF, only the initial ECHO OFF was displayed.

With DOS versions 3.3 and later, putting an at sign (@) before any command in a batch file also suppresses the echo. Any line starting with the @ symbol-even the first line-is not displayed as the batch file runs.

The command

```
ECHO ON
```

switches ECHO back on, causing the echoing of commands in the batch file. This command is rarely used. Using ECHO after the DOS prompt results; in the display of the current status of the ECHO command:

```
C> ECHO
ECHO IS ON
C>
```

The primary use for ECHO is to display lines of text as a batch file is executing. For example, the command

```
ECHO GOOD MORNING!
```

results in "Good morning!" on the display. You can spice up many batch files with ECHO, using it to display helpful messages, warnings, and other information as the batch file executes.

GOTO: The GOTO command branches batch file execution from one line to another line elsewhere in the file. Normally, each line is executed one after the other, in the order they were created. However, by using GOTO, you can make the batch file commands execute in any order. GOTO is used with a label. A label is any line in the batch file that starts with a colon. For example:

```
:BRANDX
```

The preceding label is named BRANDX. If DOS encounters the batch file command

```
GOTO BRANDX
```

DOS scans the batch file for the line starting with a colon followed by BRANDX. After DOS finds it, DOS executes the batch file at the line after :BRANDX.

Normally, DOS ignores any line in the batch file that starts with a colon. So, you can also use colons to put comments into your batch file. Note that DOS uses only the first eight letters of a label or any letters less than eight up to the space character. Any character after the first eight or the first space is ignored.

The following batch file uses GOTO:

```
ECHO OFF
GOTO SECOND
: F I R S T
ECHO AT THE FIRST LABEL
GOTO END
 :SECOND
ECHO AT THE SECOND LABEL
 GOTO FIRST
: END
```

```
ECHO ALL DONE
```

The preceding batch file contains three labels: FIRST, SECOND, and END.

The final output of the batch file is

```
AT THE SECOND LABEL

AT THE FIRST LABEL

ALL DONE!
```

Normally, GOTO is used with the IF batch file command. In that instance, DOS executes a specific part of the batch file only if a certain condition is true. Without IF, using GOTO to hop around a batch file is a real time waster, as the preceding program shows.

PAUSE. The *PAUSE* command does exactly what it says. When encountered in a batch file, PAUSE halts execution and displays a message like "Strike a key when ready." For example, the batch file containing

```
ECHO OFF

ECHO HANG ON A MINUTE ...
PAUSE

ECHO THANKS!
```

has the following effect:

```
HANG ON A MINUTE..

STRIKE A KEY WHEN  READY...
```

At this point the user strikes any key and the batch file supplies

```
THANKS!
```

on the screen.

PAUSE comes in handy, allowing you to warn users about activity that could be dangerous or giving them a chance to read a few ECHO lines before continuing. CTRL-C or CTRL BREAK cancels the pause or stops a batch file. When you enter CTRL-C or CTRL-BREAK a "^C" is displayed, along with the following message.

```
TERMINATE BATCH JOB (Y/N)?

PRESS Y TO CANCEL THE BATCH FILE, OR N TO CONTINUE.
```

REM. The REM command is used to insert remarks, or comments, into a batch file. When REM followed by space starts a line, DOS ignores everything following them on that fine. Remarks may contain the date the file was created and commentary on what the batch file is doing. For example:

```
ECHO OFF
REM This batch file copies all the files in
Drive A to Drive B
REM Written by Dan Gookin
REM November 3, 1992
ECHO Insert source diskette into Drive A
ECHO and put the target diskette into Drive B
PAUSE
COPY A:*.* B:
```

The three REM commands in the preceding program allow the comments to be used at the top of the batch file. DOS does not attempt to interpret the comments as commands. Because ECHO is OFF, comments are not displayed.

Before moving on, note how the two ECHO commands are followed by the PAUSE command. The program produces the following display:

```
Insert source diskette into Drive A
and put the target diskette into Drive B
Strike a key when ready . . .
```

Notice how "Strike a key when ready . . . " blends right in with the previous comments. The PAUSE command is often used to produce this effect.

Not-so-simple commands

The batch file commands CALL, FOR, and IF are a little more complex than the commands previously covered. Each offers several options that make them not as straightforward as the more common commands. The section that follows briefly introduces the three commands. Another not-so-simple command, SHIFT, is described later in this chapter.

CALL: Since batch files are programs like any others, one batch file can execute another. However, DOS does not usually return to the first batch file after it executes the second. To return control to the first batch file from the second, you must use the CALL command.

The format for the CALL command is

```
CALL BATCHFILE
```

where "batchfile" is the name of the batch file CALL runs. Once the called batch file is done, DOS picks up again with the first batch file.

CALL is available only with DOS 3.3 or later. In earlier versions of DOS, you can substitute COMMAND /C for CALL

FOR: The FOR command is used to perform a single DOS command on a specific group of files. The format is FOR %%variable in (filespec1, fiLespec2,...) DO command

where "%%variable" is a letter from A to Z. The letter represents each of the files ("filespec 1 " and so on) listed in parentheses. The "command" is a DOS command that acts upon each file, using "%%variable" as a place holder. For example:

```
FOR %%A IN (*.TXT *.DOC) DO TYPE %%A
```

The variable %%A takes on the value of each file with the extension TXT or DOC. The TYPE command is then performed on each of those files. This way, you can "batch-type" those files, listing their contents on the screen. Consider another example:

```
FOR %%A IN (ALPHA BETA GAMMA DELTA) DO COPY %%A B:
```

This FOR command uses %%A to represent each of the four files, ALPHA, BETA, GAMMA, and DELTA. For each one of those files, FOR issues the COPY command, copying the file to drive B. The preceding FOR command has the same result as

```
COPY ALPHA B:
COPY BETA B:
COPY GAMMA B:
COPY DELTA B:
```

Note that, if you use FOR as a DOS command, you need specify only one percent sign with the variable

IF. The IF command allows you to perform a specific command if the condition is true. The general format of an IF statement is

```
IF CONDITION COMMAND
```

where "condition" is an evaluation. The possible conditions are

- environment variable==string
- ERRORLEVEL value
- EXIST filename

The place holder "environment variable" stands for an environment variable or some variable defined with the SET command. The environment variable is compared to a string constant by IF. If both match, then the command is executed. Note that this form of the IF command uses double equals signs (==). If a batch file using IF errors, it's probably because you've used a single equals sign instead. ERRORLEVEL is a value returned from certain programs. If that value is greater than or equal to the value specified, then the command is executed. "EXIST filename" tests to see if a specific filename exists. If so, the command is executed.

The following is an example of the environment variable format of an IF command:

```
IF %DISPLAY%==COLOR GRAPHICS
```

This command tests the environment variable DISPLAY, comparing it with the string COLOR. The percent signs identify the environment variable. When the batch file is executed, %DISPLAY% is replaced by whatever string it's set equal to in the environment. If that string is equal to COLOR, then the DOS command GRAPHICS is executed.

The following is an example of an ERRORLEVEL test:

```
IF ERRORLEVEL 1 ECHO BAD EXIT
```

ERRORLEVEL tests if the value returned by a program is 1. If so,"Bad exit"is echoed to the display.

The following is an example of an EXIST test.

```
IF EXIST *.TXT ECHO THERE ARE TEXT FILES HERE
```

EXIST tests for any files with the extension TXT. If there are files with that extension, then the condition is true and "Mere are text files here" is echoed to the display.

NOT can be used before a condition test to make the IF statement true when the condition is not true. For example:

```
IF NOT EXIST *.TXT ECHO There are no text files here
```

The preceding IF command is true only if there are no files with the extension TXT in the current directory.

IF comes in very handy in certain advanced forms of batch files. But normally, for running programs-doing backups or performing other simple duties-IF is rarely used.

Batch file variables

There are two types of batch rite variables, that can be used in batch files. They are

- system variables, or environment variables
- command line variables

These variables work like most variables in common computer languages; they store temporary information that can be referenced, evaluated, or changed by the batch file. Note, however, that these variables work only in a batch file—not on the DOS command line.

System variables

System variables come from the environment. They're placed there by the SET command. Some applications can use the variables, but so can batch files. In that case, the variable name is surrounded by percent signs. For example:

```
%COMSPEC%
```

When the batch file interpreter encounters an environment variable such as %COMSPEC%, it immediately translates it into whatever the variable is set equal to. There's no messing around. For example:

```
ECHO Your COMSPEC  is %COMSPEC%
```

This command, when encountered in a batch file, is changed to

```
ECHO  Your COMSPEC  is C:\COMMAND.COM
```

The final result is

```
Your COMSPEC IS C:\COMMAND.COM
```

You can set environment variables in batch files as well as reference them. Just remember to enclose the variable in percent signs.

Command line variables

Command line variables are numbered %0 through %9. Each number stands for an item entered on the command line. For example:

```
C> WP CHAPTER3
```

In this example, the command line variables take on the following values:

```
%0  = WP.EXE
%1  = CHAPTER3
%2=
%3-%9  =
```

As you can see, the command line variables %2 through %9 remain empty. You can use command variables to reference data typed after a batch file. For example, most applications give you the option of specifying a filename after the application name on the command line:

```
C> DBASE ACCOUNTS
```

The preceding command loads the DBASE program and DBASE loads the ACCOUNTS database file. If you are writing a batch file that does the same thing, you can use the command line variable % I to represent anything typed after the name of the batch file:

```
ECHO OFF

CD \DBASE

DBASE %1
```

Suppose the preceding batch file is named DB.BAT and the following is entered on the command line:

```
C> DB CUST
```

CUST becomes the % I command line variable. It's used in the batch file, just as an environment variable would be used. The batch file then becomes

```
ECHO OFF

CD \DBASE

DBASE CUST
```

Anything you type after DB on the command line becomes %I in the batch file. Command line variables are commonly used in the IF command. IF can be used to test if a command line variable exists or not. For example, the IF test.

```
IF %1X==X ECHO No first command Line variable found
```

checks to see if there is a first command-line variable. If so and if the variable is TEST, then the IF statement is expanded by the batch file interpreter.

```
IF TESTX==X ECHO No first command Line

variable found
```

The preceding IF text is false. Since the first commandline variable does exist, TEXTX is not equal to X. Had no command line variable been included, then the IF statement would have been

```
IF X==X ECHO No first command Line variable found
```

The preceding IF text is true, since %1 didn't exist.

Remember that you can use NOT to reverse the results of the text:

```
IF NOT TEXTX==X ECHO A command Line variable was found
```

The not-so-simple command *SHIFT* is used with command line variables in batch files. Command line variables differ from environment variables in that they follow the batch file name on the command line—they're not in the environment.

What the SHIFT command does is to rotate the command line variables, moving the second position to the first, the third to the second, and so on. In other words, the variable values change as follows:

%1 becomes %0

%2 becomes%1
%3 becomes %2
%4 becomes %3
%5 becomes %4
%6 becomes %5
%7 becomes %6
%8 becomes %7
%9 becomes %8

Using SHIFT, you can sift through the command line variables in a batch file, examining each of them in a loop, without having to reference them by number.

Hardware manager

The individuals who need hard disk utilities most probably don't realize it. These less technical users need utilities that simplify the day-to-day use of a microcomputer. Any number of good utilities can be found for improving the performance of a hard disk system, for dealing with disasters, and so on. After all, it only takes one accidental formatting of a 10-MB disk to be convinced that everyone ought to have at least one trustworthy utilities package. However, utilities as powerful as these are not always for the fainthearted; the user may have to be prepared to decipher a screen full of hexidecimal values or to interpret all kinds of system and error messages.

The *Hard Disk Manager* is a disk package for both new and serious computer users. It provides a comprehensive library of utility programs and illustrates techniques on which to build additional utilities. The *Hard Disk Manager* contains the following features:

- easily installed utility programs that provide users with an integrated hard disk management system
- DISK/DIRECTORY UTILITIES: Menu creation tools and utilities for directory and disk setups
- DISPLAY UTILITIES: Utilities to change the color of the display foreground and background, and to enhance certain aspects of the display screen through-use of highlighting, reverse video images, etc.
- DESIGN UTILITY An EDLIN-based screen design tool
- BACKUP/RESTORE UTILITIES: Various options for backing up and restoring data files according to date, files last modified, etc.
- FILE MANAGEMENT UTILITIES: Utilities to write-protect data files, archive unused files, conduct text searches, find files, move files from one directory to another, etc.
- HELP SCREEN UTILITIES: Ten HELP facilities that provide basic information on using many features of the operating system

- explanations for the use and modification of the utility programs and ideas for creating new utilities
- information on little-known capabilities of DOS
- reference guides for DOS, EDLIN, and batch file commands

What does the hard disk manager do for you?

The *Hard Disk Manager* is a utility software package that can be installed as is. It is used to *organize* and *customize* your hard disk to meet your individual needs:

- It is used to establish your own hierarchical directory and file structure.
- It provides greater security around your hard disk system.
- Its menu-driven environment is used to perform routine housekeeping tasks but does not require a working knowledge of DOS.

As your knowledge and requirements grow, your disk management system can be modified to meet your changing needs. Since the program is written entirely with DOS, it is easy to modify. It is not written in a higher-level language nor is it compiled code. This means that it can be modified by you or any other user. Or, since it is built within DOS, programs in the *Hard Disk Manager* can also be incorporated into other, larger micro-based systems.

The *Hard Disk Manager* utilities are written for two types of users:

- NEW BUSINESS USERS who need and will use a menu management system but have no desire to program.
- EXPERIENCED USERS who know computers and create systems for end users--those who will incorporate the *Hard Disk Manager* an its ideas into bundled systems.

For less experienced users who wish to read about the program before beginning, "Behind the Utilities," is a good place to start. This chapter provides an overview of those DOS features that make up the guts of the utilities. It includes information on: DOS command files, DOS's file management capabilities, DOS's built-in utility commands, programming with DOS, and programming with DOS's advanced features.

Each type of utility (e.g., Disk/Directory, File Management, etc.) is described in a separate chapter. In these chapters, you will find documentation on the batch files or program files that make up each utility. You also will find some background information on how to make optimal use of the utilities and how various DOS features were used in the construction of specific utilities. Finally, you will find ideas on how to add to and modify the utilities. If you are the adventurous type and wish to try your own hand at creating utilities, separate chapters are devoted to this topic.

This package contains 25 different DOS-based utilities for organizing and customizing your hard disk system. Some are just short batch files. Others are more complex routines that employ programming techniques such as conditional logic, subroutines, validation of user input, and concatenation. All are understandable and modifiable by nonprogrammers.

Some of these routines are available through generic "desk top" applications. These "desk top" applications, however, leave you with little individual choices and lock you into certain limitations. In contrast, the *Hard Disk Manager* utilities can be tailored to individual requirements. For the novice user, the programs can be installed as is. For the more experienced user, you can have the satisfaction of knowing that you designed and installed your own hard disk management system. And, any time the need arises, you can change them again... and again.

For hard disk users, interacting with the operating system is a fact of life. It is the operating system that coordinates and integrates all aspects of one's hardware and software. The Disk Operating System (DOS) is a highly powerful tool that controls a computer's input and output, that loads and executes programs, and that is responsible for managing files in a floppy or hard disk environment.

DOS also can be viewed as a programming language for setting up and managing a hard disk system. Behind DOS's basic commands lies the ability to combine various commands and advanced features of DOS into powerful utility programs. The point of these utilities is that you, the user, can install them as is, customize them to your own system, or use them as a basis for creating new ones.

This chapter is an overview of those features of DOS that make up the guts of the utilities. A quick scan of the chapter before you install the utilities will give you some insight into their design and construction. This chapter is relevant particularly for the individual who wants to know what is behind the utilities. On the other hand, when you're convinced that you want to write some on your own, this summary is perhaps the best place to begin.

number of versions of PC-DOS have been released. The earliest versions of DOS (1.0 and 1.1) were written exclusively for the PC. Many features were added to versions 2.0 and greater so that later versions of DOS could accommodate the needs of hard disk users.

The DOS Command Files

At the heart of DOS are three command files: IBMBIO.COM, IBMDOS.COM, and COMMAND.COM. At the time a system is first set up, DOS is installed on the hard disk. During this process, some files are copied onto the hard disk automatically, and others must be copied manually by the user. The three files mentioned above are automatically copied. In addition, every time DOS is loaded or the system is initialized, these three files are placed in memory.

IBMBIO.COM establishes the system's Basic Input/Output System (BIOS) that is located in the computer's ROM (Read-Only Memory) chips. In doing so, it determines how the system is configured and initializes the system's peripherals (e.g., the printer, display, and so on). IBMBIO.COM in turn loads COMMAND.COM into memory.

IBMDOS.COM is DOS's file management system. It initializes the internal working tables of DOS. These internal working tables are established each time a disk is formatted and serve as an index of disk files and file status.

COMMAND.COM is the DOS file most users are familiar with. Also known as the command processor, it is the largest of the three essential operating system files and is the guts of DOS's programming capabilities. The COMMAND.COM file contains the DOS internal commands. These are fundamental DOS commands that are placed in resident memory since they are frequently accessed by the user.

DOS's file management capabilities

Certain aspects of DOS not only determine where data are physically held on a hard disk, but also where they are logically located. DOS organizes the disk storage space into physical locations and provides a mechanism for indexing data stored in those locations. At the same time, multiple indices, hierarchically arranged, can be established to group data into logical locations.

Physical data storage

During the formatting process, DOS marks the hard disk, dividing it into a number of concentric circles called tracks. These tracks are further divided into sectors, each containing up to 512 bytes, or characters of information. The formatting process also establishes a directory and a File Allocation Table (FAT). The directory contains an index of what is stored on the disk and the FAT contains pointers to the sectors in which information is stored.

Each time a file is saved, DOS searches for free sectors and places the file contents in them. It is interesting to note that this file organization process is quite a bit different from a manual filing system. Instead of placing like information in a single area, DOS places information in any available sector; one large file could be spread all over the disk. It is up to the FAT to keep track of the pointers to each sector.

Logical data storage

Perhaps the most useful feature added to the hard disk versions of DOS was the inclusion of hierarchical directories. As mentioned above, a directory is an index. It contains a list of files stored on a disk along with reference information that tells DOS where each file is physically stored. This index can contain references to sub-indices; that is, directories may be arranged in a hierarchy in which directory entries contain names of lower-level directories. The feature allows the user to logically group data into a number of levels of subdirectories. In the jargon of the operating system, this is termed setting up a "tree-structured directory." The starting point for all hierarchical directories is the DOS master directory (the Root Directory) that is established during the initial setup of the hard disk.

Although the operating system can keep track of where any file is stored, it is not nearly so easy for the user to search through a single index of hundreds of files. Logically grouping files with like contents into a number of subdirectories is essential for the efficient management of a hard disk system.

DOS's built-in utilities and commands

A number of useful utilities are provided with the operating system. These utilities can be used as stand-alone routines. Or, by using DOS as a programming language, a number of DOS utility commands can be combined to create multifaceted utility programs. Included in the DOS programs are some 50 commands. Included in these are utilities for disk management; utilities for manipulating files and directories; utilities for searching, sorting, and combining the contents of files; and a text editor called EDLIN.

Each utility is activated by using a DOS command. Activation of a DOS command can take one of two forms: Commands can be entered by the user, one by one, or commands can be programmed into sequences and entered in a batch mode through use of a DOS batch file.

Programming with DOS

There are any number of reasons why one might want to program with DOS using batch file sequences. For example, it may not be necessary or practical for users to enter DOS commands individually. One might be building an integrated application in which a number of DOS commands must be chained together with other applications software. Or one might be dealing with a user who has little or no understanding of DOS.

For example, a File Archive program could be written that allows the user to: Copy an infrequently used file from the current directory to a floppy disk; erase the file in the current directory; and in an Archive Log File, add an entry that includes the name of the file and the date it was archived. All the user would have to type is the command ARCHIVE and the filename, as in:

```
ARCHIVE [filename.ext]
```

Behind that simple English command would be DOS commands that copy the file from the current directory to a floppy disk, delete the file from the current directory, capture the archival information, and append the archival information to the end of a log file.

Batch files are extraordinarily versatile. Ranging from several lines of code to more elaborate programs with decision-making logic, they can be written and modified by nonprogrammers.

Batch file characteristics

Batch files are programs written in ASCII text format, and they can be written with any text editor. One does not have to go out and buy a special text editor; EDLIN, included with the DOS program files, will suffice.

As is the case with any other DOS file, batch file names must be eight characters or less. In addition, a unique requirement of batch files is that they must have the extension BAT. This is because all files with the extension BAT are automatically executed by DOS when the filename is typed. For example, if the user creates a batch file named ARCHIVE.BAT, a batch routine will be activated any time the user types the word ARCHIVE at the DOS prompt.

As batch files are executed, each line of the program is displayed on the screen unless the display is suppressed by using a special batch file command.

Depending on the technical sophistication of the user and the need for complex command routines, batch files can be created to perform most any disk or file management task. In general, batch files can be categorized into two types, based upon their complexity:

1. Batch files that contain only the usual DOS commands.
2. Batch files that also use a special set of DOS batch file commands; some of these have decision-making capabilities and permit the use of higher-level programming techniques, including conditional statements and subroutines.

Batch file contents

Any DOS command that can be typed interactively by the user may be placed in a batch file. This includes both DOS internal commands (commands loaded into memory when DOS is initialized) and DOS external commands (those that must be loaded into memory at the time of use). Batch files also may contain non-DOS program names such as BASICA, LOTUS, etc. These are programs that use DOS to communicate with the computer. In addition, batch files can also contain names of other batch files, allowing the user to chain together one batch file after another.

A useful feature of batch files is the ability to use variables. These variables, known as replaceable parameters or dummy parameters, allow the user to construct a generic batch file that can accept different input each time it is executed.

Batch file uses

Perhaps the most common use of batch files is to insulate the user from the operating system. Any command or operation that someone might want to perform on his or her hard disk can be programmed as a batch file. With minimal knowledge of the operating system, the user can make maximal use of DOS's file and disk management utilities. For example, the likelihood of a user backing up files on a routine basis can be greatly enhanced by providing menu-driven batch file backup routines.

Batch files also can be used to standardize certain routines that must be performed. By programming all command sequences into a batch file, one can ensure that the same routine is followed regardless of the user or the situation. Such a use of batch files might be required in order to maintain an organized hard disk when several users are sharing a hard disk system.

Efficiency is another major advantage of using batch files. Preprogrammed command sequences eliminate the need to perform the same commands over and over again.

Lastly, batch files greatly simplify the use of a hard disk system. Once command sequences are programmed into a batch file, it is no longer necessary to remember elaborate command sequences or arcane syntax.

DOS programming commands for batch files

A number of DOS's commands are used exclusively in batch files. These commands include:

```
REM
ECHO
PAUSE
IF
GOTO
FOR
SHIFT
```

The user may recognize several of these commands such as IF, GOTO, and FOR as commands frequently found in other more sophisticated programming languages. It is these commands in particular that permit DOS to be a powerful tool to both programmers and nonprogrammers.

Programming with DOS'S advanced features

In addition to a number of utility-oriented commands, DOS contains a number of features that allow the user to alter the computer's basic input/output system to suit individual needs. These features include the setup of a configuration file (CONFIG.SYS), redirection of the traditional modes of input and output, and the ability to alter characteristics of the display.

Configuration Files (CONFIG.SYS)

A configuration file, just like a batch file, is an ASCII file (text file) created by the user. DOS requires that such a file be called CONFIG.SYS, and that this file be located in the root directory. This allows the file to be checked by DOS when the system is booted; thus, the file tells DOS how the user has configured his or her system.

Configuration file format

The format of a CONFIG.SYS file is always the same. Each configurational feature is listed on a line of the file, followed by an equal (=) sign, and a value or filename. For example, a CONFIG.SYS file might have the following entry:

```
BUFFERS = 10
```

This entry means that the number of buffers or memory blocks has been set to 10.

Configuration file contents

Five to eight different configurational features can be used with the CONFIG.SYS file, depending on the version of DOS. These include features that are beneficial to the average user as well as features typically needed only by programmers. The three features utilized by the average user are:

BUFFERS = The ability to set the size of memory blocks from I to 99. Whenever a file is written to or read, DOS brings portions of the file into the memory buffer. Increasing the buffer size increases the amount of that file that can be held in the buffer. Up to a point, increasing the buffer size will speed up processing. By having this information at the point of initialization, DOS will always use a buffer size of 10 unless the number of buffers is reconfigured by modifying the CONFIG.SYS file.

DEVICE = The ability to specify files containing device drivers. Device drivers are hardware-specific programs to which DOS transfers control when accessing that particular hardware device or peripheral.

The device driver of most interest to users is ANSI.SYS, which is included in DOS's program contents. ANSI.SYS contains the American National Standards Institute (ANSI) set of terminal codes. These are standard codes for controlling a system's display or video screen. It is only through use of this device driver that the user can access DOS's extended screen and keyboard functions. For example, to change the display's background color or to highlight a character by making it blink, this device driver must be set. Other enhanced keyboard features accessible by setting ANSI.SYS are: character (or foreground) color, reverse video capabilities, intensified characters, invisible characters, and underscored characters.

It should be noted that when the *Hard Disk Manager* utilities are installed, a CONFIG.SYS file is automatically installed if one does not exist on the hard disk. This file contains the command:

```
device=ansi.sys
```

FILES = The ability to set the maximum number of files that may be open at any one time.

Although the default value of FILES= is 8, this value might have to be increased if the user is working with an application that requires more than 8 files to be opened at a time (such as dBASE III).

Redirection of input and output

DOS allows the user to alter a system's standard input and output devices. Typically, input is via the keyboard, whereas output is directed toward the display screen. By using DOS's redirection capabilities, for example, input can come from a file and the output can be redirected to a file, a printer, or to a device called "nul" in which the output is suppressed. Redirection of output is signified in DOS by a greater-than sign (>) followed by the output device name. For example, to obtain a printout of the contents of a directory, redirection might be used as follows

```
C:\ DIR>PRN
```

in which PRN is the DOS device name for the printer. Redirection of input is signified by a lesser-than sign (<).

DOS's redirection capabilities give the DOS programmer a good deal of flexibility. For example, whenever log files or audit trails are required for a particular operation, the output can be sent automatically to another file or to the printer. The ability to save information in a file and then use that file as input to another operation also is quite useful. For example, a batch file could prompt the user for input, save that information in a temporary file, and then refer to the contents of that file later on in the program.

Key reassignment

A lesser-known form of redirected input is the ability to reassign the meaning of various keys. In this case, it is the ANSI.SYS device driver that gives the user the ability to assign new values or functions to the keys on the computer's keyboard. Unfortunately, most users assume that it is necessary to purchase special software packages to do this.

Entire operations can be assigned to a single function key in which the function key activates a batch file. For example, in the *Hard Disk Manager* utilities, this process is used to make the < F1 > key redisplay the *Hard Disk Manager* utilities menu (or the Main Menu if one has been installed). The process is simple. When < F1 > is pressed, it activates a batch file that in turn redisplays; the menu.

Using DOS's extended screen and keyboard functions

DOS uses special character sequences, known as control codes or character control sequences, to manipulate various aspects of the video screen and terminal. For example, these control codes can be used to accentuate various attributes of a screen's design, to change the cursor position, or to alter the color of the display.

Control character sequences

All of DOS's extended screen and keyboard control functions must be activated by using a special control code known as an escape character (ASCII 27). This escape character either can be typed at the keyboard or placed within a text file. Control codes that are preceded by an escape character are intercepted by the file ANSI.SYS. As mentioned earlier, the ANSI.SYS file, which must be resident in memory, contains the American National Standard Institute set of terminal codes for altering display attributes.

Changing display attributes

Control character sequences can be used to alter or enhance many attributes of the display. They can be used in screen design to make characters typed on the screen invisible; to make portions of the display screen blink, to increase the intensity of display characters, to reverse the video screen image, to underscore display characters, to set the cursor position, and to change the color of the screen foreground and/or background.

Using the ASCII extended character set

In addition to regular text characters (letters, numerals, etc.) and control character sequences, DOS text files may contain the ASCII (American Standard Code for Information Interchange) extended character set as well. These are ASCII symbols with numeric values from ASCII 128 through ASCII 255. These characters can be used to design professional-looking informational and menu-screens. A number of the ASCII extended character set values are intended specifically for border designs.

Characters forming the ASCII extended character set are entered into a text file by depressing the Alt key and typing the ASCII value *on the numeric keypad.* The most frequently used of these characters can be found in the ASCII Help screen on the accompanying disk.

DOS features behind the utilities

1. DOS has three essential system files that are sent to memory every time DOS is loaded. These files control the system's basic input and output, initialize the system, and serve as a file management system.
2. Formatting a disk divides it into tracks and sectors and establishes a directory and File Allocation Table (FAT). The directory contains an inventory of the disk. The FAT contains pointers to sectors where each file is stored.
3. DOS's subdirectory capabilities allow the user to hierarchically organize the directories and files on his or her disk.
4. DOS's commands can be entered interactively from the keyboard. Or DOS commands can be entered automatically in a batch mode through the creation of batch files.

5. DOS programs can be written that include special batch file commands with decision-making capabilities.
6. DOS programs are written as batch files. They must be written in ASCII format (using any text editor or EDLIN). They also must have the extension BAT.
7. DOS programs can be written with variables called "replaceable parameters." These variables permit the construction of generic batch file utilities.
8. Batch files are used to insulate the user from the operating system, to standardize certain routines, and to make a hard disk system more efficient and easier to use.
9. A configuration file (CONFIG.SYS) is created to tailor a computer's basic input and output system to the user's needs. It is used to activate the DOS device driver ANSI.SYS.
10. DEVICE= ANSI.SYS can be set in the configuration file. When the device driver ANSI.SYS is called, the user can gain far greater control over attributes of the video display. These attributes include the ability to alter the color of both the display foreground and background.
11. The ANSI.SYS device driver gives the user the ability to perform key reassignment functions. This is particularly useful for assigning specific routines to the function keys.
12. Control character sequences are used to manipulate various aspects of the display. An escape character precedes all character sequences for DOS's extended screen and keyboard control functions.
13. The ASCII extended character set (ASCII values 128 to 255) can be used for generating graphic designs. These characters are generated by holding down the <Alt > key and typing the ASCII value on the numeric keypad.

Advanced DOS

When it comes right down to it, hard disk management is simply knowing DOS. You can know DOS at two levels: that of the beginner and that of the advanced DOS user. The majority of computer users are beginners. They can COPY files, delete files, maybe pull a few tricks. But nothing more. This chapter is about advanced DOS, or "tricks," if you want to put it that way. It takes you from knowing basic DOS commands up to knowing nearly the full extent of what DOS can do.

The DOS environment

You've probably made a few assumptions about what environmental issues are: Don't litter your hard drive; create the right type of environment! Instead, the DOS environment is a scratch pad of sorts. It's a place in memory where DOS stores miscellaneous information.

If you're familiar with the way programming languages use variables, then you should easily understand the DOS environment. The DOS environment is where DOS stores variables. Variables are strings of text that DOS needs in order to function. In many cases the values are assigned by you.

If you're not familiar with a programming language, then consider the DOS environment as a place for storing special code words. Those words are assigned values, usually in the form of text. When you or DOS makes a reference to a code word kept in the environment, DOS substitutes the assigned value. The DOS environment is a form of storage and also a reference source for DOS and programs that use the environment.

Think of each special code word, or variable, as being stored like this:

```
NAME = what NAME represents
```

NAME is the name of the environment item. It's referred to as the environment variable. Think of "what NAME represents" as a string of characters represented by NAME. These characters are referred to as the variable's assignment, or parameter. Each part of the item, the variable name and parameter, is separated by an equals sign.

The items in the DOS environment

You can put whatever you want into the environment. Most often, information used by batch files is stored there. However, DOS uses the environment to store the following three things:

Environment Variable Name	Stores this information:
COMSPEC	the location of COMMAND.COM
PATH	the system's PATH
PROMPT	the DOS PROMPT

COMSPEC supplies the location of COMMAND.COM, one of the three basic programs that make up DOS. COMMAND.COM is, in fact, the program you see on the screen as DOS. Since this program always needs to be accessed-for example, when you return from applications software back to DOS-the location of COMMAND.COM is kept in the COMSPEC environment variable.

PATH refers to the system's search PATH—the subdirectories through which DOS will search for programs. Normally, PATH is set to nothing, meaning DOS looks only in the current subdirectory for the file you request. However, you can set it to list several popular subdirectories, allowing you to access the files in them without changing to that subdirectory.

PROMPT is a description of your DOS PROMPT. Unlike PATH, which is always present but which you may not ever declare, you must assign the PATH parameter;

DOS does not create it automatically. The PROMPT variable describes what your DOS PROMPT looks like; what color it is; whether or not it shows you the date, time, or currently logged directory; and so forth.

These three variables-COMSPEC, PATH, and PROMPT-can be altered by you, using the SET command which is covered in the next section. PATH and PROMPT can also be set by the PATH and PROMPT commands, respectively. Normally, when you turn the computer on, DOS assigns the location of COMMAND.COM to the COMSPEC variable and sets the PATH and PROMPT equal to nothing. It's up to you to set those variables to whatever you think will work best.

How to set environment variables

You can put variables into the environment. These variables might be used in a batch file program or by an applications program. They are created by using the SET command.

SET has two "faces." When you type SET and press ENTER, you see a list of environment variables used by your system. The second face of SET allows you to create an environment variable and assign it a string of characters.

Had you just started your computer, not set any environment variables, and entered SET, this would be what you'd see:

```
COMSPEC=C:\COMMAND.COM
  PATH=
```

The place for the PATH parameter is blank. PROMPT isn't shown unless you specify a PROMPT.

The sample that follows shows a few more variables.

```
COMSPEC=C:\COMMAND.COM
PROMPT=$P$G
PATH=C:\DOS;C:\BATCH;C:\UTIL
MASM=/V /Z
```

All three of the standards are there: COMSPEC, PROMPT, and PATH. The fourth variable is MASM. It's set to the string /V /Z. This variable is used by an assembly language program to set certain options. When the program,runs, it looks in the DOS environment for the MASM variable and then uses the options it finds there. You set that variable into the environment by using the second face of the SET command.

To create an environment variable, use the SET command in the following format:

```
SET variable=parameter
```

In the preceding, "variable" is the name of the environment variable you're creating. It can be upper -or lowercase, though DOS translates it to ALL CAPS when it puts it in the environment. The variable name can be as long as you like, though short descriptive names are always best. Also, use only letters and numbers in the name-no spaces.

In the equation, "parameter" is what the variable name should represent. All characters immediately after the equals sign and before you press ENTER are included: letters, numbers, spaces, symbols-everything.

Setting an environment variable

The purpose of this lab is to give you a realistic example of what it's like to set an environment variable. Place the data diskette in drive A of your computer. Boot the computer, using the diskette as the source of DOS. Enter the date and time.

1. At the PROMPT, type LAB51 and press ENTER.
2. You've just received a new application to install on your computer. It requires that you enter an environment variable that describes the location of the new application's main program. You know two things:
   a. The name of the variable you need to create is VANGUARD.
   b. The main program should be in the VAN subdirectory, which is in the BIN subdirectory in drive C.

   Enter the environment variable at the DOS PROMPT, using the SET command. Assign to the variable a parameter that indicates the location of the program, its full PATHname.
3. Type the SET command by itself to see a description of your computer's environment.
4. Press PRINT SCREEN to get a hard COPY of the screen display to document your work.
5. If possible, keep the diskette in the drive for the next lab.

Devices

DOS is a device-oriented operating system. It passes data between various devices. As long as DOS recognizes some part of the computer as a device, it can send data to the device or from it. What does this mean? It means that DOS is quite flexible in how it deals with data.

Common devices available to DOS

Device	*Device Name*	*Capable of*
Firs floppy drive	A	input ad output
First serial port	AUX	input and output
Second floppy drive	B	input and output
Hard drive	C	input and output
Cassette Tape	CAS	input and output

First serial port	COM1	input and output
Second serial port	COM2	input and output
Console	CON	input and output
First printer	LPT1	output only
Second printer	LPT2	output only
Null device	NUL	input and output
First printer	PRN	output only

What is a device?

A device is

- a peripheral or storage hardware
- capable of input, output, or both

The disk drive is the device that most people think of first. It is capable of input and output. DOS sends data to the disk drive for storage on the disk. DOS can also receive data from the disk drive.

The printer is an example of an output-only device. DOS can send data to the printer, but it cannot receive data back. However, all other devices are used for input and output. Yes, that means that DOS can treat a device, such as a serial port or the printer, just as it does a disk drive. You can actually "save" or "load" data to or from any device.

A special case is the CON device, the computer console. The console consists of your keyboard and monitor. When DOS accesses the console device for input, it gets the input from the keyboard. When DOS sends output to the console device, it sends it to the monitor.

DOS Devices

It's said that DOS is device-oriented, which means that DOS treats an devices in the same way. When you save a file on disk, you're really telling DOS to take all the characters in that file and send them to the disk device. Since all devices are treated alike, you can also send that file to the printer. This is done by specifying the printer device instead of a disk device. For example, if you specify PRN, DOS sends the file to the printer. If you specify CON, DOS sends the file to your monitor.

Devices can be specified in standard file manipulation commands. Say, for example, you want to print the contents of a text file. You type

```
C> COPY AUTOEXEC.BAT PRN ENTER
```

This command says "COPY the contents of the file AUTOEXEC.BAT by sending it to the PRN device." Note that the disk drive device is always implied unless another device is specified; the command could have been C> COPY AUTOEXEC.BAT ENTER. You don't need to specify a filename for a device other than a disk drive.

The console device (CON) is often specified in the COPY command to create little text files on disk quickly. Since the input part of the CON device is the keyboard, the net effect is that you can type directly to a file on disk. For example:

```
C> COPY CON MESSAGE.TXT ENTER
```

The preceding command means "COPY output from the CON device to a file named MESSAGE.TXT." DOS can even create MESSAGE.TXT in the current directory, placing the characters you enter at the keyboard into that file. All characters you type are put into the file, including the ENTER you use to end a line. To stop sending characters to MESSAGE.TXT, press CTRL-Z. CTRL-Z is the end-of-file marker according to DOS. After you tell DOS to end file MESSAGE.TXT, DOS quits COPYing and displays the DOS PROMPT.

CTRL-Z ENTER ends input from the CON device.

When the CON device is used for output, the output appears on the screen. For example, to display the contents of a file, you need only COPY it to the CON device:

```
C> COPY MESSAGE.TXT CON
```

This command means "COPY the contents of the file MESSAGE.TXT to the CON device." After pressing ENTER, you see the contents of that file. To stop the display or to cancel input from the CON device, press CTRL-BREAK. This halts the COPYing.

CTRL-BREAK cancels the COPY command.

You can COPY data between any two DOS devices. For example, the command

```
C> COPY CON PRN
```

means "COPY all data from the CON device to the PRN device." Each time you press ENTER to end a line of data, DOS sends the data to the printer. To stop sending data to the printer, press CTRL-Z and ENTER.

Remember that DOS can COPY data between devices, as well as specify devices other than the disk drives for output.

I/O Redirection

You now know that to DOS, all peripherals and storage hardware are devices. More important than memorizing the various device names and the tricks you can pull with the COPY command is knowing that, except for the printer, all devices are capable of input and output. Because of that fact, DOS can alter data in those devices and send it away to any other device.

I/O redirection is meddling with the places DOS normally gets input and sends output.

Standard input and output

DOS uses standard devices for input and output. There are three standard devices: one for input, one for output, and a special output device used to output error messages only. By maintaining a device for error messages only, DOS can output error messages on the screen, even if you redirect data output to some other device.

The standard input device is the keyboard. All DOS commands and PROMPTs "expect" input to come from the keyboard. The standard output device is the monitor. All DOS commands usually display their output on the monitor. So, it's proper to say that the CON device is the standard input and output device. All DOS commands receive their input from the CON device and send their output to the CON device. But, remembering that DOS is device-oriented, it's reasonable to assume that you can change this device.

Before moving on, note that most major applications—word processors, spreadsheets, databases, communications programs, and so forth—read input directly and write directly; most applications don't use DOS as a go-between. Why? Because DOS is just too slow. So, you cannot use I/O redirection with most major applications, only with DOS.

I/O redirection commands

There are two commands that redirect input from and redirect output away from the standard devices. They are: > and <.

Command	For
>	redirecting output
<	redirecting input

Another symbol, >>, is used to redirect output and append it to an indicated device.

Command	For
>>	redirecting output and appending it.

Note that it helps if You think of the symbols as arrows: > points to the output of a command; < points back to the command, redirecting input.

Redirecting output. Remember that, unless otherwise specified, the output of a DOS command heads straight for the standard output device, the console. For example:

```
C> TYPE TINA.TXT
```

causes the file TINA.TXT to be typed to the standard output device. In effect, the command is the same as:

```
C> COPY TINA.TXT CON
```

However, the TYPE command is designed to deal directly with the CON device-unless you tell DOS to do otherwise with the output redirection symbol,

```
C> TYPE TINA.TXT > PRN
```

This command sends output to the printer instead of the CON device. It means "Type the contents of the file TINA.TXT, redirecting the output to the PRN device." Yes, the TYPE command still functions. You've only changed the destination of the output from the standard device to a new device, the printer.

Here's another example:

```
C> DIR > PRN
```

The DIR command, like all DOS commands, usually sends its output to the CON device. However, the output redirection symbol in the preceding example routes the output of the DIR command to the printer instead. The result is a hard COPY of your directory listing.

How about this:

```
C> DIR > DIRTXT
```

What do you suppose this command does? Yes, it redirects the output of the DIR command-but to where? Since DIRTXT isn't the name of a device, DOS assumes that it's a filename. After you enter the preceding command, DOS creates a file named DIRTXT in the current directory. In that file is the output of the DIR command. All DOS commands and all the programs that use DOS to output to the standard output device can have their output redirected by the output redirection symbol, >.

Redirecting and appending output. When you use > to redirect output to a file, DOS creates the file. If the file already exists, DOS overwrites the file so it contains the new data. But, sometimes, you do not want this to happen. In those instances you can use >> to redirect output and append it to the end of an existing file. Consider

```
C> DIR >> DIRTXT
```

The preceding command sends the output of the DIR command to a file on disk named DIRTXT. If DIRTXT doesn't exist, DOS creates it. If it does exist, DOS appends the output of DIR to that file.

Note that the >> symbol has significance only for the disk drive devices. Appending output to the console or printer device doesn't really make much sense.

Redirecting input. Redirecting input is a little bit trickier than redirecting output. When you redirect output, you redirect the result of a DOS command. When you redirect input, you're supplying all the keystrokes for a DOS program. If you miss a keystroke or something happens that you don't anticipate, DOS continues to look for the keystrokes from the input device you specified not the console. The net effect may be that your system locks up, or hangs. This brings up an important note about redirecting input: Know *what the program needs as input before you redirect input.* Because of the potential for system lock, redirecting input is rarely done.

Suppose you want to use redirection to provide input for the DOS command TIME, which is used to set the time on your computer. To do this, you must take two steps. First, you must create a file on disk to be used as input. Normally, input comes from the keyboard. In this case, however, you want to have DOS obtain input from a file. Second, you must enter the DOS command along with the input redirection symbol and the name of the file that contains the keystrokes. Remember, if the input isn't keyed just right, you could loose control of the computer.

Here's how it's done.

1. Create the file to hold the input. In this case, the input will be only Create the file by using the COPY command:

   ```
   C> COPY CON INPUT ENTER
   ENTER
   ```

   Then signal the end of the file by using the end-of-file marker, CTRL-Z.

   ```
   CTRL-Z ENTER
   ```

   The computer responds by displaying

   I File(s) copied

2. Now that ENTER is in a file on disk, tell the computer to get the input for the TIME command from the file by typing

   ```
   C>TIME < INPUT ENTER
   ```

   This instructs DOS to execute the TIME command, but accept input from the INPUT file on disk-not the keyboard. After pressing ENTER you'll see the following:

   ```
   Current time IS 12:59:20.96
   Enter new time:
   C>
   ```

   DOS accepted the ENTER from the file INPUT and placed it after "Enter new time:". You have, in effect, chosen not to reset the computer's internal clock.

There are several circumstances in which you can use input redirection, so don't write it off as something too scary to bother with. For example, some programs are modified by using the DEBUG program and input redirection. A programmer places in a file all the keystrokes needed to modify the program. All you do to modify the program is to use < to input the new keystrokes.

Filter programs

A filter is a special type of program. Its purpose is to check or modify data passed between two devices. Since DOS *deals with data* on a character-by-character basis, a filter program simply intercepts characters, checks and possibly modifies them, then sends them along.

Filter programs are unique in that they require input and provide modified output. You don't run them like normal programs. Instead, you use DOS to supply the input and then send the output to the standard output device or direct it some place else.

DOS includes three filters: SORT, MORE, and FIND. The SORT filter is used to sort a text file. The input is the contents of a text file. The output is the same text sorted alphabetically in ascending or desending order or according to other options of the SORT filter.

The MORE filter is used to stop the output of a long display. For example, when you type a document in DOS, it usually scrolls on up the screen without stopping. To cause the output to pause, you must press CTRL-S. However, if you send the output of the TYPE command through the MORE filter, it automatically pauses every 24 lines, giving you a full screen to look at before pressing any key to continue. The FIND filter is used to locate text within a text file or to find text in the output of some DOS command. FIND locates *the text,* displaying the line on which it appears.

A computer user may add other filters. For example, I've written a filter that adds line feeds to text files that don't have them. But SORT, MORE, and FIND all come with DOS. And remember that all filters work on the same principle: They intercept output, check or modify it, and then pass it along.

The hard part about understanding what filters do is remembering that they need input to function. Input is supplied by output from a DOS command. This output is provided primarily via the pipe, but it can be provided by output redirection. For example:

```
C> MORE < TEXTFILE
```

The preceding example uses the MORE filter. The input for the MORE filter comes from the text in the file TEXTFILE. The input redirection symbol, <, establishes TEXTFILE as the input. This isn't the normal way things happen with filters, but it does show how input is provided for the filter. The net effect is that the contents of TEXTFILE are displayed on the screen, but the MORE filter stops the output every 24 lines, displaying "MORE" and waiting for you to press any key to continue.

Pipes

The pipe symbol is the vertical bar, |. On some displays it may have a small gap between the upper and lower parts of the bar. Other displays may show it as a solid vertical line. A pipe directs the output of a DOS command through a filter. Remember, a filter requires input. You can provide that input by using input redirection. For example, suppose you want to use the filter SORT on the output of the command DIR. You type

```
C> SORT < DIR ENTER
```

In this case, DOS looks for a file named DIR to use as input for the SORT filter. The DIR file is not the DIR command. Next you type

```
C> DIR > SORT ENTER
```

In this case, DOS sends the output of the DIR command to a file it names SORT. That still doesn't cut it.

To achieve your purpose, you must use a pipe to send output from a DOS command directly through the filter. The needed command is

```
C> DIR | SORT
```

which means, "Read a directory of the disk and pipe (1) its output through the SORT filter." The output still goes to the standard output device. You may see something like the following:

```
9 FILE(S) 18870272 BYTES FREE
DIRECTORY OF C:\
VOLUME IN DRIVE C IS TOO LOUD
AUTOEXEC  BAT        864      7-21-89     2:59P
COM             <DIR>         9-24-88     6:16P
CONFIG          SYS    156   11-07-88    10:48P
GRAPHICS         <DIR>        9-25-88    11:26A
MISC             <DIR>        9-28-88    11:37P
SYSTEM           <DIR>        9-24-88    12:49A
TEMP             <DIR>        9-24-88    12:26P
```

The display shows a sorted directory listing. Even the drive name, volume, and directory statistics are sorted.

You can further use I/O redirection to send the output to a file or to the printer

```
C>DIR | SORT > PRN
```

The pipe simply takes the output of the DOS command and pumps it through a filter. Here's another example:

```
C> TYPE FILENAME | MORE
```

This pipe takes the output of the TYPE command and pumps it through MORE filter

Practical application of advanced DOS concepts

All the examples in this chapter involved the command line. By typing in the command fine the command associated with the advanced DOS concept, you can enhance efficiency and convenience.

Batch files are programs that you can write in DOS. They consist of lines of DOS commands, one listed after another in a text file. The text file has the extension BAT, which tells DOS that it's a batch file. When you type the name of the batch file, DOS reads each line of the batch file, executing that line as if you had typed it at the command PROMPT.

The advantage batch files is that they make doing repetitive things easier. For example, if you always type the same three commands to start your word processor, you can put them into a batch file. Then you simply type the name of the batch file at the command PROMPT. DOS executes those three lines for you.

DOS allows itself to be customized in a number of manners, allowing you to make the system look and behave exactly as you see fit. Since each user is different and each system must meet different needs, configuring your system is all part of hard disk management. This chapter is about configuring your system. It covers background information about how DOS sets itself up and then goes into detail about how you can modify and augment that setup. There are three topics to cover:

- how DOS starts
- CONFIG.SYS
- AUTOEXEC.BAT

The first topic concerns what happens to get a PC up and running. The other two relate to configuration programs you can use to customize DOS.

How DOS gets up in the morning

When you turn your computer on, you're setting into motion a chain of events. These events end with your computer up and running, with the sunshiny face of DOS greeting you and with the ugly command prompt. But everything starts when you flip the switch to the "on" position.

There are seven steps to getting your computer ready to use:

1. the system ROM BIOS check
2. disk bootstrapping
3. the loading of IBMBIO.COM (or 10. SYS)
4. the loading of the DOS kernel, IBMDOS.COM (or MSDOS.SYS)
5. system configuration (CONFIG.SYS)
6. the loading of the command interpreter (COMMAND.COM)
7. execution of an AUTOEXEC.BAT file, if found

   Of the seven steps, you have direct control over two: system configuration and execution of AUTOEXEC.BAT. Continue reading to get an overview of what happens in each step.

The ROM BIOS check

When your computer is turned on, power rushes through all the circuits, including the microprocessor. When Intel designed the microprocessor, it designed it with a kick-start mechanism, a built-in method of automatically getting the computer off and running. Your PC microprocessor is set up to run the routines stored in your computer's BIOS.

BIOS is the "guts" of the PC. It's also called ROM or, sometimes, ROM BIOS. It provides the low-level interfaces to the PC's hardware, controls the video, reads the keyboard, and does other "primitive" functions. One BIOS function is to do a memory check and make a list of everything in the computer. BIOS does this when you boot the system. The BIOS routine ends by looking for a diskette in either drive A or drive C. If a diskette is found, then the bootstrapping step takes place. Otherwise, an error message is displayed on the screen.

Bootstrapping

In bootstrapping, BIOS reads the first 512 bytes from a disk, either in drive A or drive C. Those 512 -bytes contain a program. If the disk is a DOS disk, then the program loads another chunk of data from the disk and executes it as a program. If the disk isn't a DOS disk, then the 512byte program does one thing: It causes displays of a message telling you that the disk is a "non-DOS" or "non-System" diskette.

This method of starting by loading a tiny chunk of data from disk is referred to as bootstrapping. Figuratively speaking, the computer is pulling itself up by its bootstraps. If the first 512 bytes BIOS loads from disk are DOS, BIOS loads another, larger portion. That portion contains a program that looks for the DOS program IBMBIO.COM on disk.

This section refers to the PC-DOS files IBMBIO.COM and IBMDOS.COM. If you're using MS-DOS, the files are named IO.SYS and MSDOS.SYS, respectively. Whether PC-DOS or MS-DOS, the files serve the same purpose.

Loading DOS's BIOS

If the bootstrapping is successful, the program IBMBIO.COM is loaded from disk and executed IBMBIO.COM does two things.

First, it's responsible for the low-level interaction between DOS and your computer's hardware. For example, if you made an IBM-compatible PC and wanted Microsoft Corporation to write you a custom version of DOS, Microsoft would customize IBMBIO.COM to your system's specific hardware.

Second, IBMBIO.COM initiates a series of programs referred to under the general title of SYSINIT. These programs do various housekeeping duties, all related to getting your system up and running. One of the main functions of SYSINIT is to load and execute the second DOS program from disk, IBMDOS.C0M.

The DOS Kernel

IBMDOS.COM is the main part of DOS. It's the DOS kernel, the main core of routines that manage files on disk; control memory; and deal with DOS input and output, the environment, and all the basic stuff.

Once the kernel, IBMDOS.COM, is loaded, the SYSINIT program looks for a file named CONFIG.SYS in the root directory of the disk you're using for booting. If found, SYSINIT reads CONFIG.SYS and performs whatever duties are outlined there. Otherwise, SYSINIT looks for the file COMMAND.COM in your root directory.

System Configuration

If the root directory of your boot disk contains the file CONFIG.SYS, SYSINIT reads and executes the commands in the file. CONFIG.SYS contains two types of commands: The first sets up the DOS environment, telling how many buffers it can have, how to deal with certain types of files, and so on. The second part of CONFIG.SYS loads special programs called drivers. These are programs, but they're special in that they actually become a part of DOS, directly affecting the way DOS functions.

The command interpreter

SYSINIT finishes its job by loading and running the DOS command interpreter, COMMAND.COM. At this point SYSINIT stops running and COMMAND.COM takes control of your computer, presenting itself as DOS.

COMMAND.COM is normally found in the boot disk's root directory. However, you can use a command in the CONFIG.SYS file to place it else-where-even to rename it or use another command interpreter.

COMMAND.COM is called the command interpreter because it's the part of DOS into which you issue commands; it's the part of DOS you see when you use your computer. This is why, if COMMAND.COM isn't found, your system won't boot. With SYSINIT's dying breath, you'll see a message such as "Bad or missing command interpreter."

Execution of AUTOEXEC.BAT

COMMAND.COM is set up to look for a file named AUTOEXEC.BAT and execute the commands in that batch file if it's found. Note that, unlike COMMAND.COM, AUTOEXEC.BAT must be in your root directory.

AUTOEXEC.BAT is the last file executed in the startup process. It's also one of the two files you have direct control over. You can do a number of things with AUTOEXEC.BAT: configure your system, set the clock, set various modes, and run your own startup programs.

Once AUTOEXEC.BAT is done, you're sitting at the ugly ol' C> prompt and COMMAND.COM is awaiting your input.

Now that you've been introduced to the startup process as a whole, consider in detail the two files you can affect: CONFIG.SYS and AUTOEXEC.BAT.

CONFIG.SYS

CONFIG.SYS is a text file on disk. You create it by using a word processor or text editor and saving the file's contents in text, ASCII, format. The computer reads the contents of CONFIG.SYS when it boots, setting various elements of your system accordingly.

When it comes to CONFIG.SYS, you should know

- its purpose
- the associated configuration commands
- the associated device drivers

The purpose of CONFIG.SYS

The purpose of CONFIG.SYS is to set certain options for DOS and to load special programs that modify and customize your system. Basically, CONFIG.SYS does two things: It establishes the way DOS uses the system and loads device drivers.

CONFIG.SYS is the only sanctioned way you can get control over some of the primary aspects of DOS. Using CONFIG.SYS, you can tell DOS how much memory to set aside for dealing with files, set certain disk options, and control how DOS interacts with various parts of the computer.

Using CONFIG.SYS you can also load device drivers. These modify the way the computer behaves, giving direct control over the screen, setting aside memory for a RAM disk drive, controlling external devices such as mice and scanners, and controlling expanded memory in your system.

Before moving into the details, note that what you put into CONFIG.SYS becomes part of your computer's operating system. If you change CONFIG.SYS by adding new items, changing items, or removing items, you must also reset your computer. You must reboot your computer after changes to CONFIG.SYS.

The CONFIG.SYS Commands

Command	*Function/Comments*
BREAK	monitors the CTRL-Break key to cancel certain commands
BUFFERS	sets aside space for file I/O
COUNTRY	sets date, time, and currency formatting
DEVICE	loads a device driver
FCBS	controls the number of open files (used with file sharing)
FILES	allows you to set the maximum number of files that DOS can have open at one time.
INSTALL	runs and loads a memory-resident program (DOS 4 only)
LASTDRIVE	determines the highest drive letter allowed in your system (used for the SUBST command, network computers, etc).

REM	allow you to use REM to insert comments in to the CONFIG.SYS file (DOS 4.0 only)
SHELL	specifies the location of the DOS command interpreter or the location and name of an alternative command interpreter
STACKS	sets the space required for DOS stack storage
SWITCHES	allow programs that can't deal with extended keyboard functions to be more compatible

Configuration commands

There are only 12 commands used by the CONFIG.SYS file. Careful and appropriate use of these commands will give you a computer that runs at optimum performance.

You don't need to use all these commands. In fact, with the typical system, you'll use maybe six at the most. The commands you'll use most often in the CONFIG.SYS file are BREAK, BUFFER, DEVICE, and FILES.

BREAK

The BREAK command controls how DOS interprets the keystroke combination CTRL-BREAK. It's followed by an equals sign and either the ON or OFF determining how you want DOS and applications to interpret CTRL-BREAK

Normally, when you press CTRL-BREAK during the execution of any DOS command, it halts the command, returning you to the DOS prompt However, CTRL-BREAK can also act on some applications programs. If you set BREAK to ON in CONFIG.SYS, CTRL-BREAK stops those applications also. Setting BREAK to OFF causes the computer to ignore CTRL-BREAK. Normally, BREAK is set to OFF.

DOS also offers a BREAK command you can use to set BREAK to ON or OFF at the command prompt.

BUFFERS

BUFFERS is one of two most common commands that find the way into CONFIG.SYS files. What BUFFERS does is to set the number of file buffers DOS uses. You follow the BUFFERS command in your CONFIG.SYS file with an equals sign and the number of buffers you want. For example:

```
BUFFERS=15
```

The preceding command sets aside space in memory for 15 buffers for use by DOS in file input/output. Normally, BUFFERS is set to the value 15, which is appropriate for most applications. If your system has less than 512K, set BUFFERS to 10 or less.

If you're using a database program or an application that needs to have several files open at a time, then the higher the BUFFERS value, the better. As a rule of thumb, if you have the memory, set BUFFERS equal to 32.

FILES

The command FILES lets DOS know how many files to keep open at a time. As with BUFFERS, the FILES command is followed by an equals sign and a value. The value indicates the maximum number of files you want to have open at a time. For example:

```
FILES = 15
```

Normally, if you don't include a FILES command in your CONFIG.SYS file, DOS sets the value to 8. The number is rather deceptive because five of those file values are used for standard 1/0 and other devices preset in DOS. So, a value of 8 really means you can have only three files open at a time.

Most users set the FILES value to 20 or more. Some database programs request that you set it to 32. Since each value above 8 takes up only 48 bytes, there's no sense in not listing a value over 20. I personally recommend

```
FILES =40
```

a command that practically guarantees you'll never run into an error message like "Too many files are open."

DEVICE

The command DEVICE is the third most popular CONFIG.SYS command. It's used to load a device driver into low-level memory. The device driver either modifies the way part of your computer behaves or gives you control over an extra peripheral. The format of the DEVICE command is

```
DEVICE = PATHNAME
```

in which "pathname" is the full pathname of a device driver. When SYSINIT encounters a DEVICE command in CONFIG.SYS, it locates that device and loads it into memory, executing the device driver's code.

DOS comes with about half a dozen device drivers. Additional device drivers are available commercially, generally when you purchase some type of hardware that requires them. Note that all device drivers end with the extension SYS.

Other commands

Two additional commands that you may see in the CONFIG.SYS file are COUNTRY and SHELL. The COUNTRY command allows you to use DOS in an environment that does not use American-English. For example, if you want the date to be day/month/year instead of month/day/year or the currency symbol to refer to the British pound instead of the American dollar, then use COUNTRY to specify formatting. For example:

```
COUNTRY=033,863
```

The preceding command, when found by DOS in CONFIG.SYS, sets up the computer to operate a *la francaise.* The date and time will be in the French format and the currency symbol will be for francs. If a COUNTRY command isn't, specified in

CONFIG.SYS, then DOS assumes you want to speak American. The SHELL command is used in two ways. First, it allows you to Specify a location other than the root directory for COMMAND.COM. Second, it allows you to specify a command interpreter besides COMMAND.COM. The following is an example:

```
SHELL = C:\DOS\COMMAND.COM /P
```

tells DOS to load COMMAND.COM in the DOS subdirectory. Note that if you use the preceding command, you must set the COMSPEC environment variable to indicate the proper location of COMMAND.COM. For example:

```
SET COMSPEC = C:\DOS\COMMAND.COM
```

Unless the SHELL command is in your CONFIG.SYS file, DOS loads COMMAND.COM in your boot disk's root directory.

Device drivers

As you know, DEVICE loads device drivers into low-level memory, adding extra capability to your system. The most common device driver loaded in CONFIG.SYS is the ANSI.SYS screen driver. It gives extra control of your display and keyboard to certain DOS commands. The ANSI.SYS driver allows you to have color in DOS commands, to manipulate the location of the cursor, and even to assign values to the function keys.

To load the ANSI.SYS, use the DEVICE command in CONFIG.SYS. For example:

```
DEVICE = C:\DOS\ANSI.SYS
```

Note that the full pathname is specified. When SYSINIT executes the preceding command, it loads the ANSI.SYS driver found in the DOS subdirectory. After that, you can use the ANSI commands to control the screen display or modify the keyboard.

Another common device driver is MOUSE.SYS, which is used with most of the electronic mouse devices you can buy for your computer. For example:

```
DEVICE = C:\MOUSE\MOUSE.SYS
```

loads the MOUSE.SYS driver into memory. Note that most mouse drivers come in two "flavors": MOUSE.COM and MOUSE.SYS. The MOUSE.COM program is a memory-resident program. MOUSE.SYS is a device driver. It's better to load the device driver, primarily because DOS 'puts it in low-level memory, where it is more effective. Also, since it's a part of your CONFIG.SYS file, it will always be loaded each time you start the computer. MOUSE.SYS comes with the mouse hardware, not DOS.

The most popular of these, after ANSI.SYS, is VDISK.SYS. VDISK.SYS sets aside part of your computer's RAM for use as an electronic disk drive. What's the advantage? Electronic drives, or RAM disks, are much faster that traditional mechanical disks. By performing certain disk-intensive operations on a RAM disk, you can really move through a pile of work.

Note that two SYS files that come with DOS, KEYBOARD.SYS and COUNTRY.SYS, are not device drivers. You shouldn't use them as such or you may damage your system.

Dos drivers offered by dos 4

Device Driver	Function
ANSI.SYS	controls the display and keyboard
DISPLAY.SYS	allows laptops and EGA monitors to display foreign language character set
DRIVER.SYS	drives
PRINTER.SYS	modifies the printer the way DISPLAY.SYS modifies an EGA display
VDISK.SYS	sets up a RAM drive
XMAEM.SYS	allows you to change the extended memory of an IBM PC AT into expanded memory
XMA2EMS.SYS	controls expanded memory and allows certain DOS commands to take advantage of that memory

AUTOEXEC.BAT

AUTOEXEC.BAT is a text file on disk. Because it has the BAT extension, DOS treats it as a batch file, executing each line of the file as if it were typed at the command prompt. Since AUTOEXEC.BAT is the last program in the chain that starts your computer and one you have direct control over—it's a pretty good place to continue determining how your system operates.

AUTOEXEC.BAT sets up your system when you turn the computer on. It can set environment variables and run startup programs—all automatically, when your computer starts.

AUTOEXEC.BAT is a batch file, which means it contains a series of commands you could type on the DOS command line. In fact, DOS executes each line of the AUTOEXEC.BAT file just as if you had typed it on the command line. Amazingly enough, though AUTOEXEC.BAT is the most important batch file in your system, it's usually the one with the fewest number of tricks in it.

The average DOS user usually uses AUTOEXEC.BAT to

- configure the system
- configure the environment
- load startup programs
- run applications

System Configuration

Configuring the system with AUTOEXEC.BAT file is different from doing it with

CONFIG.SYS. With AUTOEXEC.BAT you can enter commands you'd normally issue from DOS. Usually, you must perform three tasks to configure your system:

- set the system clock
- set the screen mode
- set the printer

Setting the system clock involves telling DOS the date and time. DOS needs this information to time-stamp the files you create on disk. The TIME and DATE commands are used to set the time and date, respectively. If you omit an AUTOEXEC.BAT file, DOS automatically asks you for the time and date.

Nearly every PC sold today comes with an internal clock. The IBM PC AT and compatible systems have a built-in automatic clock. The date and time are preset on those systems. Other PCs have internal clocks that come with clock-setting software. It's that type of program that you run in AUTOEXEC.BAT to set the time and date for DOS. The users of AT systems need not bother with setting the clock.

You must set the screen mode if your system uses two types of monitors. The DOS command MODE is used to determine which monitor is to be used as the startup monitor. On single-monitor systems, MODE can be used to establish the screen mode.

You might want to use additional commands to set the screen mode. For example, if you have an EGA or VGA monitor, you may want to set the multiline options. For Hercules monochrome monitors, you may want to issue the command that uses the Hercules Graphics Card to its full capacity. Or you may want to run a program diat allows your color monitor to display DOS in color.

You must set up the printer only if the device is a serial printer, plotter, and laser printer. If you're using a serial printer connected to the COM1. port, you must issue the following MODE command to make that printer work as the PRN device:

```
MODE COM1:9600,N,8,1
MODE LPT1=COM1
```

The first MODE command sets the serial port to 9,600 bits per second (bps), no parity, 8 bits, 1 stop bit. The second MODE command assigns LPTI to the first serial port. This allows you to use a serial printer as your fast printer.

Environment Configuration

Your system's AUTOEXEC.BAT file is the place where you can set certain *environment variables,* Those variables can be for the system or for certain applications. Since they're being set in the AUTOEXEC.BAT file, you won't have to type them in later; everything will be set as the computer starts.

There are three environment items that you normally set in AUTOEXEC.BAT'

- search path
- system prompt
- SET application and other environment variables

Setting a path

Setting a search path is one of the most important things AUTOEXEC.BAT can,,', do. The search path is a list of drives and subdirectories where you want DOS to look for files.

Normally, DOS looks only in the current directory. However, if a PATH variable exists in the environment, DOS examines the subdirectories listed, looking for files there as well. Only after DOS has exhausted all those possibilities do you see the "Bad command or filename" message.

To set a path you can use the PATH or SET commands. The format of the PATH command is

```
PATH = pathname;pathname;.......
```

in which "pathname" is the full name of a subdirectory you wish DOS to scan for files. If you want to list more than one subdirectory, separate each with a semicolon. You can list as many subdirectories as will fit on one line in DOS, about 127 characters. But you really don't want to list any more than three subdirectories: Remember, DOS scans through each one for files. If you type BLECH and press ENTER, DOS looks for BLECH.COM, BLECH.EXE, and BLECH.BAT in the current subdirectory, then in every subdirectory listed in the path. If you have several subdirectories listed, it can take quite a while for DOS to figure out the file doesn't exist.

The format of the SET command is

```
SET PATH = pathname;pathname
```

PATH is the preferred command. If you enter PATH at the DOS prompt,

```
C> PATH ENTER
```

the current path is displayed:

If you want to reset the path to nothing, just enter PATH followed by a single semicolon and ENTER

```
C> PATH;
```

PATH should always list subdirectories that contain the programs you use the most. Since nearly every subdirectory will have program files in it, it's up to you to decide which subdirectories you use all the time and which you want to be able to access from anywhere on the disk. Most often these include

- the DOS subdirectory (which is nearly always listed first)
- utility subdirectory

- subdirectory containing batch files that run other programs
- subdirectories that contain programs you use most often: word processors, spreadsheets, databases, integrated software, menu programs, and so on.

Remember to be frugal with the path. The shorter the path, the fewer subdirectories listed, the better. Also, remember to include drive letters so you can access the subdirectories from other disk drivers.

Setting the system prompt

Next to PATH the most common command in AUTOEXEC.BAT is PROMPT. The PROMPT command is used to set your system prompt, tile way the DOS Prompt appears. Yes, you aren't limited to the boring old C> prompt.

The format of the PROMPT command is

```
PROMPT = commands
```

Commands to use with prompt

PROMPT Command	Displays
$$	the dollar sign character, $
$b	the pipe character, |
$d	the current date
$e	nothing; it's a special escape character prefix
$g	the greater-than symbol, >
$h	nothing; it backspaces and erases the previous character
$l	the less-than symbol, <
$n	the current disk drive letter
$p	the full pathname of the currently logged drive and directory
$q	the equals sign character,=
$t	the current time
$v	the version of DOS
$_	nothing; the carriage return character

in which "commands" are special characters and normal text characters used to define your system prompt. As with PATH, you can use SET to set the system prompt:

```
SET PROMPT = commands
```

However, unlike PATH, entering PROMPT on the command line resets the PROMPT back to nothing.

Note that each command is prefixed by a dollar sign. Any other character you specify with the PROMPT command becomes part of the system prompt.

The most common PROMPT set in the AUTOEXEC.BAT file is

```
PROMPT = $P$G
```

which sets the prompt to the full pathnarne ($p) and the greaterthan symbol (>) For example:

```
C:\SYSTEM\DOS>
```

This way, you don't need to type CD all the time to get the current directory.

Another popular PROMPT command is

```
PROMPT = $T$_$D$_$P$G
```

which sets the prompt to the current time ($d) and, on a new line ($), displays the current date ($d). On another new line ($_) the current path ($p) is displayed along with the greater than symbol ($g). The resulting display looks like this:

```
05:47:00.00
WED 101988
C:\WP\DATA>
```

The time and date are frozen once the prompt is displayed; DOS does not automatically update it on your screen. Only by pressing ENTER or having DOS redisplay the prompt can you see the current date and time.

The PROMPT command $e is the escape character. It's primary purpose is to enter ANSI commands into die DOS prompt. ANSI commands can add color to the prompt or move the cursor around the display.

Setting other environment variables

There are environment variables you can set in Your AUTOEXEC.BAT file aside from those you set with PATH and PROMPT. These could be variables for applications programs or environment variables you'll use in batch files.

For example, suppose the program FOOFY.EXE is in the SMURF subdirectory of MISC. FOOFY requires an environment variable, FOOF, that gives the location of FOOFY.EXE's home directory. The command

```
SET FOOF=C:\MISC\SMURF
```

in AUTOEXEC.BAT does the job for you. In the same way you can set any environment variables required by your applications.

Another important environment variable you may have to set is COMSPEC. COMSPEC gives the location of COMMAND.COM in your system. However, if you've moved COMMAND.COM by using the SHELL command in your CONFIG.SYS file, then you need to specify its location in the environment. To do this, use the SET command in AUTOEXEC.BAT to set the proper location of COMMAND.COM.

```
SET COMSPEC=C:\DOS
```

Once COMSPEC is set in this manner, your system can operate as normal.

Otherwise, you may receive the message "Bad or missing COMMAND.COM" or "Insert system disk into Drive C."

Startup applications

AUTOEXEC.BAT can also be used to load special startup Programs that is, applications you always want to start before you run any other program on your system, and utilities. There are three types of startup applications:

- memory-resident software
- non-SYS device drivers
- utility programs

Memory-resident software includes programs such as pop-up calculators, notepads, and alarm clocks. These Programs load into memory and stay there. You can then activate them by pressing a special key combination or, in the case of clock displays, they may always appear on the screen. The only drawback to these programs is that they eat up a lot of memory and some of them don't work right in all situations.

Certain device drivers can also be loaded by using AUTOEXEC.BAT. For example, AUTOEXEC.BAT allows you to load and set up drivers that control a mouse or change part of memory into a RAM disk drive or a printer spooler.

A startup utility program is a program you run each time you start your system. For example, you may want to run a program that checks the disk for corrupted files. Or a program that backs up your files in case you accidentally delete any.

A startup utility program may also be DOS commands in your AUTOEXEC.BAT file. The commands may copy files from one directory to your RAM drive. Or they may back up certain applications, move files around, or delete files from JUNK and BACKUP subdirectories. Remember, AUTOEXEC.BAT is a batch file and you can put any commands into it that you would normally issue under DOS.

5

Documentation

Documentation is the essential element for defining user-oriented software systems and providing independence from the original authors. A major source of software problems arises when users associate "comments in the code" with documentation.

The documentation standards defined in this chapter cover the external documentation library defined within the software product. This dichotomy is essential to the software design process that is embodied in evolving the layers of detail that make up the external documentation library. The software documentation standards offered here provide a framework to support a highly structured approach to the design, construction, support, and use of a software product over its lifecycle. The purpose of a documentation standard is to aid software developers in providing clear and concise descriptions of the system and of individual programs as they relate to the end user, operating personnel, and persons who must technically support the, system. In particular, a documentation standard should be aimed at producing the following attributes in a documentation library:

- Providing a clear understanding between user and developer about what the system will do before detailed software design
- Providing a clear understanding between designers and programmers about what the program modules will do before coding
- Allowing the end user to initiate requests and interpret outputs without the aid of a computer technician
- Allowing operators to execute instruction from the end user without the aid of an analyst or programmer
- Allowing the system to be supported or enhanced independent of the original authors
- Allowing other programs or systems to be integrated without assistance from the original authors

It is important to observe that software development support typically requires that a large portion of man-hours be spent clarifying how processes are invoked, how they work, and how they interact with other processes in the system. Experience has demonstrated that understanding can be gained most quickly by reading well-structured documents in plain English, annotated with good diagrams and tables. Nothing is more time consuming and frustrating than trying to derive such information from program listings. Program listings cannot be organized in a hierarchical structure and don't lend themselves to descriptive writing that can be supplemented with pictures. Internal program documentation should be limited to comments that explain unreadable source code and change history. All higher level documentation must reside in the external documentation library.

The documentation library for a particular application must be self-contained to the maximum extent possible. It should not refer to other documentation except when disjoint from the application. In particular, it should contain the detailed description of the entire database that it references. Because this standard is concerned with large user-oriented systems and because these generally are database oriented, it is convenient to organize the documentation with direct access to the database. In many cases, it is similarly convenient to have direct access to human readable output formats, communications formats, and input formats, so this material also must be provided. Incorporating these items into separate documents within an overall library results in the following advantages:

- The assigning of identical common names and descriptions within each program to all external program references
- The elimination of redundant descriptions of identical data from individual program documentation via a symbolic file/record reference system or a similar heirarchical structure
- Ease of considering any changes to the database structure in light of how they affect the total system
- The availability of a simple procedure for ensuring that any database changes are properly reflected throughout the system
- Availability of the complete database description in one condensed document for handy reference

For the purpose of instructing and guiding the user, or as an aid to gaining a clear understanding of the system, it is generally convenient to break the software into functional parts. In many software systems, particularly interactive systems in which the user is on-line to the database, the software functional structure is very different from the functional structure that a user sees. For example, in a word processing system, the user may want to insert text into an existing paragraph. The user's manual would describe the insert function from a user's standpoint. The structure of the software functions that must be implemented to perform the insert function (for example, reading the keyboard, controlling the screen, updating the data files) bears little resemblance to the structure of the insert function the user perceives.

When designing or supporting software, one must be able to translate easily from user functions to software functions, particularly when tracing problems. A convenient rule to establish for fault isolation is that a subprogram will not span (perform) more than one major software function. In fact, many subprograms may be used to perform one software function. In these cases it will be convenient to break each function into subfunctions that correspond to subprograms or groups of subprograms. When subprograms are used in more than one subfunction, they will be termed utility programs and combined under a separate utilities section. In such cases the subfunction can be defined by specifying its external references to the corresponding utility and by referring to the utility subfunction for further detail.

External documentation outline

The following items make up the external documentation library. Brief explanations accompany each.

Operating procedures documents

User's manual. This is the most important item in the documentation set, it completely defines the system from a user functional standpoint, with the aid of the human interface document. It should provide sufficient instruction so that the user can use (or direct operators to use) the system and interpret output without the aid of a computer technician.

Operating procedures manual. This manual should instruct the operator on the interpretation of directions from the user and should describe the corresponding procedures to be followed so that operations can be performed without assistance from an analyst or programmer. In some applications the end user and operator may be the same person, in which case the user and operating manuals can be combined.

Technical support documents

System overview. This document provides the road map to all of the software functions in the system. The overview can be accomplished using software functional block diagrams, modified HIPO diagrams, and brief narrative descriptions of all of the software functions in the system. When the user functional specifications are complete, the system overview can be used as the top-level software design document.

Program descriptions. These must contain descriptions of the individual subsystems, with corresponding programs in sufficient detail to allow modification or enhancement of the system without assistance from the original authors. These descriptions also contain the details of each utility used in the system and the details of standard procedures that are incorporated into more than one subfunction.

Interface documents

Human interface specifications. This document depicts the visible output and input formats in a form that should closely resemble the display format, or provide a good visual likeness. It should contain a sample for each format, with references to specify display formats or provide all display information directly on the sample.

Database specifications. This document describes all internal (intraprogram) and external (interprogram) databases in a hierarchical structure.

Communications interface specifications. This document describes the communication protocols—that is, the form in which the applications programs must present information to the communications system.

Management planning and milestones

Documentation should start at the earliest possible stages in the development cycle and be formally completed, except for the most detailed internal program module descriptions, before coding unless subsystems can be completed and tested on an independent basis. The first item to be completed will be the user's manual, which should be reviewed and approved by the user before other dependent parts of the documentation are finalized. Generally, all other items in the documentation library may be worked on concurrently. Any documents referenced in the user's manual, however, should be finalized along with that manual.

The level of effort required to complete the user's manual will depend on the following:

- Degree of complexity of the system
- Effectiveness of the analysis phase and quality of the resulting documentation
- Automation experience existing for the application
- User's level of understanding of functional requirements and user's ability to organize and communicate them

It is organized with respect to the phases within the incremental method. The chart is not intended to be used for precise time scaling. Rather, it should be used as a guide for the following points:

1. The individual items should start to take shape as documents at the approximate position of the tail of the arrow.
2. All items should be brought to a final-form version before the end of certain phases, as indicated by the large circles. In particular, the operating procedures manual and the system overview and interface documents must be in final form before the end of Phase III. These are the "design to" documents for Phase IV; they will be referred to as the preliminary documentation set. The subsystem descriptions must be completed before the end of Phase IV. Thus a complete final version of the external documentation is prepared before initiation of the program (source code) development, Phase V.
3. All items should be finalized before the end of the phase containing the head of the arrow. From the finalized version of each documentation item forward (point 2 above), originals and a working copy should be kept under tight control.

Procedures manuals

The procedures manuals, together with the human interface document, must explain the use and operation of the system in clear terms without need for assistance from analysts, programmers, or original authors. In some systems the "user" functions will be separate from the "operator" functions and must be split into separate manuals. In other systems these functions may be combined, and a single manual will suffice.

User's manual

The user's manual must completely define the system from a user functional standpoint, with the aid of the human interface document. It should provide sufficient instruction so that the end user can direct operators to query and update the system as well as interpret output without the aid of a computer technician. The User's manual can contain instructions that deal with functions other than those directly controlled by software. Often this can be done to provide a convenient reference within one manual. The willingness of the user to accept a system and utilize it on a long-term basis will depend heavily on how well this manual is written.

Organization. The user's manual should be organized functionally into contiguous steps as would be performed under normal operation. It should start with an overview of the system and should describe its basic approach and philosophies where applicable. Sections concerned with editing and validating inputs should come first, followed by construction and control of the database. A separate section describing the organization of the database from a user's point of view may be desirable. Query and report facilities should come next, followed by utilities and standard procedures. If the sections and subsections of this manual can be labeled according to the standard numbering system that holds throughout the documentation, this will greatly aid the user to communicate with operators and support personnel.

The contents of each function and subfunction section should follow a pattern if possible, with the following items contained under each section when applicable.

1. *Input information.* The user must be told precisely what input information he must provide, and in what format, to properly execute a system function. If input is edited by the system, the user should be told what edit and validation checks are performed and the data limitations that exist. The user should be provided with sample display depicting how he would have to prepare or view the edit and validation checks. It may be possible to reference the human interface document for this purpose.
2. *Control options.* Any options available to the user and their controls should be fully explained.
3. *Scheduling.* If frequency of operation or deadlines are applicable to a given function, they should be explained.

4. *System resource estimates.* If an estimation of utilization of system resources is required, this should be explained so that the user can make the estimates and pass control to the operator.
5. *Monitor information.* If information can be provided so that the user can alert the operator early regarding possible malfunctions, the manual should provide these hints. Timing estimates and key output words can be helpful here.
6 *Interpretation of output.* Interpretation of output should be clearly specified through the use of sample displays or reports. The use of reference numbers next to circled data samples that are explained on a separate sheet are helpful. The human interface document can also be used as a reference. All anticipated error or exception conditions should be fully explained.
7. *Disposition of output.* Routing or disposing of communications output or hard copy should be specific where applicable.
8. *Recovery.* If recovery procedures have been developed for certain possible malfunctions, these should be explained to the extent required for the user's understanding.

Operator's manual

The operating procedures manual should provide sufficient direction for the operator to execute user instructions without any programming knowledge or assistance.

Organization. The operating procedures manual should be organized functionally into the same contiguous steps as is the user's manual. The use of a standard numbering system will greatly assist the operator in communicating with user and support personnel. Because an operator is dealing with the same set of devices to perform each function or subfunction, organizing instructions onto standard forms can be convenient. If this application is one of a number being performed at a given site, standard forms already may be available or imposed. If the hardware system to be used exists in other previously developed applications, one should investigate their forms and take advantage of refinements learned from experience. Independent of how input data and instructions are passed to the operator, it is desirable to reduce operator directions to a set standard forms that can be interpreted for each function to be performed. Normally these would be covered in the operations standard at a given installation.

The contents of each function or subfunction section should follow a pattern if possible. If standard forms are used, they will impose a pattern that operators will learn. The following items should be explained where applicable.

1. Function/subfunction description
   Designation
   Organization control

Classification
Priority

2. *Scheduling*
   Timing
   Frequency
   Duration
3. *Resource requirements*
   Software
   Devices/units/channels
   Modes/volume
   Forms/alignment
4. *Inputs*
   Source
   Description
   Format
   Volume
5. *Initialization procedures*
   Storage media
   Forms
   Recording of starting data
6. *Monitor instructions*
   Alert conditions
   Messages
   Errors/exceptions
7. *Termination procedures*
   Normal termination
   Recovery
   Restart
   Abort
   Recording of termination data
8. *Outputs*
   Source
   Description
   Interpretation
   Volume
   Disposition

9. *Special instructions*

   Anything not covered conveniently elsewhere

   Anything requiring special attention

Technical support documents

The technical support documents, in conjunction with the procedures documents, interface documents, and source listings, must allow the system to be maintained or enhanced without the aid of the original authors. They should also allow other programs or systems to be integrated independently. These documents assume that the reader has Sufficient programming knowledge to understand standard techniques and terminology easily referenced elsewhere. Special technique terminology peculiar to this application or a small class of applications should be explained. Borderline cases should be referenced if not explained.

System overview

The system overview provides a technical as well as software functional overview of the system. It should be initiated early in Phase III along with the environment specifications.

Organization. The system overview should be organized around software functions that correspond to the physical software design, starting with an overview of the entire system. At its most detailed layer, this document must identify the bottom-level software modules. Actual descriptions of these modules would be contained in the program description document. Figure 6.3 provides a pictorial representation of a typical "software system tree." The purpose of this diagram is to show the hierarchical relationship of physical software elements that make up the system. It is important to understand that the software functional boxes typically bear little or no resemblance to the system functions from a user standpoint. For example, bottom-level modules typically will be utilities, such as file handlers.

The organization of the system overview should follow the block diagram, starting at the top (level 0), which describes the system as being comprised of subsystems. The document would then be broken into sections corresponding to these subsystems. Each subsystem would be described in terms of its programs, with corresponding sections broken into subsections describing each program. This type of breakdown would continue to the level just above the bottom module. The number of levels needed would depend on the size of the system.

Starting at level 0 with a description of the system, each section should contain a software functional block diagram, a HIPO, and a brief narrative description of that particular software element. Note that a software element as defined here corresponds to a block on the software functional block diagram. The modules at the bottom level are not described separately, only as part of the level above.

The block diagram need only cover two levels for any particular software element. For example, when describing the system (level 0), one need only show the top level system block and the next level (level 1) subsystem blocks. When describing a program, one need only show the program block and the corresponding module blocks. Other levels can be described similarly.

Inputs and outputs contain entries that must reference the database specification. This is best accomplished by assigning a unique code to each file and record in the data base. Additional details are given in the data-base specification section later in this chapter. Each entry in the input and output section contains a database reference that is shared between at least two modules in the system. These will be interprogram, databases (external files) or intraprogram databases (common areas of main memory shared by an executable task). The processing portion of the HIPO contains the names of processes that make up the particular software element being described. In a large system convenient to assign a unique code to each of these processes. Many of these processes will be utilities that will be used in at least two different HIPOs. The brief narrative should contain enough information to help the reader understand the organization of the system, subsystem, program, and so forth. The narrative should not go into the functional properties of the system from a software standpoint, other than those that can be helpful as a road map. It should contain information that helps relate how the user functions are implemented in the software. Thus system overview provides a road map from user functions to software functions.

Program descriptions

The program descriptions provide the detailed descriptions of each subsystem, program, and corresponding bottom-level modules. They must bridge the gap between the procedures manuals and the source listings to provide a clear understanding of the details of each software module in the system.

The program descriptions document should follow the same organization as the system overview, except that it should contain a separate section for each bottom-level module. Whereas the system overview ends one level above the bottom modules, the major part of the program descriptions is the detailed module descriptions. Therefore, within each program description section there must be a subsection corresponding to each program module contained in that program.

Each software element above the module level should contain the same set of software functional block diagrams and HIPOs as the system overview. The narratives for these elements should contain all the information necessary to understand how that particular software element is organized. All the software properties of that element should be clearly specified so that anyone who must change or enhance the software related to that element can easily read the description and determine how to proceed. Each bottom-level module should be described in enough detail so that a programmer can independently write the code required to make that module perform its expected software functions. This description should provide the following information:

- How this module is called and controlled and how it calls and controls other modules
- A list of all modules called by this module
- For utility modules (those called from at least two different software elements), a list of all the calling modules to determine the effects of any changes
- Difficult areas of code (for example, special algorithms or data manipulation processes)
- Modifications to shared databases (for example, common memory areas or files), along with any conditions that affect these changes
- Abort procedures, operator messages, or debug features

If a module is a utility module, then its detailed module description should be contained in the utilities section as described in the following paragraphs. References to a utility from any program in the system need only specify the name and unique code of that utility. The reader then can refer to the common utilities section to obtain the detailed description of that module.

Utilities

The utilities section contains the detailed descriptions of each utility used in the system. A software element is a utility if it is used by two or more higher level software elements. Note that a utility may be a module or a combination of modules (for example, a program). The program descriptions should not redundantly explain the details of a utility but should emphasize the particular aspects of applying and controlling the utility, and should reference the utilities section for more detail.

If a utility is a "system" utility (that is, a standard program supplied with the system support software) and it is explained elsewhere, then reference may be made directly to the support software documentation as long as it will be as readily available as the system documentation.

Organization. The utilities section should be organized in the same manner as the program descriptions, being an extension of them. It should be included at the end of the program descriptions.

The content should be the same as for the program descriptions. Particular care must be taken to document utility modules (bottom level) because they may do different things for different calling modules.

Interface specifications

The interface specifications provide direct access to detailed descriptions of the following: (1) human inputs and outputs, (2) databases, and (3) communications protocols. Because these specifications are referenced by most of the other documentation, it is convenient if a common framework can be used for reference identifiers. For example, a combination of letters and numbers can be used for codes that tell the reader if the specification is part of a database and whether it is a file or a record. Hierarchical numbering schemes can be used to show what program or module originates the records of outputs being referenced. Such a numbering scheme can be derived directly from the software functional block diagram or the HIPO.

The particular indexing scheme used is not nearly as important as having a scheme. In the software design phase many interface specifications will be created and destroyed. Therefore, during this period, it is most helpful if their reference identifiers carry pertinent information. The need for this information is just as important when new personnel are called on to support the system after the original authors have departed. The interface specifications are described in the succeeding sections.

Human interface specifications

Output formats. The output formats contain descriptions of all of the outputs visible to a human. These should be depicted in a form that is as close as possible to the actual display or print format. Complete detail must be provided on all display options so that devices or forms can be specified, and the programs coded. It is helpful to tag each field on a display output specification whose meaning is not obvious. These tags then can provide an index on a separate sheet, with explanations of each corresponding field. Because it is convenient to reference the output formats from the users manual, they should be explained in a manner the user can understand.

Input formats. The input formats must depict the visible input ormats in a manner that closely resembles the display format or provides a good visual likeness. Because the input formats are likely to be referenced from the users manual, they should be presented in manner the user can understand. Explanations should include descriptions of all the fields for insertion, allowed codes and their translations, and any editing that is to be performed automatically.

Many times the human interface specifications can be described using standard forms. Doing this can be helpful in that much of the specification is contained on the form itself and needs to be understood only once.

Database specifications

Before we describe the database specification, it must be noted that we are not describing a database management system. We are merely describing the means for documenting a database. By database we mean all of the data shared by two or more modules or programs. This includes external files shared by separate executable tasks and common memory areas shared by modules within a single task. Both can be described in a common data record format. The main purpose of the database specification is to provide all information required to properly access, utilize, and update the database with programs or modules other than those originating it. This document must provide the common specification of data that is shared by different processes in the system. Changes to this specification must be carefully controlled, because they must be compatible with all modules sharing the changed data.

Elements of the database can be viewed in a hierarchical structure, starting with bits, characters, and fields. Fields may take on the special property of being keys, in which case they are used by processing programs to search, sort, and merge information. However, one can dispense with this special consideration and think of all fields as keys, a more human-oriented approach. Fields can then be grouped into records. In fact, the basic data description element most commonly used is the data record. Records can then be grouped into blocks and blocks into files. It is convenient to record descriptions of data in two ways simultaneously: (1) a file or record format description and (2) a data element dictionary. Both are described in the following paragraphs.

File-Record format descriptions. The purpose of the file-record format descriptions is to define file and record layouts in a simple, concise way. A common and convenient approach is to list all fields in the order they occur in the record. The list should include the field mnemonic, field name, field type and length, and the starting character position of the field. Files can be described in terms of the records they contain, along with any special information (for example, format, maximum record size, and so forth). In the case of internal data records--that is, common areas of main memory that are shared--the same record format descriptions can easily apply to each.

Data element dictionary. This dictionary is an alphabetical listing of each element in the database, with its corresponding definition. The definitions should be simple to understand and user oriented, because the data element dictionary can be helpful to a user as well as a software technician. The dictionary should be used to define internal memory data areas as well as external files.

Communications interface specifications

The communications interface specifications must describe all of the communications protocols that directly interface any of the software in the system. These descriptions must be sufficiently complete to allow integration with other systems. If descriptions of communications protocols are adequately explained in other documentation that is readily available, then these documents can be referenced. This is an area in which reduncancy should not be avoided.

An existing framework for describing communications protocols has evolved over many years of practical implementation in tile field of international communications. The framework provides the basis for describing individual protocol standards and the manner in which various protocol standards interrelate. This framework, known as the Reference Model for open Systems Interconnection (OSI/TC97/SC16), is promulgated by the International Standardization Organization (ISO). The approach taken is to address each layer as a separate and independent protocol layer, starting with the application or presentation (human interface) layer and working to the physical media layer. This approach has provided a framework for easily specifying what heretofore was a difficult problem to describe. Anyone building software for the international market is well advised to contact ISO to obtain a description of the Reference Model for OSI.

Revision process

As each documentation item is completed at the solid black circle on the milestone chart it should be put under a rigid revision control process. It is important that all changes be strictly controlled and recorded as a permanent record. This is absolutely necessary when large volumes of documentation are distributed to the customer base as well as to support personnel. Pages can then be replaced individually when updating is done. The control process also provides the means for checking the congruence of outstanding copies with the latest version.

Source listings

The internal program documentation (source listing) is as important as the external documentation just described--particularly when maintaining or improving the system. Generally, the source code should be clearly structured functionally. Depending on the source language used, the extensive use of notes (in English) may be necessary.

Well-documented FORTRAN code usually requires a minimum of 50% comment statements. Many other languages require a substantially higher ratio of comments to code for readability. COBOL, properly used, requires little need for program comment because the language itself provides the structure and facilities for writing highly readable code.

Index